The psvcholog

This book

the

The psychological complex
Psychology, politics and society in England, 1869–1939

Nikolas Rose

Routledge & Kegan Paul
London, Boston, Melbourne and Henley

First published in 1985
by Routledge & Kegan Paul plc

14 Leicester Square, London WC2H 7PH, England

9 Park Street, Boston, Mass. 02108, USA

464 St Kilda Road, Melbourne,
Victoria 3004, Australia and

Broadway House, Newtown Road,
Henley-on-Thames, Oxon RG9 1EN, England

Set in Sabon, 10 on 12pt
by Columns Ltd, Reading
and printed in Great Britain
by Billings and Son Ltd,
Worcester.

Library of Congress Cataloging in Publication Data

Rose, Nikolas S.
The psychological complex.
Bibliography: p.
Includes index.
1. Psychology. 2. Social psychology. 3. Environmental
psychology. I. Title. [DNLM: 1. Behavior. 2. Psychology.
3. Social Environment. BF 121 R797p]
BF57.R56 1985   150   84-29814

ISBN 0-7100-9808-1 (pb)

Contents

Acknowledgments

This work has taken a long time to bring to some sort of a conclusion, and in the course of it I have incurred many debts. I owe most to the many other works of research, scholarship and analysis which I have plundered so unceremoniously in constructing my own account, no doubt distorting their arguments to suit my own ends. These other texts are the conditions of possibility for my own; their specific contributions are evident on every page. The work was carried out under the auspices of the Department of the Sociology of Education at the University of London Institute of Education where, from 1975 to 1978, I was the recipient of a grant from the Social Science Research Council.

Tony Green showed patience and good humour as my supervisor over the many incarnations of the thesis on which this book is based, and gave me much sound advice. Graham Burchell and Colin Gordon talked to me at a very early stage in the work, enabled me to think of the form which it should take, and encouraged me to write a paper, published in the journal *Ideology & Consciousness* in 1979, which was an early version of the account which appears here in Chapters 2 to 5. Anna Wynne helped considerably, by putting much of the text on to a word processor when time was short. Hilary Allen read all the drafts at least once, and with great care and kindness showed me where spelling, grammar and argument went astray. Diana Adlam has discussed psychology with me over many years and in many ways, helped me clarify my ideas and made me feel this work had some interest when I had lost all sense of it. To my other friends who suffered some of the burden of this study, my thanks; I am sorry to disappoint your expectations.

Introduction

In studying the psychology of the individual, sleep, madness,
delirium, somnambulism, hallucination offer a far more
favourable field of experience than the normal state.
Phenomena which in the normal state are almost effaced
because of their tenuousness appear more palpable in
extraordinary crises because they are exaggerated . . . human
psychology will have to be constructed by studying the madness
of mankind, the dreams and hallucinations to be found on
every page of the history of the human spirit.

Ernest Renan, 1890[1]

Since the end of the Second World War, psychological expertise
has been increasingly deployed around a range of practical
problems and within a large number of administrative and
reformatory practices. Psychological agents and techniques are
involved in assessment and diagnosis of problems of individual
conduct in institutional sites such as hospitals, schools, prisons,
factories and in the army. An analogous range of psychological
specialisms has arisen – clinical psychology, educational psychology, criminal psychology, industrial psychology, military psychology and so forth. How is one to account for the emergence and
functioning of these new knowledges and techniques for the
conceptualisation, regulation and amelioration of the problems of
personal and social life?

In the authoritative histories of psychology, the discipline is
considered to be fundamentally the science of the normal mental
functioning of human beings, and the accounts of the origins of

the modern psychological enterprise are constructed in this light. The roots of psychological modernity appear to be traceable through a long tradition of reflections on the human psyche, stretching back across the span of written history. A history which takes as its organising principle the normal human mind can order the ideas it examines along a continuous path, in terms of the extent to which they grasped, enabled us to grasp, or were obstacles to the grasping in thought of this real object of knowledge. Considered from this perspective, the social deployment of psychological expertise can only be seen as a by-product, often unexpected and unintended, of the advances of our knowledge of the functioning of the normal mind and its role in behaviour. Hence the various aspects of psychology which concern themselves with practical and technical questions can be conceived of as the application to specific problems of the knowledge gained in the study of the normal mind. The practical issues with which psychology is bound up are thus pertinent only to this penumbra of applied psychology; the central core of psychological discourse has a history which is indifferent to them.

Even where it is allowed that there are links in this field of 'application' between social questions and psychological developments, these concern only the pressing need to *derive* useful techniques from our knowledge of psychological normality. Whilst it is indeed the fortunate status of psychology to be enlivened by, and relevant to, questions of everyday life, its status as a knowledge is independent of them. Thus if the constitution of psychology as a scientific discipline was quickened or even induced by certain practical problems, even if it allowed of an application of this scientific knowledge to certain technical tasks, it was nonetheless an occurrence in a pure theoretical space, in which a union was achieved at last between a discourse motivated only by a desire to know and its object, the human individual, which pre-existed it and awaited it.

So if, in this practical field, psychology has been chiefly concerned with problems of pathology, of those who for some reason are failing to function normally, it is implied that psychology can recognise and diagnose such pathology because of the knowledge which it already possesses of the normal mind. A knowledge of normal mental processes thus appears to be the condition and basis for the application of scientific techniques to the problems posed by abnormality.

The present study contests such an analysis. Modern scientific psychology in England was not born in the quiet and reflective atmosphere of the academy. The place now occupied by psychology within the practices of social administration and regulation has not been established through the application of established psychological doctrines to pressing practical problems. Nor have we seen a knowledge of the normal mind turned to account in the understanding of pathology. If anything, the issue is more usefully posed the other way round. The conditions which made possible the formation of the modern psychological enterprise in England were established in all those fields where psychological expertise could be deployed in relation to problems of the abnormal functioning of individuals.

Whilst most histories of psychology trace the roots of psychology back through a continuous series of speculations about the mental life of humans from time immemorial, there is a common acceptance that something significant occurred in a period from about 1875 to about 1925. Both from the standpoint of the historian, and that of contemporary participants, something appears to happen over this fifty-year period, in Britain and Western Europe as well as in the United States, which has the character of an 'event'. This event appears to consist of the translation or extension of certain recurrent questions about the nature of humans from the closed space of philosophy to a domain of positive knowledge: the formation of psychology as a coherent and individuated scientific discourse.

Obviously there is nothing definite about the boundaries of this period of transition: they can be drawn differently according to the criteria brought to bear upon the historical record. Nonetheless one can trace over this period a shift within the organisation of disciplines in the universities, and the progressive institutional delineation of psychology from philosophy and logic on the one hand and from biology and medicine on the other. One can see the establishment of institutions and departments specific to psychology – psychological laboratories for example. One can see the formation of groupings of individuals who identify themselves as psychologists, who are trained by psychologists and who have qualifications as psychologists. And one can observe the establishment of a professional apparatus of psychology, and a network of psychological journals which define the characteristics of the discipline through their criteria for selection of articles for publication, and reconfirm them through the nature, as well as the results, of the psychological research which they disseminate.

Thus in England, under the influence of Alexander Bain, a journal entitled *Mind* appeared in January 1876, declaring itself in its opening editorial 'the first English journal devoted to Psychology and Philosophy' and setting itself no less an aim than 'to procure a decision as to the scientific standing of psychology'. James Sully, Grote Professor of Philosophy of Mind and Logic, established the first English laboratory for experimental psychology at University College London in October 1897, and in the same year a similar laboratory was founded in Cambridge. In October 1901 the British Psychological Society was inaugurated, in 1904 the *British Journal of Psychology* first appeared – the list of similar developments could be considerably extended.[2]

Yet, as Hearnshaw points out in his *Short History of British Psychology*, the subsequent growth of academic psychology in Great Britain was remarkably slow. At the outbreak of the Second World War there were only six university chairs in psychology, and a total lecturing staff of about thirty. The central subject matter of university psychology, the science of mental life, was consciousness or experience. Philosophers disputed psychology's claim to this domain, and psychologists disagreed as to the merits of different theories. But the analysis of the conscious experiencing self defined the space of controversy and its principal terms. However, Hearnshaw argues that the impetus for the development of psychology in England did not come from this field of debate. It came, rather, from those practices where psychology was deployed – in particular, medicine, education and industry. 'Here indubitably, and beyond the boundaries of philosophical controversy, progress was being made, new disciplines were being forged, new professions created. The academic world could not indefinitely refuse to recognise these developments.'[3] It was outside the academy that the claims to truth which psychology made were first recognised, it was here that psychologists first gained social recognition, professional status and a practical role, it was this that powered the lift-off of psychology in the post-war period.

The psychology which began to establish itself in these social apparatuses prior to the Second World War characterised itself in a particular way. Its proponents termed it 'the psychology of the individual' and claimed that if psychology was to become a scientific discipline it must become a science of the individual.[4] The psychology of the individual had as its object, not the general laws of functioning of the human psyche, but the specific mental capacities and attributes of human individuals. It particularly concerned itself with the variation of these capacities and attributes among individuals and the causes and consequences of such variations. The psychology of the individual was, that is to say, a psychology of individual differences, of their conceptualisation and their measurement, of the interpretation of past conduct in the light of them, and of the prognosis of future conduct in terms of them. A psychological science of the individual emerged through this act of differentiation and quantification.

The issues around which the psychology of the individual formed were not, however, produced in the laboratory or in the study. They were those prioritised by the objectives and mode of functioning of particular social practices. The school, the reformatory, the court, the army and the factory were the surfaces upon which the problems emerged which individual psychology sought to make its own. The problems posed for the functioning of these apparatuses set the conditions which would have to be fulfilled if there were to be a socially effective science of the individual psyche. It was not a question of external stimuli to the development of knowledge. The conditions which made individual psychology possible established the issues to be resolved, and the functions which its techniques would have to fulfil: they set the terms which individual psychology would have to abide by if it were to establish its claims to truth.

The problems around which individual psychology formed had one thing in common – they were phenomena deemed to be pathological. Psychological knowledge of the individual was constituted around the pole of abnormality. Far from knowledge of the pathological being an unlooked for and advantageous consequence of a science seeking only a knowledge of the normal, the opposite is closer to the truth. Practices whose object was the identification and administration of abnormality were more than merely external conditions for the development of the psychology of the individual. This psychology sought to establish itself by claiming its ability to deal with the problems posed for social apparatuses by dysfunctional conduct. No doubt it would be too much to make the general claim that psychology conceives of the normal as no more than the absence of abnormality. But in this field at least, psychological normality was conceived of as merely a lack of socially disturbing symptoms, an absence of social inefficiency: *that which did not need to be regulated.* This mode of conceiving and dividing normality and pathology is a constitutive feature of modern psychological knowledge of the individual and the technologies which it operates.

To understand the psychology of the individual in this light enables us to place its emergence as a scientific discourse, not within a history of reflections upon the nature of the soul, but within the changing conceptions of pathologies of thought, belief, intellect, emotion and conduct. It is to these conceptions and the practices of government, regulation, surveillance, segregation, and therapy within which they were deployed, that we must look if we are to begin to identify the conditions which made such a psychology possible. Not a history of ideas, then, but a history of practices, techniques, institutions and agencies, of the forms of knowledge which made them thinkable and which they, in their turn, transformed. And a history of the categories and problems around which such complex apparatuses formed, which provided the motivation for their emergence and the targets of their tactics. The feeble-minded individual, the shell-shocked soldier, the inefficient worker, the maladjusted child, the juvenile delinquent – no doubt these are simply the ones which have been most obvious in this particular study.

To trace the emergence of the formation and functioning of this type of psychological knowledge from such a perspective is to introduce discontinuity into the history of psychology. Where the standard histories see a progressive evolution of knowledge from past to present, we can now discern radical shifts, the elimination of certain themes, the rise and decline of others, the eruption of new questions from unexpected quarters. We can, for instance, both appreciate the significance of the issue of the feeble-minded for about three decades at the turn of the nineteenth and twentieth centuries, and understand why it is that the debates around this problem are so foreign to our contemporary concerns with the mentally handicapped. We can no longer trace a single line through all those discourses which address the mental functioning of man, for the development of the science of psychology is no longer ordered around the apparently reassuring stability of the normal human psyche. We now seek the conditions for the formation of the psychology of the individual within a history of the emergence and transformation of concerns over the pathologies of mind and conduct and their consequences.

We cannot, therefore, relegate the social conditions within which psychology emerged and functioned to a domain external to that of its concepts and theories. But we must also avoid committing the opposite error. Psychological knowledge of the individual was no mere function or effect of its social conditions. There were specifiable discursive conditions for the ways in which social problems were conceptualised at particular times, the measures which were directed towards them, the evidence gathered as to the consequences of such measures and the conclusions drawn. The scientific discourse of individual psychology did not form in a pure space of knowledge, but neither was it called into existence through the force of social exigencies. It was made possible by the existence of certain ways of thinking about populations, statistics, evolution and heredity, by certain theories of the nature, origin and treatment of mental pathology, and by certain conceptions of the role and objectives of good government and the laws of economic and social life. An analysis of these conditions will be necessary if we are to understand how psychological conceptions of individual variability were to be able to play their part in techniques of social administration.

A scientific discourse is not a mere register of effects from elsewhere. It consists of a complex set of ways of conceptualising the objects of its attention, naming them, theorising about them and explaining them.[5] We have to consider how the psychology of the individual was organised as a specific and distinctive discourse: the ways in which its objects of investigation were classified and analysed; the manner in which certain events and observations were drawn together into a domain of relevant evidence; the formulation of certain concepts, models and theories to represent human psychology and its variability; the types of experiments and active interventions into reality which were undertaken in order to evaluate these representations; the development of particular conceptions of demonstration and proof. In other words, the psychology of the individual consisted in complex explanatory techniques which need to be described and accounted for if we are to understand its formation and functioning.

Scientific discourses seek to produce explanations that are true, contain means by which that truth is demonstrable, and deploy and evaluate statements in terms of a division between the true and the false. Their systematicity is regulated by this fundamental relationship with truth, and that systematicity establishes the conditions which theories and explanations will have to fulfil if they are to be 'in the true'. To characterise a scientific discourse as truthful is not to imply any commitment to its epistemological status. For the present analysis the point is not that scientific discourses are true, or that some are truer than others, but that they seek truth, establish criteria for what is to count as truth and contest among one another according to the opposition between truth and error. The psychology of the individual could become an effective field of knowledge, only to the extent that it could define and defend a particular regime of truth.

Scientific discourses do not only *seek* truth, they also *claim* truth. The extent to which a scientific discourse can establish its claims to truth, can command acceptance of the veracity of its explanations of certain phenomena, is crucial for the relations which can obtain between that discourse and the various social practices within which it circulates. Firstly, within the field of scientific practice itself. But furthermore within the various other practices – technical, judicial, pedagogic, governmental and so forth – within which that discourse or the explanations which it produces may be deployed. The social functioning and consequences of the psychology of the individual were conditioned by the ways in which its explanations laid claim to truthfulness and the extent to which their veracity was accepted.

The psychology of the individual existed as more than merely a set of arguments and explanations of problems embodied in books, articles, reports of experiments and so forth. It also consisted in a set of practical instruments and techniques which embodied the explanations proposed and deployed them in relation to the practical problems which had occasioned them. A whole technology was constructed, consisting in manuals of instruction, testing and assessment procedures, rules of diagnostic practice and classification, techniques of therapy and reformation. The psychology of the individual entailed a quite new set of relationships between psychologists and those who were the subjects of their investigation and experimentation. These new practices were carried out by agents designated competent to pronounce the explanations of the psychology of the individual and to utilise its practical skills, by virtue of their training, qualifications and experience. They formed professional bodies to designate who was competent to speak and practise as a psychologist, to control teaching, training and admission to the ranks of the professionally qualified, to regulate standards of professional conduct, and to give voice to the claims of psychology as a professional instance. These psychologists sought to locate problems of individual conduct within the jurisdiction of the psychology of the individual, and hence to claim the right to adjudicate upon them. The social destiny of the psychology of the individual was consequent upon these events and the outcome of the contestations around them.

This study seeks to chart the conditions for the emergence of the psychology of the individual as a scientific discourse and a body of social practices, in England from 1869 to 1939. It was the existence of this psychology – as a complex of discourses, practices, agents and techniques, deployed within schools, clinics, the judicial and penal processes, the factories and the army – which provided the basis for the generalisation and development of 'applied' and 'clinical' psychology during and after the Second World War. For it had become possible to think scientifically about the mental capacities and attributes of human individuals, to understand their conduct in these terms, to conceive of their problems and potentials in terms of these psychological capacities, and to construct techniques of regulation and reformation with reference to this psychological domain.

Two further points should be made in introduction. Firstly, this study neither seeks nor pretends to provide an exhaustive account of psychological happenings in England over the period in question. There were certainly many questions raised in academic discussions whose relationship to the concerns, methods and theories of individual psychology was tenuous. In addition, there was one significant area of 'applied psychology' in England during and after the First World War which is barely touched upon here. This concerned the psychologisation of problems of industrial organisation and efficiency, carried out in the Health of Munitions Workers Committee, the Industrial Fatigue Research Board and the National Institute of Industrial Psychology. This was a substantial field for the employment of psychologists. Questions raised in psychophysiology were transformed in these concerns, and new questions were posed concerning the psychology of sensation, discrimination, attention and co-ordination in relation to industrial fatigue and accidents, industrial training and skills and the technical organisation of the production process. A large proportion of papers to the psychological journals were directly or indirectly indebted to this work.

Questions of individual differences certainly did emerge in relation to the psychology of industry, in particular the issues of job selection and vocational guidance. But by and large, the new means of conceptualisation which constituted the psychology of the individual were forged in relation to the problems of social life rather than industrial labour. The principle of selection which has guided this study is this: In what ways, and with what consequences, did it become possible to think psychologically about the variations of capacities and attributes amongst individuals?

Finally, to avoid misunderstanding, I must point out that this study is not a *critique* of the psychology of the individual. It is not written in favour of one sort of psychology as against another sort of psychology, nor against psychology and in favour of the absence of psychology.[6] It does not seek to show the falsity of individual psychology, nor to discredit it by revealing its association with reprehensible social interests or political ideologies. The study simply seeks to uncover what made it possible to think psychologically about individual differences, how this was connected up with other social, political and theoretical events, and what this psychological individualisation, in its turn, permitted.

1
The moral subject
of psychology

I cut out with scissors the names of these objects [stick,
bellows, brush, glass, knife] and thus transformed into labels
they were placed in Victor's hands; thus returning to our first
steps in this experiment, I required him to place on each object
the word which served to indicate it. It was in vain; and I
experienced the inexpressible chagrin of seeing my pupil fail to
recognise any of these objects, or rather the relationships which
linked them to these signs, and with an air of indescribable
stupefaction move his uncomprehending eyes over these
characters, all at once again suddenly meaningless to him. I felt
my heart sink with impatience and discouragement.

I went and sat down at the far end of the room and
considered bitterly this unfortunate creature whose strange
condition reduced him to such sad alternatives: he could either
be sent to one of our asylums as a down right idiot or spend his
life striving to achieve an education which would hardly serve
to increase his happiness. 'Unhappy creature', I said with a sad
heart, as though he could hear me, 'since my labours are
wasted and your efforts fruitless, go back to your forests and
the wild life of yore; or if your new needs now leave you
dependent on a society which you cannot serve, then go and die
of poverty at Bicetre.' Had I not known the limitations of his
intelligence, I could have believed myself understood; for barely
had I uttered these words than I saw an expression of great
sorrow on his face, his chest heaved with sobs, his eyes closed
and tears streamed down his cheeks.

Jean Itard, 1806[1]

Picture a child, male, about twelve or thirteen years old. Four and a half feet high, brown hair, round face, slightly stooped shoulders, a rocking gait. Scars on his body, a long horizontal scar across his throat. He does not speak, although he emits certain guttural noises. There is some doubt as to whether he can hear, though he has a sense of smell and taste, and apparently normal eyesight. He has little sensitivity to heat or cold, relieves himself wherever he happens to be, is indifferent to childish amusements and has no ideas of modesty or property.[2]

An unfortunate being, perhaps. But nothing, you would think, to mark him out for an historical role, especially in a country experiencing momentous political events. Yet this child, discovered living wild in the Department of Aveyron in Central France in the closing years of the eighteenth century, was to become the focus of an extensive popular and scientific debate. The leading scientists of the revolution – Bonnaterre, Virey, Sicard, Pinel – were to subject him to their scrutiny. The state was to provide funds for an experiment lasting some six years, in which every facet of this little child's soul and conduct was to be probed. His tastes in food and drink, his cries and the expressions of his face, his senses and sensitivities, his pleasures and pains, his sexual difficulties – all these were the object of scrutiny, documentation and reform. He became the focus of academic texts and disputes which continue up until today. He occasioned the invention of a range of practical techniques of reformation whose successors may be seen in our modern schools and laboratories. His fame – Victor, the Wild Boy of Aveyron – and that of his governor, teacher and doctor – Jean Marc Gaspard Itard – would last as long as that of the actors in the 'event' of the French Revolution which inaugurated our present. Victor too, in his modest way, marked a shift into modernity. For Victor, as a new object of knowledge and a new target of reformation, was the first psychological subject.

What is psychology? Any student of psychology knows the variety of ways in which the discipline defines and individuates itself. But, to the extent that these are disputes over the proper characterisation of a psychological science, they operate on the premise that such a science is possible; that there are facts of a psychological order and theories of a psychological order. The minimum condition for a scientific discipline of psychology is that it can separate out a field of phenomena and explanations not subsumed within any other discipline, pertinent to a psychological domain. And before there can be a psychological conception of individual variability, and a scientific discourse and practice which seeks to differentiate individuals on the basis of their psychological capacities, the individual must have a psychology. This psychological domain emerges between the organism – which is a biological system of organs and physiological processes of body and brain – and the person – whose conduct is the concern of ethics and politics. It is here that the origins of volition, emotion, speech and action are proposed to lie. Here is the locus of thought, the site of conscience and judgment. And here is a domain with its own systematicity, its own laws, processes and idiosyncrasies, irreducible to those of any other order.

But we cannot identify psychology simply with the emergence of such a theoretical object. Psychology consists not only in a set of theories, concepts and models, but also in a set of procedures of observation, investigation and experimentation, which will elicit psychological facts and evidence and provide the testing ground for explanations through the effects which they produce. Those enterprises which claim the status of positive sciences consist in interlocking projects of representation and intervention.[4] Speculations, calculations, predictions and the construction of models organise existing observations and stimulate new ones. They are also the occasion for the invention of technologies which are capable of regularly producing effects already observed and the creation of new phenomena. Psychology was born through just such a combination of representing and intervening. At one and the same time there emerged a conception of a psychological domain, and new techniques and procedures for eliciting psychological phenomena through acting upon that domain. What is born with this combination of theoretical object and experimental target is a new entity: the psychological subject.

The first subjects of psychology

From the tales of Romulus and Remus, through the Wild Boy of Aveyron and the Wolf Children of Midnapore, to the Gazelle boy of the Sahara, the discovery of children living in the company of animals and outside human society has been the object of myth, of disbelief, of romanticisation, of anthropological and scientific debate.[5] Malson, writing in 1964, lists fifty-three cases of such children reported in sources available to him. The earliest of these dated from 1344, the most recent from three years prior to the date his book was published; the scientific discussion of such cases spans the period from 1672 to the present.

The scientific imagination has repeatedly returned to these unfortunate children and sought to utilise them to resolve theoretical controversies. The Wild Boy of Aveyron, perhaps by virtue of the documentation that surrounds him, occupies a key place in such disputes. Each author seeks to rework the evidence, to re-examine the results, to answer finally, once more, the question of how his condition should correctly be diagnosed, of what conclusions can truly be drawn from his case, of who Victor really was. No doubt one is seeing here an example of a more general phenomenon in which the reconstruction and interpretation of history plays an important part in scientific debates.

In his detailed reconstruction of the event, Harlan Lane explains the importance accorded to the Wild Boy of Aveyron at the beginning of the nineteenth century in terms of the 'central question of the Enlightenment, What is the nature of man?'[6] Wild children, he argues, formed a key test in relation to three questions: the distinction between man and the beasts; the existence of innate ideas; the nature of man in a state of nature. Itard brought together diverse strands of Enlightenment thought: the sensationalist philosophy of Etienne Bonnot, Abbé de Condillac; the moral treatment of insanity as expounded by Philippe Pinel; the techniques of training the deaf and dumb devised by Abbé R.A. Sicard. Synthesising these strands with originality and invention, he established the very foundations of modern psychology, and originated a range of investigative and pedagogic techniques which remain with us until today:[7]

> Itard had set out to train an *enfant sauvage*; by his journey's end he had become the originator of instructional devices, the inventor of behaviour modification, the first speech and hearing specialist, founder of otolaryngology, creator of oral education for the deaf and father of special education for the mentally and physically handicapped.

And Malson too finds in Itard a precursor of the modern scientific enterprise, and writes 'A hundred and thirty years before the Kelloggs, Itard was already talking like a modern psychologist.'[8]

No doubt there is much truth in such accounts. But perhaps one should be a little wary of such an historical analysis which operates through the identification of precursors of modernity, and which reads past events through the eyes of the present – in terms of what they would become. As Georges Canguilhem has pointed out, the writing of such continuous histories is dependent upon a conception of the unity of the object of a scientific discourse across its history:[9]

> the precursor is a thinker whom the historian believes he can extract from one cultural frame in order to insert him into another, which amounts to considering concepts, discourses and speculative experimental acts as capable of displacement or replacement in an intellectual space in which reversibility of relations has been obtained by forgetting the historical aspect of the object dealt with.

So perhaps here we can pose our question slightly differently. What was this new object of scientific investigation, this new target for systematic reformation? What made its formation possible? What is the subject of psychology?

The sensationalist individual

> If it was proposed to resolve the following metaphysical problem viz 'to determine what would be the degree of understanding, and the nature of the ideas of a youth, who, deprived, from his infancy, of all education, should have lived entirely separated from individuals of his species'; I am strongly deceived or the solution of the problem would give to this individual an understanding connected only with a small number of his wants, and deprived, by his isolated condition, of all those simple and complex ideas which we receive from education, and which are combined in our minds in so many different ways, by means only of our knowledge of signs. Well! the moral picture of this youth would be the Savage of Aveyron, and the solution of the problem would give the measure and the cause of his intellectual state.
>
> Jean Itard, 1801[10]

In the last decades of the eighteenth century, philosophers began

to concern themselves with discussions of sorts of individuals who
might appear marginal to modern eyes. On the one hand, there
were those who were deprived of one or more of the senses – the
blind, the deaf and the dumb. On the other hand, there were those
who were deprived of normal experience by virtue of their
isolation from civilisation – members of primitive tribes, wild
children. Discussions of these figures – speculative or based upon
observations and reports – found their way into the writings of
Rousseau, Montesquieu, Voltaire, Buffon and La Mettrie.[11]
Diderot wrote studies of the deaf and dumb and of the blind.[12]
And Condillac attended public demonstrations of the use of sign
language which were given by deaf mutes instructed by the Abbé
de l'Epée.[13]

It was the sensationalist philosophy of Condillac and his
followers that unified these diverse figures and gave them their
significance. To found an epistemology exclusively upon the senses
was to accord a demonstrative function in philosophical discourse
to those who, for some reason, were deprived of one or more of
the full complement of the senses. It gave an even more important
place to those who, having been deprived of a particular faculty,
were enabled to regain it by an act of man or God: the deaf who
hear again; the dumb taught to communicate; the blind given
sight. No longer simply freaks of nature, accidents or marvels of
medicine, such events now could be used to justify or dispute
philosophical theses. The empirical subject and its vicissitudes
now could provide the means of demonstration and elucidation of
the epistemology of sensationalism. But simultaneously, a new
importance was conferred upon these events themselves, and a
new object of scientific investigation began to take shape. As
philosophy began to order itself around the problem of 'the theory
of knowledge', to pose this question as one of the relation of
representations to be represented, and to conceive of this relation
on the model of vision, occurring through the mediation of the
senses, a surface formed upon which the psychological subject
could begin to find a foothold.

Condillac described his 1746 *Essai sur l'origine des connaissances humaines*, in a subtitle, as a supplement to Locke's *Essay
Concerning Human Understanding*.[14] As is well known, Locke
opened his essay by arguing against the proposition that the mind
contained innate ideas. Ideas – which mediated between the
mind and the rest of the world – were derived from sensation

and experience and were constructed through the activity of an inner faculty of reflection. Ideas were the focus of a kind of mental vision, and could be signified by words. Words were secondary and derivative marks, invented by men and formalised by convention in order to serve the technical function of communication – though some words, of uncertain or unclear signification, could perplex thought.

Condillac reversed the priority which Locke accorded to ideas over signs, and in doing so shifted the study of the ordering and combination of signs, of the nature of language in its development, to the centre of the project to understand the method of operation of the mind. Whilst simple sensations gave rise directly to simple ideas, the soul only acquired the ability to recall ideas and reflect upon them by annexing these ideas to signs. The human understanding worked with these representations of ideas. Further, complex ideas were made up from simple ones through signs which acted as chains to the different combinations of simple ideas. It was thus to language that man owed the possibility of knowing, of establishing relations between elements and combining them into various sequences:[15]

> how simple and admirable are the springs of human
> knowledge. The soul has felt various sensations and operations:
> how then shall it dispose of these materials? By gestures, by
> signs, by sounds, by ciphers, by letter; by instruments so
> foreign as these from our ideas, we set them to work, in order
> to raise ourselves even to the sublime knowledge. The materials
> are the same in all men; but the art of making use of signs
> varies; and from thence the inequality which may be observed
> among mankind.

But our natural languages are imperfect knowledge. Many signs are not clearly attached to ideas; others annex no ideas at all; the relations amongst signs are inexact. This lack of correlation between signs and ideas gives rise to confusion both in daily life and in the abstract sciences. Hence science must reform language, adjust the relations between signs and ideas and establish clear chains from the simple to the complex. Scientific procedures consisted in the rational and logical ordering of representations so that they might conform with the facts of experience, which were all that man could ever know of truth.[16] Sense data were to be analysed into their simplest elements, to each element was to be ascribed an unambiguous and distinctive sign, the signs were to be recombined and ordered into a hierarchy from simple to complex within a logical and rational structure. Thus the work of science was that of constructing a well-made language.

Simultaneously a pedagogic project was inscribed at the heart of sensationalist epistemology. It was in its very nature to be prescriptive, to identify that – in signs, their ordering, or their relations to objects – which misled understanding and to prescribe corrective action. Problems concerning the validity of knowledge could now be shifted from a philosophical to an empirical terrain. The subject of knowledge was an empirical individual, and epistemological questions could be resolved by a judicious combination of observation, experimentation and attempts at individual reformation. The psychological conception of the individual begins to form when a philosophy of the subject casts itself in a mode which is amenable to observational elaboration, open to practical verification, and utilisable for individual transformation.

In outlining the objective of the *Origin*, Condillac sets out his wish to reduce whatever related to the human understanding to a single principle. In his *Traité des sensations* he achieved the promise of finally eliminating the residual dualism of Locke's ascription of certain key epistemological functions to faculties of the human mind.[17] Condillac's argument proceeded through a thought experiment which drew upon recent medical advances and observations on the restoration of vision to the blind.[18] He imagined a statue, complete with all the organic structures of the human body but initially deprived of all its sensory faculties. By examining the forms of knowledge, the ideas which the statue would develop if one sense after the other were successively awakened, he purported to derive all the features of human knowledge from a single sufficient source – experience conceived as sensory impressions upon the body. From a consideration of a subject limited to the sense of smell alone, Condillac demonstrated that, even limited to a single mode, sensation could generate all the faculties of the soul – the faculties of attention (including remembering, comparing, judging, discerning, imagining, forming abstract ideas, ideas of number and duration and knowing general and particular truths – all modes of attention), the different modes of desire (expression of passions, loving, hating, willing, the capabilities of hope, fear and wonder) and contracting habits.

But the senses alone would not generate knowledge. We attend to objects and order our ideas in relation to them because we are creatures with needs that must be satisfied, and are capable of experiencing pleasure and pain. The derivation of the faculties from the sensations occurred at the price of assuming that no sensation was indifferent in regard to the pleasure or pain which it produced in the mind. The distinction between pleasure and pain, and the tendency of the subject to seek to repeat the former and avoid the latter, was the single principle to which Condillac believed he had reduced all the attributes of man: 'the different degrees of pleasure and pain are the laws by which the germ of all we are is developed, and that they have produced all our faculties.'[19] This was a principle which was to have considerable pedagogic and reformatory consequences. It would also be the basis for the development of an elaborated system of utilitarian ethics; an analysis in these terms would have a powerful social destiny in England.

For Condillac the argument was important for another reason: it allows the construction of a developmental epistemology. At the moment of its inception, such a project encounters its inescapable problem – how to account for the birth of the subject: the idea of the body as the discrete and unified seat of the self and the distinction between self and object.[20] Condillac's solution, like so many which have followed it, assumed that very unity between sensations, needs, wants and judgments which it purported to explain. Subjects had the ability to take the totality of their present and past states as an object of reflection, and to make a judgment as to their coherence, when motivated by wants and according to the natural and universal calculus of pleasures and pains. And the subject's knowledge of itself as both separate from the external world and the unified subject of sensations, needs, wants, desires and passions was the condition for the attribution of the source of sensations to objects in that external world.[21] The sensing subject must be capable of taking itself as an object before it becomes an 'I'; its understanding must already be organised towards the satisfaction of its bodily wants.

In the often repeated gesture of developmental epistemology, the empirical subject – the child, its needs, its passage through the world – was called in to resolve the philosophical problem. Thus Condillac asked, rhetorically, 'How could a new born babe be occupied with its needs if it had no knowledge of its body, and if it could not as easily acquire some ideas of bodies able to take care of it?'[22] The watchful eye and prior arrangement of nature and the body were accorded the ability to resolve the problem, that epistemological discourse has itself constructed, of the adequacy of knowledge to its object. Philosophy had begun to cede its epistemological rights to the space of positive science through the notion of the subject which it had constructed. But paradoxically, in seeking to resolve its metaphysical difficulties through an appeal to the empirical, philosophy merely succeeds in transferring its accumulated baggage of presuppositions concerning the nature of the human subject on to that empirical individual who is supposed to relieve it of them.

This was the birth of a subject which a positive science of man could take as its object. There were no innate ideas or faculties, just a subject form which could support self-consciousness, awareness of others, simple and complex ideas, attention and acts of judgment, given only possession of the senses, natural wants, the ability to distinguish pleasure and pain and the possibility of experience. All ideas developed from sensations as directed by needs, wants and desires to produce experience. Simple experiences could be directly annexed to simple ideas; the more complex must be analysed, classified and combined through signs. Knowledge consisted in a regular, rational and systematic relation between signs and ideas. And epistemology was immediately a pedagogic activity, in that it recognised this as the condition of knowledge, sought to reform other sciences such that they too possessed such a structure, and to instruct others in the correct methods for gaining knowledge.

It is evident how such a theory of the human understanding should accord an important demonstrative function to subjects born lacking one or more of the senses, and to subjects enabled to regain them. What would be the degree of understanding of the objects of vision possessed by a man who was first enabled to see at the age of thirteen years?[23] How did ideas come to be linked to sensations, how were complex ideas, judgments and analyses made? Similarly, if words are merely marks attached to ideas in order to allow their combination and communication, no necessary privilege need be attached to verbal signs. Hence if the deaf and dumb can be taught to use a language of gestures to represent their ideas, they too can learn to analyse and develop abstract ideas.[24] Thus the epistemopedagogy of sensationalism can

make of the deaf and dumb a simultaneous target of reformation
and an object of experimentation and demonstration of its theses.
If sensationalism could be the basis for the first positive science of
man, this is because it allowed such a combination of representation and intervention, of speculation, theorisation, technical
invention, experimentation and reformation.

But we can also see how such an epistemology can attend to
another type of individual. The Wild Boy of Aveyron was its
subject, not on the grounds of his lack of senses but on the
grounds of his lack of experience. His limited understanding could
be conceptualised as a consequence of the lack of those
requirements for the development of knowledge which are
dependent upon society and education: signs by which to
combine, represent and analyse; wants to stimulate the ordering
and combination of ideas. We attend to nature and order our
ideas only because we require to satisfy our wants. As children,
our wants, and hence the ordering of our ideas, are concerned
merely with the satisfaction of our basic, pressing needs. They are
under the control of our appetites, our habits and our inclinations.
But in our progress through society, under the stimulus of our
education, our senses are constantly awakened, stimulated, made
more sensitive, new wants are constantly created. It is the pressure
of these new wants which drives us forward to form new ideas
concerning the new objects to which we have become attached.
Hence we feel the necessity of using signs and increasing their
number, of using them to form complex ideas and to analyse, in
order to satisfy our desires. It is this, too, which leads us to
speech, for a word is initially merely a sign for a want, a means of
communicating that want to others who may have the ability to
satisfy it.[25]

Thus we can understand how the Wild Boy of Aveyron becomes
a possible subject for a positive science. Itard seeks to realise
through his observation, experimentation, technical innovation
and manipulation, the phenomena predicted by the theses of
sensationalist epistemology. The programme for the treatment of
Victor sought to awaken the sensitivity of his organs by hot baths,
massages and even pain, and to provoke strong emotions of joy,
anger and fear. It sought to discover his pleasures, his favourite
foods for instance, and to derive from them new means of reward,
punishment, encouragement and instruction. As Itard commented,
having 'found out a *pleasure* for him, I had only to repeat it a

certain number of times in order to convert it into a *want*. . .'[26] Once wants had been constructed, deprivation of their satisfaction could be used as an incentive for the young savage to express them in speech rather than in the language of action and pantomime which was sufficient for him to communicate simple needs. Similar means could be used to direct the operations of the understanding 'to a new order of things which have no original connection with them. From this application flow all his knowledge, all the improvement of his mind, and even the conceptions of the most sublime genius.'[27]

Itard placed between Victor and his wants a series of obstacles which continually changed and became more difficult, so that, in order to surmount them, he had perpetually to exercise his attention, his memory, his judgment, and all the functions of his senses. Itard reproduced, in experimental form, all those techniques of the subject which have given birth to the modern soul. But by simultaneously expanding wants and manipulating their satisfaction, this soul had become the object and target of a new scientific practice. Victor had become the first psychological subject. A link was beginning to be systematised, certainly not without precedent but now organised, generalised and provided with a methodological rationale, between the formulation of true propositions about subjects, their systematic observation, experimental manipulation and therapeutic socialisation. And these latter mundane operations thus acquired a scientific status because of their philosophical significance.

It was not simply a question of what Victor could do for science. It was also a question of what science could do for Victor. Central to the medical psychology and scientific pedagogy of the early nineteenth century was the simultaneous constitution of an object to be known and a target to be transformed. Theory and practice combined in a sort of phenomenotechnics of the subject, a process in which the abstract object of a theory of the subject was concretised, in which theory was materialised.[28] Psychological theory was, from the moment of its inception, always a theory 'in action', and the 'theory of the subject' always operated in and through a set of technical and practical procedures for its 'realisation'. A positive science of man produces its object within a set of practices in which it is to be known through its transformation. Hence the founding moments of psychology always concern the pathological, as that which is to be normalised and known through the procedures and results of reformatory tactics. Itard's treatment of Victor was the reproduction in microcosm of the major institutional sites within which such a science of man would be elaborated – the asylum, the prison and the school were only the first of these. And the domain in which such a science operated was not delimited by the understanding – it was a domain designated *moral*. It owed its possibility not simply to sensationalist epistemology, but also to a different type of pedagogy with a different type of object – moral medicine and the reformation of the mad.

The moral space

> Indeed, when we consider the little time he has been in society, the Savage of Aveyron is much less like a simple youth, than an infant of ten or twelve months old, and an infant who should have against him anti-social habits, an obstinate inattention, organs scarcely flexible, and a very blunted sensibility. In this last point of view his situation became a case purely medical; and the treatment of it belonged to moral medicine – to that sublime art created by the Willis's and the Crichton's of England, and lately introduced into France by the success and writings of Professor Pinel.
>
> Jean Itard, 1801[29]

There have been many discussions, in histories of psychology and psychiatry, of the emergence at the end of the eighteenth century of forms of 'moral management' of the mad. The moral medicine and moral treatment developed and promoted by Willis, Crichton, Pinel and Tuke is counterposed to the use of physical coercion and constraint which supposedly preceded it. There is less discussion, however, of the significance of the term 'moral' as it was used in texts of this period, although some authors remark upon its ambiguity.[30] On the one hand, 'moral' appears to make reference to the register of ethics, of evaluation of the correctness of conduct and the rules of right living. On the other hand, it appears to refer to the mental as opposed to the physical, to the emotions and the will rather than the body, its organs and fluids. Hence it is used to designate causes of insanity other than physical ones, and treatment of the mentally deranged through kindness, appeal to conscience and to the will of the insane person. To the writers of the nineteenth century, there was nothing ambiguous about the relations existing between moral conduct, moral processes and moral derangement – indeed the systematic relationships between them constituted the moral domain. Let us map out these relationships, focussing upon the practice within which they first took shape – the 'sublime art' of moral medicine.

For the eighteenth century, conduct, in the case of madness at any rate, existed in very close proximity to the ducts of the body and their contents – the nerve fibres, the blood, the bowels, the humours. The contacts between medicine and madness (initially limited to those with money to pay, and occurring within the family or in one of a small number of private establishments for the deranged of the wealthier classes) had the objective of the restoration of these bodily fluids to their proper states. Thus, for example, a range of noxious substances was administered in an attempt to strengthen the spirits or fibres which had been weakened in madness. And techniques of purification – blood transfusions, bleedings, purges – were utilised, linked to a theory of madness involving the clogging of the fibres of the mind or viscera. A third set of treatments involved the use of immersions – hot or cold baths, showers or douches – with the aim of restoring suppleness to the fibres and the added advantage of cooling or shock to bring sufferers to their senses. Fourthly, the movements of the body could be regulated – through the use of restraints or of specialised pieces of apparatus for spinning or revolving the lunatic – partially with the aim of adjusting the movements of the bodily fluids, partly in an attempt to restore the links between the deranged internal time of the body and the real external time of the world.[31]

It was, paradoxically, the very intractability of madness to these physical cures, and the conclusions that were drawn from this that madness was beyond cure, which provided the conditions under which, towards the end of the eighteenth century, a space could begin to open between the body and the ravings, delusions, hallucinations and melancholias of the mad. This space would be designated *moral*. Having argued that there is no cure for original madness – though the physician may treat consequential madness with some success – Battie concluded that the chief function of the physician was that of 'management' – general care of the patient, confinement away from friends or families, the checking of unruly

appetites and the pursuit of a quiet, well ordered life.[32] Pargeter's
Observations on Maniacal Disorders (1792) reversed this connection between madness and a well-ordered life: whilst we cannot
search for the real causes of insanity, one thing we can conclude is
the part played by immoderate passions in its genesis – sudden
emotions, luxury, the reversal of the proper functions of day and
night, fanaticism – indeed a range of conditions arising not so
much from the fibres as from the morals. And while the physician
should apply the full armoury of physical treatments – bleeding,
cupping, cathartics, emetics, cold and hot bathing, drugs – since of
the ultimate causes of these disorders we must remain ignorant
'chief reliance in the care of insanity must be rather on
management than on medicine'. Further, since the maniacal
disorders originated with moral excess, they could be governed
and subdued by moral domination. The physician was to become
an expert in the art of governing maniacs through the exercise of
moral mastery.[33] Pinel described how, in the gaze of Reverend
Doctor Francis Willis:[34]

> Penetrating eyes seem to read [the madman's] heart and to
> divine his thoughts as soon as they come into being. Over them
> he exercises something resembling sovereign authority, which
> subsequently becomes a therapeutic instrument and which in
> no way contravenes the employment of gentler instruments.

The domination involved in moral treatment was thus the most
powerful of all – not force ensuring submission but authority
assuming mastery – a contestation in a moral space in which the
madman is bent to the will of the doctor and comes to accept this
will as his own.

The rise of moral treatment is habitually identified with Tuke's
foundation of the York Retreat in 1792, and Pinel striking the
chains from the insane in Bicêtre in 1793.[35] It defined itself
through oppositions along a number of axes. It opposed physical
with moral causes of insanity – passions, vices, lusts, griefs and
desires rather than humours, spirits, fibres, lesions in the brain. It
constructed moral classifications and characterisations of insanity,
as opposed to physical nosologies. And it deployed moral rather
than physical treatments of insanity – the management of the
moral life, relations and milieu of the madman rather than his
purging, bleeding, bathing or rotation.

The treatment required the creation, around the patient, of a domain of pure morality. Hence the asylum became the right place, and the family became the wrong place, for curing insanity. Firstly, of course, because the institution provided the appropriate conditions for the realisation of the dominance/dependence relation which successful treatment required. But secondly because treatment depended upon the possibility of manipulating the experiences, pleasures, pains, movements and timetable of the insane. The family environment was unsuitable not only because within it the mad were constantly reminded of their past, of the exciting causes of their indisposition, but also because the family milieu was inherently unprogrammable. The new asylum was to become a moral domain, but not one that sought to activate the principles of morality associated with religion – love, piety, brotherhood, asceticism – but rather one which deployed a set of moral principles purely social in origin and orientation: deference, modesty, compliance, industriousness, regularity of habits.[36] Drunkenness, promiscuity, laziness, apathy, misconduct of any sort were to find their antidote in the extension to the inmates of the homogeneous and unbroken rule of morality.

But how was this rule of morality to prevail over the deranged, the melancholic, the manic, the perverse? Firstly, because insofar as the mad, for all their moral transgressions, remained human, there existed within them some core to which treatment could direct itself. It was the lack of this possibility which made idiots, for Pinel and Esquirol, impervious to the action of moral treatment. But lodged deep in the interior of the mad lay an essential nature, a primitive morality which was both the condition of treatment and that which manifested itself during such treatment. Secondly, this core was accessible to a therapeutics because it was organised by principles which governed any sentient organism – the pursuit of pleasure, the avoidance of pain, the ability to form associations. Thus the moral order could be constructed, shaped, organised and re-educated through disciplining the body, imposing habits and regularities through the tactical utilisation of this utilitarian calculus.

Hence the asylum was not merely a domain of morality, but a domain of the enforcement of morality, by virtue of the principle of punishment for transgression and reward for obedience. Thus Reil wrote:[37]

Rewards that bring pleasure and punishments that bring

displeasure should be meted out in a proportion calculated to
lead patients back to the path which is necessary and proper for
them and which will cause them to be submissive and to
practice strict obedience.

Punishment was not given in anger, nor as the appropriate means
for the subduing of those who partake in the nature of the beast.
It was given coolly, dispassionately, according to a pedagogic
calculus that sought to form and shape conduct in morally
desirable directions. All aspects of the asylum were informed by
such a calculus and organised around the constant evaluation of
the behaviour of the insane individual. The giving or withholding
of anything which the inmate might require, or any object that
might be desired, could be integrated within this calculus – isolation, hunger, thirst, defamation, humiliation, chastisement – but,
in addition, moral treatment created the conditions where the old
medical treatments – the douche, bleeding, spinning, restraints –
could be reactivated, outside their original therapeutic rationale,
as threats or punishments for transgression. The asylum, with its
perpetual surveillance, was certainly a moral regime, but it was a
juridicalised morality. It was a morality in which the law
transgressed was only secondly the law of God, but firstly the law
of the social space of the asylum, the assemblage of norms which
the mad had to make their own if they were to return to
normality.

Hence the necessity of continuous monitoring of moral rules, of
continuous assessment of behaviour in relation to transgression.
The violation of a norm became an offence; hence the institution
of a frankly juridical regime. The inmate had to be aware that all
behaviour was judged according to a rule, and that the
transgression of any rule would be known and punished. But the
function of this surveillance and judgment was not the simple one
of the production of a well-ordered institutional regime, as it
would become later in the nineteenth century. On the contrary,
the conduct of the asylum, all those harsh words and unsym-
pathetic responses which we have just been documenting, had a
specific therapeutic rationale. This continual play of judgment had
the objective of forcing the inmate to take into himself the role of
judge, to internalise that moral order which constituted the
asylum, to incorporate the rules and principles of that institutional
space of morals into the moral space of his own character.[38]

The moral space of the asylum reduplicated, in material form, the contours of the domain that had begun to form between the body and its conducts – the formation of this moral space of the soul was thus the condition, referent, target and product of the regime of moral treatment. This particular domain, at once mental, medical and ethical, made possible more than just the reformation of the insane. Indeed, despite the rapid building of asylums during the nineteenth century, moral treatment in its original form lasted but a few decades. It gave way before the massive overloading and underfinancing of the asylums, and a critique of the therapeutic disappointments of moral management. But the conceptual counterpart of this institutional site – a particular way of constructing objects for investigation and an explanatory structure consisting in a specific way of conceptualising those objects – was destined to play a fundamental role in the social and political debates of the nineteenth century, and in the formation of individual psychology.

The inventories of the causes of insanity produced at the turn of the eighteenth/nineteenth century form a strange amalgam to our eyes: excesses of joy, grief, fright, fear, anger or love; religious fanaticism; intemperance; immoderation in food; gambling; vices of all sorts; onanism; shock; disappointment or sudden success in personal or business affairs; rapid changes of fortune; extremes of heat or cold; excessive vanity or ambition; failures of management in the nursery, especially early indulgences; fever; blows to the head – the possibilities proliferated.[39] But to the early nineteenth century, the intermixing of the physical, the emotional, the physiological, the financial, the intellectual, the accidental, the unethical and the vicious formed a rational distribution. The conception of a moral domain had allowed the systematisation of elements which were previously evaluated in distinct spheres into a single register. It consisted in a nexus of relations between predispositions, experiences and conduct, between desires, understandings and actions. Yet for all its complexity, this moral space remained two-dimensional, a space without hidden depths or secret laws. It was certainly structured historically – things past were laid down and affected things future – but it had no thickness to it. In it things remained exactly what they were and what they seemed. It integrated the flows of the body, the effects of passion and vice, the excesses of will and the exigencies of fortune. Here the forces of the body were mustered and directed,

channelled towards particular objects, good or ill, vicious or
virtuous. And here these forces could be neutralised or blocked,
or, on the other hand, amplified and intensified.

Itard's systematic programme for the treatment of Victor
exemplifies the analyses and techniques which such a moral space
made possible. The causes of Victor's plight were not an original
idiocy but the lack of all the virtuous influences of society and
education; the treatment sought to reproduce these in microcosm
through an all-embracing regulation and utilisation of all that the
Wild Boy desired and all that affected him; the object was to fill
out the moral domain with those aptitudes and controls on
conduct which presently had to be externally supplied. Thus
Victor's treatment operated through the emotions and the will,
through the systematic regulation of pleasures and pains, through
the pedagogic use of access to food, drink and other wants,
through provoking the emotions of joy and sorrow, through the
incitement of tender feelings for those close to him and the use of
their embraces and reprimands to mould conduct. The object was
for Victor to internalise these within his own conscience, to open
his soul to the noble feelings which are the happiness and glory of
the human heart and the foundation of society.

Towards the end of his final report, Itard records how he
ascertained his success in equipping Victor with the inner
sentiment of justice. After some hours of work in which Victor
had demonstrated intelligence and obedience, he was clearly
expecting praise and reward. In a 'truly painful experiment'
however, Itard put on a severe and threatening expression, seized
him by the arm and dragged him roughly towards the little dark
room which had sometimes served him as a prison. Victor
resisted, furiously and indignantly, finally biting his master on the
hand. Itard records his satisfaction:[40]

> It could only delight me, for the bite was a legitimate act of
> vengeance; it was incontestable proof that the idea of justice
> and injustice, the permanent basis of the social order, was no
> longer foreign to my pupil's mind. By giving this feeling to him,
> or rather by stimulating its development, I had raised savage
> man to the full stature of moral man through the most striking
> of his characteristics and the most noble of his powers.

Moral treatment was made possible by a belief in the common
nature of man. Firstly, all individuals alike had their faculties

formed through the effects of circumstances and education. Secondly, the deranged shared with all others a common core of reason, to which the treatment was directed, and which it could use as its first foothold on the pathological condition. But the practice of moral treatment enabled these issues to be reformulated. For the treatment paid attention to the asylum inmates not *en masse* but individually – the specific characteristics of the individual had to be attended to in detail, for they were to be systematically exploited for the purposes of reformation. And when observed and utilised in the course of treatment, one thing became evident – psychological man was not a universal being, he had his individual differences.

The educability of idiots

> It is not among outstanding and gifted individuals . . . that we should look for the benefits and disadvantages of our routine education but among those that this same education has barely shaped . . .; among the idiots, for example, or among those who we frequently call slow witted . . . The gaps or these faults of the human mind are much more the result than we realise of the defective management of education, whose principal fault is that it is essentially the same for all children and never adapted to the innumerable variations in the intellectual make-up of individuals. Let us take one hundred children of the same age and subject their intellectual state to an analytical examination. We will be convinced that there are as many points of dissimilarity as of similarity among them. . . Thus psychological man more than physical man has his idiosyncrasies or individual differences. . .
>
> Jean Itard, 1802[41]

It is widely recognised that the sensationalist philosophies of the eighteenth century stressed the essentially common nature of the human mind, spirit and understanding, and attributed individual variations to differences in 'experience'. It is also usual to note a shift which occurred at the end of the eighteenth century from such a belief in universal reason and the unity of man to the study and documentation of individual differences. This is frequently attributed to the rise of the Romantic movement, and the supplanting of Enlightenment rationalism by organicism and historicism.[42] In his study of medical psychology in the early nineteenth century, Michael Donnelly eschews such global strategies of explanation in terms of changes in world view.[43] He argues that the critics of the universalist theses, in particular Cabanis and other students of physiology, systematised and generalised a growing number of 'observations' of differences amongst individuals, in particular those derived from medicine and medical psychology. These began to be deployed in questioning whether human individuals were all equivalent prior to differences contributed by circumstances and education. The article on equality in the *Dictionnaire Philosophique* had proclaimed that all men enjoying their natural faculties were equal. Idiots, the blind, the deaf and the grossly deformed represented merely boundary cases which defined the limits of humanity.[44] Cabanis disputed this claim, arguing that there was no common human type, but that individuals varied in their nature and capacity to feel. And he supported his argument with evidence from the new clinical medicine.[45] What was it about clinical medicine that made possible a conception of individual variability?

The medical nosologies of the eighteenth century had sought to establish a classificatory table, in which the types and varieties of disease were displayed in a clear and ordered fashion. Medicine, like other sciences, sought to establish a clear and unambiguous language of disease, in which the apparent disharmony of illness could be reduced to the harmony of a taxonomy. The problem for the physician was to identify the species of the disease which had occupied the body of the patient, a problem which required the peculiarities of the person to be subtracted, as it were, in order to reveal the true nature of the disease. The physician had to know his patient, his particular characteristics and idiosyncrasies, in order to be able to perform this act of abstraction; illness was best treated in the home, for to place the patient in an artificial setting would further complicate the business of discovery of the essential disease.[46] To place a particular phenomenon in a certain class was not merely to systematise it, but to establish a certain knowledge of it. The construction of a classification was thus an activity which was at once epistemological and therapeutic.

The transformation of conceptions of illness which occurred at the end of the eighteenth century did not emerge from a philosophical overturning of this project of classification; indeed the medical nosologies produced over this period were entirely conventional. The formation of the new medicine of the clinic – a new mode of medical knowledge and a new site of medical practice – was made possible by a complex of political, social, technical and theoretical shifts which took place at the end of the eighteenth and the beginning of the nineteenth centuries. Amongst these were the emergence of the hospital as the principal site for the practice of medicine, as a result of increasing urbanisation and industrialisation coupled with a change in the laws of assistance which made institutionalisation a condition of medical treatment for those on relief. This entailed a change in relations between doctors and patients, for doctors now observed a whole series of instances of a particular condition. This made possible the tabulation and statisticalisation of diseases. New systems of record keeping, developed in the hospitals and introduced into the asylums by Pinel, could be used to demonstrate links between symptoms and prognoses, between symptoms and individuals and between successive events in any one condition. Medical norms could now be established on the basis of the observation and accumulation of data on large numbers of individuals. It was partly these statistical norms that made possible the clinical conception of the *case* – the unique intersection between a body and a life history, as the proper object for medical knowledge and for the practice of the cure. The case was unique but intelligible, for its individuality could be charted in terms of its conformity to, or deviation from, the general standards of functioning which were now available for comparison.[47]

But clinical medicine entailed a conception of the normativity of life in a rather different sense. Pathological phenomena now begin to be conceived in terms of the organism as a living system. They are disruptions in the vital processes themselves, and what diseases reveal is the essential normativity of life. A disease is no longer an essence which comes to inhabit a body, which can only disguise its true character. But nor is it a mere concatenation of observable coincidences and successions in bodily functioning, a bundle of characters bound together by statistical relations. The norms of clinical medicine were made possible by the statisticalisation of disease, but they are not merely statistical in character: they refer to the fundamentally normatised existence of the vital order. It is the body itself which has become ill. Hence the role of pathological anatomy: the observation of the sequence of illness until death followed by the opening up of the corpse allows the observable symptoms to be linked to hidden disturbances in the tissues and organs. The visible symptom now becomes diagnostically significant and medically meaningful because of the link which can be forged between it and the underlying organisation of the body as a living system. The new method of transmitting medical knowledge, involving lengthy tuition at the bedside, turns the hospital into a pedagogic apparatus, in which the poor, benefiting from the care which they receive for free, repay through the medical lesson which they provide. But this change in methods of medical instruction is necessary in order to introduce the medical apprentice to the techniques of diagnosis, of utilising the visible signs of temperature, pulse, flushing, and the techniques of palpation and the stethoscope to map out the complex volume of the body as a living system. Whilst the norms of clinical medicine were established through the examination of large numbers of bodies, their role in diagnosis and treatment entails an attention to the specifics of the case history and life processes of the individual sick body. Thus the act of establishing such norms simultaneously reveals the variability of individuals in relation to them. When disease becomes a process of life, and the sick person becomes a case, the essential normativity and variability of life processes brings the individual within the scope of knowledge in a way which the medicine of classification and ontological conceptions of disease entities had precluded.[48]

But if the new moral medicine was to be a part of this transformation, its diagnostic attention to mental derangement was initially untouched by it. When Pinel's *Nosographie Philosophique* was published in three volumes in 1798 it was very much in the spirit of the old classificatory medicine.[49] Mental illness was divided into four classes: mania, melancholia, dementia and idiocy. There was nothing original about this division, or the place of idiocy within it. Idiocy was set apart from the other forms; it was afforded a less extensive symptomatology and aetiology, but was marked by an absence of intellectual faculties, almost certainly with an organic basis, almost invariably incurable. Indeed, whilst the *Traité médico-philosophique sur l'aliénation mentale* reported 51% of cures in cases of mania, 62% in melancholia, 19% in dementia, it found none at all in cases of idiocy.[50] Thus for Pinel, whilst idiocy could pose interesting legal problems, it remained marginal to a mental medicine which centred around a therapeutic practice and depended upon the existence of a core of reason and humanity which remained within the insane. When the Wild Boy of Aveyron was brought to Paris, the Society of Observers of Man appointed a commission to study him and to report its observations: Pinel; Sicard, the Director of the Institute for Deaf Mutes; Jauffret, naturalist; de Gérando, philosopher of language and ideology; Cuvier, anatomist. At the end of December 1800, Pinel's report documented the imperfections of the senses and their dissonance, the absence of speech, the fleeting character of his ideas, the limits of his feelings. On the basis of comparison with others who had been placed in various positions in the range covered by the class of idiocy, Pinel drew the necessary conclusion: the Wild Boy was properly to be classified among the idiots, ineducable and incurable. It was as a member of this class that the child was entrusted to the Institute for Deaf Mutes. The chief physician, who was appointed just two days after Pinel's report was delivered, was Jean Marc Gaspard Itard.[51]

Deaf mutes in eighteenth century France were not merely objects of philosophical interest, they were also the focus of a philanthropic pedagogy. The Abbé de l'Epée, who founded the Institute for Deaf Mutes, had recognised the revolutionary implications for the deaf of the relationship which sensationalist epistemology proposed between ideas and the signs by which they were marked. If articulate sounds were adopted by man in the beginning simply because of the ease and variety with which they might serve to mark ideas, there was no reason why this mythical origin of language should not be replayed for those who, by virtue of physical accident, lacked the means to utilise spoken language and oral signs. Thus they too might be provided with the means to mark, recall and order their ideas. The deaf and dumb, hitherto conceived of as irremediably ignorant, were so only because of their absence of a spoken language for communication and for the organisation of their own understanding. To teach them a language then would be pedagogic in both a restricted and an expanded sense – not simply through the immediate activity, but also through the prescriptive and analytic benefits which the learning of a language conferred.

Epée had regarded gesture as the natural language of the deaf, a language of signs to which they were led directly by the intersection of nature and their wants. This natural language of gesture could be developed and conventionalised, transforming it from the immediate expression of physical needs through to signs designating objects and grammatical relations. Epée produced a conventionalised language of gesture by translating the structure of French language and grammar into signs, both gestural and written. And in his institution in Paris, he taught his pupils to communicate in gesture signs, and to translate these signs into established written words by committing the association between word and sign to memory.[52]

Sicard was no less committed to sensationalist philosophy and the methods of analysis which it proposed. But he disagreed with the techniques which Epée had utilised. Epée, he argued, had produced only copyists – the deaf mutes could translate written French into signs and vice versa, but they could not compose for themselves even simple sentences of French, nor carry out the instructions in a letter which they could translate into signs. Epée had recognised this, and considered it the inescapable limit to pedagogy for the deaf mutes. But Sicard considered that it arose from a technical and methodological error. This was the teaching of *invented* signs which corresponded to each word, rather than the elucidation of signs *from the pupils* which corresponded to particular ideas.[53]

Sicard's innovation was to make pedagogy into a practice as much clinical as educational. In the organisation of the asylum, Pinel had introduced the taking of histories, the keeping of individual records and the differentiation and individualisation of treatment in the light of them. But, further, treatment was not merely differentiated as between individuals, the peculiarities of the individual were to be used in the curative process. Subjects were no longer merely the passive recipients of sensations addressed to them, they were to be actively engaged in their own transformation. The wants and fancies of the individual were the means of their management back to normality. For Pinel, madness could be cured if the mad person recognised himself as mad, took into himself the moral lessons of the asylum and internalised a perpetual judgment of his actions within his soul. Sicard's medico-pedagogy was less juridical, but no less individualised. The child was to be engaged as an active agent in the training of the habits of body and mind. Experiences were not to be merely enjoyed or suffered, but were to become the occasion for classification and analysis. Movements were no longer to be merely the expressions of bodily states, they were to be regulated, organised, directed. Thus Sicard *individualised* his pedagogic techniques, directing them towards the particular propensities of specific individuals, adjusting them in the light of their particular requirements and orienting them in the light of a definite doctrine of the subject. The target of these practices was the soul, and the nature of that soul, the rules of the moral space, determined the techniques and their means of application.

It was these techniques, refined and developed in relation to the doctrines of moral treatment, which Itard utilised in his work with the Wild Boy of Aveyron. And less than six months after Pinel's pessimistic conclusions, the Society of Observers of Man, at the initiative of Sicard, invited Itard to submit a further report on the Savage Child, and concluded after hearing it:[54]

> These observations made by Citizen Itard, who has tried to conduct the education of this child, lead us to conclude that his faculties have been developed up to a certain point, and hope that more substantial development will be seen subsequently. The assembly applauds this effort.

But neither for Itard nor for the assembly had the traditional view of idiots as incurable and ineducable been transformed. It was by disputing Pinel's diagnosis of the Wild Boy as an idiot that Itard was able to develop his system of treatment, utilising Sicard's methods of individualised instruction within a regime modelled on moral treatment, which sought to reawaken, develop, instrumentalise and channel Victor's wants. Thus it is not surprising that Esquirol could still write, in 1818, after the results and limits of Itard's attempts at methodical education were well known:[55]

> Everything about the idiot betrays a organisation imperfect, or arrested in progress of development. We can conceive of no possibility of changing this state. Nothing teaches us how to impart, for a few moments even, to the wretched idiot, an increase of reason or intelligence. . . . It will be observed, that I have nothing to say, respecting the treatment of a constitutional condition.

Yet the incident of the Wild Boy of Aveyron, and Itard's treatment, had provided the conditions for a transformation in the place and status of the idiot in philanthropic and pedagogic practice.

In 1839 Edouard Séguin opened the first school for idiots.[56] Inspired by the philanthropic socialism of Saint-Simon, he sought a class of unfortunates to whom he could extend its benefits. He discovered idiots intermingled, without aid or hope, with convicts, epileptics and the insane. Moral treatment of the Wild Boy had only been possible for Itard on the condition that the boy was *not* an idiot. But for Séguin, Victor *was* indeed an idiot; his progress under the regime of medico-pedagogy demonstrated that, given appropriate methods, idiots could be educated; they had become improvable, a new target for philanthropy. Séguin, it should be noted, did not dispute Esquirol's belief that idiocy was incurable. What he contested was the view that was still maintained as late as 1837 in the standard *Dictionnaire de Médicine*: 'It is useless to combat idiocy. In order to establish intellectual activity, it would be necessary to change the conformation of organs which are beyond the reach of all modification.'[57] Idiots remained *incurable* for Séguin, but despite this they were not *ineducable*.

Education for the idiot had a moral function, a philosophical basis and a physiological method. The idiot was one isolated from humanity by virtue of cerebral incapacity, deprivation of stimuli to the senses or by some combination of mental and physical defect. The physiological method was a sequence to reopen the linkages between the idiot and the physical, emotional and moral world which surrounded him:[58]

> From the feeling of pressure in the tactile organs which taught prehension to our feeling of duty towards our pupils which taught them affection, from the distinction of the difference between a circle and a square and that between right and wrong we have followed a continuous path, beginning where the functions refuse to soar higher in the atmosphere of idealism.

Where sensationalism found intellectual error, it located the blame not in the senses but in the field of signs; for Séguin the abilities and senses themselves were variable and could be educated, the body and its organs, the senses and the muscles, could be systematically awakened, taught to move and to discriminate. They could be mustered, organised, governed, through a systematic programme of instruction. Further, variation had become a part of the intrinsic nature of the moral realm – it was not a case of a universal reason or intellect being present or absent but of variation of a psychological order which in interaction with experiences of certain types, in a certain sequence, produced results in the sense of both intellectual abilities and morality. The conditions were thus formed for a conception of the distinct laws of childhood moral organisation. It was from the space of pathology that the possibility of a knowledge of the normal child arose.

It was for Maria Montessori to effect this transformation in the field of pedagogy.[59] Whilst others wondered that idiots, in the schools she established for their training, did so well at examinations in relation to normal children, she wondered why the normal children did so badly. But despite Montessori's own desire to trace her heritage back to Séguin and Itard, the transformation with which she is linked occurred in a practical and discursive space very different from that within which they worked. For schooling had become universal, assessment in the form of examinations was a commonplace, idiocy had become feeble-mindedness, and feeble-mindedness had become a matter of intelligence. This transformation had occurred in the context of a field of debate that was to rack nineteenth-century social and political discourse on 'the social problem' – the problem of degeneration. And it was in this context that a new mode of theoretical and practical individualisation was to form, which called itself the psychology of the individual.

2
The psychology of populations

What man possessed of sense, curiosity or fancy, could gaze
unmoved on this mixed mass of poverty, destitution and crime
which makes up the lower stratum of our artificial society?
How resist the question, what part of all this misery is the
result of personal defects and vices – of sloth, unthrift,
incapacity; how much of what may be called inaptitude in the
State! How is it possible to resist the inquiry whether when
more than three centuries ago, our ancestors established a poor
law, they ought not rather to have given us a good police force.

William Guy, 1873[1]

The psychology of the individual formed in England at the end of
the nineteenth century around a problem of defective mental
capacities: *feeble-mindedness*. What was at issue was not the
plight of the individuals themselves, but the consequences of such
individuals for the population as a whole. It was argued that
feeble-mindedness was a hereditary phenomenon, that it was
passed down from parents to children. Since the feeble-minded
bred more rapidly than others, their proportion in the population
would increase. Feeble-mindedness produced all sorts of social
problems, and these problems were becoming increasingly evident
in the heart of the new centres of population created by the
growth of manufacture. What was occurring was a deterioration
or degeneration of the race, which would weaken the country at
home, and hamper it in competition abroad. Here was a question
of the gravest concern, and a proper matter for government
action. It was necessary as a matter of urgency to discover those
who were mentally defective and to take steps to prevent them
propagating.

The problem of the feeble-minded was posed in these terms by linking up three somewhat distinct themes in social and political argument in the mid-nineteenth century. Firstly, the doctrine that the regulation of the quality of the population was a proper and important issue for government policy and action. Secondly, the argument that the conditions of urban life were deleterious to the habits and abilities of the labouring classes, and that the effect was a cumulative demoralisation of the population. Thirdly, the theory that pathological physical and moral states were the expression of a constitutional predisposition which was transmitted by heredity and which tended to become more marked with each generation, thus forming a process of degeneracy. When these themes were linked up around the problem of the feeble-minded, each was transformed.

Government and population

> Next to the blessings which a Nation derives from excellent
> Laws ably administered, are those advantages which result
> from a well-regulated and energetic Police, conducted with
> purity, activity, vigilance and discretion.
>
> Patrick Colquhoun, 1797[2]

From the middle of the eighteenth century it is possible to identify the emergence of a recurrent theme in texts on the problems and objectives of government. It has at its core a question of the organisation of the population and the creation and maintenance of order, morality and public tranquillity, and it is posed, in part, in terms of *police*. Police in the sense in which Colquhoun wrote in 1800:[3]

> Police in this country may be considered as a new science; the
> properties of which consist not in the judicial powers which
> lead to punishment, and which belong to the magistrates alone;
> but in the prevention and detection of crimes; and in those
> other functions which relate to internal regulations for the well
> ordering and comfort of civil society.

Put simply, what police represented was a new conception of government, of its role and functions, of its objects and of its legitimate mechanisms. The Parliamentary Committee of 1822 gave voice to four decades of opposition to the programme of police, when they argued: 'It is difficult to reconcile an effective system of police, with that perfect freedom of action and exemption from interference, which are the great privileges and blessings of society in this country.'[4] It would, therefore, be wrong to see the introduction of a professional police force in 1829 as merely an extension and reorganisation of the office of constable. The constable, from the thirteenth century, was an elected officer who had as his responsibility the maintenance of the King's peace, by hue and cry and other means. But this was merely a systematisation of the duties of all subjects, as clarified in the Statute of Winchester of 1285, which laid down the principles of policing until 1829.[5] This Act, together with the Justice of the Peace Act of 1361, which established the Justices as the representatives of the King, concentrated judicial and administrative power in their hands and made constables subordinate to them, established the mechanism for the maintenance of the King's peace and removed the last elements of feudal rule in this area. This apparatus took shape within a conception of the Crown as the sole source of law with the sole right to hold courts and dispense justice. Law was a part of the relationship between a sovereign and his territory, and crime was an offence not against another subject but against the King's peace and the person of the sovereign himself. Certain acts were forbidden, but outside the infraction of a law the Sovereign had no business to interfere with the lives of his subjects. When a law was infringed, the wrong against the Sovereign was righted by a public manifestation of the power of the King. The public trial and punishment was not so much a legal as a political ritual in which the injured sovereignty was restored, and the might of the prince was re-established in the minds of his subjects.[6]

Against this, we can counterpose a different conception of government, one linked to that sense of police which was decried in the opposition to Colquhoun. Police, as Von Justi put it in 1760, was the foundation of the power and happiness of states; in Beccaria's terms it was the knowledge of the laws of education, security, good order and public tranquillity which was necessary if the products of the earth, of labour, of commerce and taxation were to be obtained with perfection and constancy.[7] In the eighteenth century Europe was a policed society, not in the sense of the realisation of all these programmes for the regulation of that space between the commands of Sovereign and the daily lives of his subjects, but in the sense that these programmes were active elements in debates and practice. For the science of police the construction of a well-ordered political machine and an enlightened administration depended upon a knowledge of the state of the population. On the one hand the population becomes a value to be maximised through its organisation; on the other it becomes a domain to be known and charted through statistics – literally the science of state.[8]

The emergence of population as the object of regulation enabled the generalisation of the knowledges and practices of social police as a new rationale for the arts of government. Mercantilism had attempted to develop a rational practice of government to be utilised by the State but nonetheless took as its instruments the very apparatus of sovereignty which it sought to oppose – laws, decrees, regulations and so forth. Further, the art of government was conceived on the model of the family. Political Oeconomy was a discourse which attempted to apply to a State a mode of government modelled upon that of a household, in particular a royal household. Thus, for Steuart:[9]

> Oeconomy, in general, is the art of providing for all the wants of a family, with prudence and frugality. If any thing necessary or useful be found wanting, if any thing provided be lost or misapplied, if any servant, any animal, be supernumerary or useless, if any one sick or infirm be neglected, we immediately perceive a want of oeconomy. . . . The whole oeconomy must be directed by the head, who is both lord and steward of the family.

A conception of government as oeconomy fails to pose either a shift in the *mechanisms* of government (which it conceives in terms of acts of a sovereign-like statesman), nor in the *object* of political government (which it conceives on the model of the household). It was first of all a transformation of this second element through a change in the conception and status of the population, which enabled the unblocking of the new art of government.

This transformation can be partially understood in terms of the operation of the discourse of statistics. Statistics, the science of state, had been initially conceived as the means of calculation to be deployed by a statesman in the determination of appropriate forms of legislation. Thus Sinclair, in 1791, defines it as enquiries 'respecting the Population, the Political Circumstances, the Productions of a Country and other Matters of State,'[10] and similar positions are advanced in the texts of Conring and Aschenwall in Germany, or the Political Arithmetic of Petty and Davenant in England. These were concerned, in the main, with the means of estimating and comparing the wealth of nations, the contribution to this wealth of the size of population and its division into those pursuing different trades, with problems of the circulation of wealth, of taxation, and of the laws which regulate all these. But these statistics themselves transformed the conception of the population which they studied, gradually revealing:[11]

> that the population had its own regularities, its own rate of death, of diseases, its cycles of scarcity, etc.; statistics shows also that the domain of population carries a range of intrinsic, aggregate effects and that its phenomena, such for instance as the great epidemics, endemic levels of mortality, and the spiral of labour and wealth, are irreducible to those of the family; lastly it shows that, through its displacements, habits, activities, etc., population causes specific economic effects: statistics, in that it makes it possible to quantify the phenomena specific to population, also shows that this specificity is irreducible to the dimension of the family.

But further, it is now this population, its welfare, the condition of its members, the increase of their health, longevity and wealth, which becomes the objective and end of government. Government now seeks to intervene in various ways into these areas, improving health, stimulating births, directing the flow of the population to various localities. These interventions require a knowledge of the immanent laws of this domain, for it is through acting upon them, rather than directly upon the consciousness of subjects, that the new art of government will operate.

If the emergence of the problem of population separated the question of its government from issues of trade, taxation, production and the creation and circulation of wealth, it simultaneously freed these elements for their independent elaboration, for them to become the object of a specific discourse now termed, in the nineteenth century, political economy.[12] This discourse had as its object a realm of the 'economy' in something like its modern sense, but also as something which *does not have to be governed.* The economy, as it began to take shape in the economic discourse of the early nineteenth century, was no longer to be managed like a household; it was no longer the role of the statesman to ensure that there was a proper distribution of labour to different tasks, and proper links and circulation between the different parts. It was a realm which governed itself, in virtue of its *internal* laws and principles, in respect to which the role of legislation is merely to provide the *external* conditions in which it can function. Hence the 'invisible hand' which regulated economic activity could be counterposed to the guiding hand of the statesman.[13]

For political economy labour, not nature, was the source of all wealth. Wealth had, as its necessary and inevitable counterpart, poverty.[14] Poverty was the outcome of differences in condition and an outcome which had considerable utility. It was a spur to those in poverty to better themselves and a warning which helped promote the industriousness of the middle classes. Thus poverty acted, on rich or poor alike, as an economic mechanism regulating the propensity of individuals to engage in labour. It provided a source of labour for the expansion of production, and a space within which such expansion could occur, through the extension of existing needs and the creation of new ones. The relation between poverty and wealth was functional and non-eliminable, and poverty was not an issue for government since it existed internal to the regulated order of the economy. Thus Colquhoun wrote:[15]

> Poverty is therefore a most necessary and indispensable
> ingredient in society without which nations and communities
> could not exist in a state of civilisation. It is the lot of men – it
> is the source of wealth, since without poverty there would be
> no labour, and without labour there could be no riches, no
> refinement, no comfort and no benefit to those who may be
> possessed of wealth. . . .

For most of the nineteenth century inadequacies of income as such, whether caused by low wages, irregular employment or sickness, could form neither a legitimate object of state intervention nor a specific problem for economy theory. No overall imbalance could exist between production and consumption, or between the supply and demand of labour. The aggregate wage fund at any given time was inelastic; if workmen were unable to obtain employment it was simply because they tried to sell their labour at too high a price. Gratuitous assistance to such workmen would therefore merely depress the general level of wages, discourage mobility of labour and encourage reckless procreation incommensurate with the true position of the labourer. Schemes of public employment were similarly futile and dangerous, for they diverted capital from private industry and thereby depleted the wage fund for privately employed workmen. Want of employment was thus either a short-term effect of transfer between jobs, for which workmen should provide out of their earnings whilst employed, or a voluntary condition wilfully incurred by those unwilling to accept the responsibilities of labour.

Pauperism, or indigence, however, was a different matter. It was a problem external to the economy and a proper matter for regulation – for police. The pauper came to represent all those conducts which were anti-social, for pauperism was a rejection of regular employment which meant also an existence outside those benign self-regulating mechanisms of the economy. Hence pauperism stood for vagrancy, promiscuity, improvidence, ignorance, insubordination – a refusal of all those relations which were so essential to a healthy, wealthy and well ordered polity. Here is Colquhoun again:[16]

> mendicity, vagrancy, female prostitution and criminal offences . . . still continue to afflict society. . . . The cause of these evils may be traced principally to one source. There exists in this country nothing in the shape of a systematic superintending police, calculated to check and prevent the growth of vicious habits, and other irregularities incidental to civil society.

The doctrine of police was unable to conceptualise pauperism as engendered by economic conditions. However, despite or rather because of this, it was able to produce a mechanism for the regulation of pauperism, at least as far as the economy was concerned. The New Poor Laws, like the laws of 1601 which they replaced, were thus not concerned with poverty at all – with categories of individuals defined in relation to the necessities of life and so forth. They were concerned with pauperism, as a particular way of conceptualising certain problems of social organisation. The different tendencies and positions within political economy all combined in their view of the Old Poor Laws as self-defeating and a cause of the very problems they sought to solve.[17] Thus Smith

condemned them as interfering with the construction of a free
market through the restrictions which the Laws of Settlement
imposed upon the mobility of labour; Malthus considered
allowances based upon family size to be an encouragement to
improvident marriage and the production of children and hence of
more pauperism; Ricardo considered that what was paid out in
relief was withdrawn from the wage fund and hence reduced
employment and threw more into pauperism. These arguments
underpinned the proposals put forward by Chadwick and Senior
in their famous Report of 1834. The central principle through
which the New Poor Laws were to restore the economy to its free
and automatic functioning was that of 'less eligibility'; it was this
which enabled Chadwick to argue that they were the first great
piece of legislation based upon scientific principles and a great
engine of social improvement. 'Less eligibility' was to solve the
problem of pauperisation, to remove the poor from the operation
of the Poor Law, and to restore the principle of work, by ensuring
that the situation of the pauper was, really or apparently, less
desirable and pleasurable than that of the independent labourer of
the lowest class.[18]

Political economy operated with a definite conception of the
determinants of individual action. The rational calculus of
pleasures and pains most clearly stated by Jeremy Bentham
underlay both its conception of economic activity and the
principle of less eligibility. Nothing specific marked out the
pauper, the criminal or any other from the mass of the people,
apart from those actions to which the operation of this universal
calculus of desires had led them. Whilst the character of those
who stood outside the social order might well have been the
subject of moral or religious criticism, or the target of reformatory
techniques, it did not have a specific status within this discourse. A
reformulation of the problem of population and the objectives and
means of its regulation; a shift in the location and formulation of
the central problem facing government; a new conception of the
determinants of socially unacceptable conduct; a new way of
posing the issue of 'want of employment' – all these would have to
take shape before a psychological conception of individual
pathology could form and play a central role in a strategy of social
regulation.

Hobsbawm writes that 'by the middle of the nineteenth century, government policy in Britain came as near laissez-faire as has ever been practicable in a modern state.'[19] But laissez-faire was not a real state of absence of governmental regulation, it was a definite political doctrine determining the form and objectives which governmental action should take and actually entailed the strengthening of government machinery.[20] However, political economy as a doctrine of government placed definite limits upon the form and extent of social regulation of the conditions of the population in the early decades of the nineteenth century. By the middle of the century the dominance of political economy was displaced as a range of problems for government emerged not in the countryside but in the towns. In this shift of focus, the order of priority of political economy and police was reversed, and the conception of population which was the object of government action was transformed. By the end of the nineteenth century a new and systematic mode of conceptualisation of the social problem was operative, one posed in terms of the danger of urban degeneracy, the key role of casual labour, the rate of reproduction of unemployables and its consequences.

Demoralisation in towns

The emergence of a social theory of urban demoralisation in the mid-nineteenth century has been well documented.[21] The concentration of the lower orders in the heart of the great cities created by industrialisation gradually came to dominate the concerns of politicians, the early social investigators organised in Statistical Societies, philanthropists and the Church. The problem was first posed as one of the loss of moral values engendered by the conditions of existence of this class. It was disease which provided the model for this analysis; to be more precise it was a particular conception of the nature and causes of epidemics. The pathology which threatened this class, and which threatened to spread from them to other sections of society, was engendered by the characteristics of the social space in which they were located, a space in which moral contagion could spread through a kind of pernicious miasma, existing within the milieu and having its deleterious effects upon those forced into contact with it.[22]

The lowest elements attracted into towns by the prospect of easy pickings, and others forced into towns by the necessity of finding work, were concentrated together into large and impenetrable masses, isolated from the beneficent influences of civilisation, losing whatever virtuous habits they might have had and contracting bad ones – intemperance, irreligion, insubordination, prostitution, idleness. In brief, they were subject to *demoralisation*.[23] In these colonies and rookeries, vice and immorality flourished without check, leading to the degradation of the worker and the transmission of these immoral habits to their offspring who were brought up in an overcrowded, insanitary atmosphere, forced at a tender age into contact with sights and experiences of corruption and crime. The solutions proposed in the early decades of the century – the programmes of William Farr, the street clearances schemes, the construction of model dwellings – were conceived in this light. They consisted of grand schemes of social hygiene which attempted to break up these enclaves, to render them accessible to the influences of civilised society and its systems of regulation and police, to disperse these teeming multiplicities, regulate the promiscuous interminglings, eliminate anti-social habits, produce an atmosphere of decency and morality within the home.[24]

But the history of these schemes, whether undertaken by philanthropy, by local administrators, or regulated centrally through legislation, was perceived as one of failure. The street clearances, the model dwellings, the sanitary regulations, whilst they reclaimed a small number of the respectable poor, actually appeared to be exacerbating the demoralisation of those others who, displaced by these very schemes, were forced into even worse conditions of life.[25] It began to be argued that schemes of social hygiene increased overcrowding through large-scale demolition whilst doing nothing to change the situation whereby honest working men, in order to obtain employment, had to reside in the centre of towns. The social problem of the towns gradually came to be posed in terms of employment, and the question of employment and its relation to socially undesirable habits and morals rapidly came to centre upon the issue of casual labour.

For the first time, in the closing decades of the nineteenth century, a conception began to develop of the unemployed as a distinct grouping with specific social characteristics.[26] And the casual labourer assumed a key role in debates about the social problems engendered by want of employment. The work of the Statistical Societies had developed the notion of 'family budgets' in the context of studies of 'the condition of the poor' and had increasingly constructed a systematic link between lack or irregularity of employment and social distress.[27] Mayhew's work in particular drew attention to the large number of families in London dependent on employment which was, to a greater or lesser extent, irregular or occasional, contingent upon particular times, seasons, fashions and accidents.[28] And casual labourers were repeatedly discovered to comprise the vast number of those applying to the various schemes of relief operated over this period.[29] Charles Booth's massive enquiry served to confirm the exemplary status of casual labour in the 'social question', and of casual labourers as the focus of practices of social administration. But in doing so it transformed the status of casual labour and its relation to urban problems. The notion of demoralisation which had lain behind the strategy of social hygiene had no cumulative implications, demoralisation being transmitted to children only through the habits which they formed or failed to form. It was hence remediable given improvements in milieu. But in Booth's work one can see emerging a new conception of demoralisation, as a cumulative process with long-term effects upon the quality of the population as a whole.

Booth operated with a conception of the population as a continuous distribution of individuals with varying characteristics. Thus the eight classes into which he divided the population of London were indications of locations upon a continuum, rather than descriptions of a fixed typology. Four classes constituted together the 35% of the population in poverty: classes D, C, B and A. Class D were the small regular earners, comprising some 14.5% of the population, 'the better end of the casual dock and water-side labour'. Class C were the intermittent earners (8%), 'on them falls with particular severity the weight of recurrent depressions of trade ... here may perhaps be found the most proper field for charitable assistance', provided, of course, that such assistance was conditional upon the thrift of the recipients. Class B were the casual earners, the very poor, making up some 11.25%, 'the ideal of such persons is to work when they like and play when they like; these it is who are rightly called the 'leisure class' among the poor – leisure bounded very closely by the pressure of want, but habitual to the extent of second nature.' The lowest class was class A – estimated at 1.25% but, 'these people are beyond number'. They were the occasional labourers, loafers and semi-criminals, 'their life is the life of savages, with vicissitudes of extreme hardship and occasional excess. . . . They render no useful service, they create no wealth: more often they destroy it. They degrade whatever they touch, and as individuals are perhaps incapable of improvement.'[30]

Booth's 'moralism' was not an idiosyncratic addendum to an otherwise objective set of social categories. Classes were defined and differentiated in terms of an amalgam of individual character and morals, income level and conditions of life. But class was not a fixed attribute of an individual. The level individuals occupied within the continuum of classes was the outcome of an interaction between character and environment, an interaction which was progressive and cumulative – nature of employment affected income which affected conditions of life which affected character, which affected nature of employment and so on – a spiral which could be either virtuous or vicious. And crucially, this spiral acted not only within a single generation but across generations.[31]

The last twenty years of the nineteenth century saw the categories of pauperism and poverty placed in a dynamic relation, and the evils of town life represented as a process; a theory, that is to say, not simply of urban vice but of the progressively deepening decay of the quality of the race. The towns, and London in particular, were acting as foci for a whole system of deterioration, as sinks down whose drains the quality of the population was fast disappearing. The stages were clear: immigration from the country to the towns . . . gradual deterioration over several generations consisting in the weakening of constitution both moral and physical . . . casual labour . . . entry to the lowest class of all, the unemployables. From pamphleteers like Arnold White to administrators like Llewellyn-Smith and economic theorists like Alfred Marshall, the theory of rural immigration and urban deterioration was the principle around which the social question was organised.[32] The result was clear – a gradual deterioration progressively increased the ranks of the lowest of all classes, that class destined to cause the maximum harm to rational life, whose individual members might be short-lived but which the very nature of urban existence was continually providing with new recruits.

Casual labour occupied a crucial place in the spiral of deterioration. Booth wrote, of his Class B, that it was 'not so much one in which men are born and live and die, so much as a deposit of those who from mental, moral and physical reasons are incapable of better work', and whilst the more industrious or capable rise again into Classes C, D or E, those who fail to find regular employment sink down into Class A.[33] Casual labour was thus the site, *par excellence*, of competition and the struggle for survival. It was also situated in the position of a relay, for it operated the critical mediation between the improvable who, through labour and appropriate charitable help, could be morally and industrially regenerated and move back up through the spiral in a reverse direction, and the unimprovable, who were hopeless and worthless – the group that came to be known as the residuum. Casual labour was thus a sort of no-man's-land between the inside and the outside of civilisation, but the current within it pulled almost irresistibly in one direction, spiralling those who entered towards unemployability.

The category of the unemployable thus began to take over from that of the pauper as the condensation of all those anti-social forms of conduct and vices which threatened good order and public tranquillity. 'Unemployable' was a series of forms of conduct, habits, behaviours – vagrancy, crime, prostitution, inebriety – and a series of physical ills and weaknesses – poor eyesight, bad hearing, small size, scrofula, phthisis. These were both the corollary of a certain position in relation to labour, and the outward and visible signs of an inward state of character. In relation to unemployability, *character* was both cause and effect. Cause to the extent that character was the explanation of why certain individuals came to be unemployable; effect to the extent that it was the consequence of dependence upon casual labour, through the effects of the casual labour market and the conditions of life associated with it.[34]

From Booth to Beveridge, the schemes of de-casualisation had as their objective the re-establishment by administrative means of the boundary between the employable and the unemployable. They sought to bring to the former the beneficent and educational discipline of regular employment whilst exposing the latter for the harsh but necessary remedy their condition demanded. Thus Beveridge argued:[35]

> It is essential to maintain the distinction between those who, however irregularly employed, are yet members, though inferior members, of the industrial army and those who are mere parasites, incapable of performing any useful service

whatever. And it is equally important to remember that degradation of character is directly traceable, not to original sin, but to industrial conditions, so that by altering the conditions of employment it is possible to check, in part at least, the supply of 'unemployables'.

The distinction made here was between membership of society and exclusion from it. The employable were to be granted full employment, average earnings, civil liberties, and political power, whilst the unemployable had to be:[36]

removed from free industry and maintained adequately in public institutions, but with the complete and permanent loss of all citizenship rights – including not only the franchise but civil freedom and fatherhood. To those, moreover, if any, who may be born personally efficient but in excess of the number for whom the country can provide, a clear choice will be offered: loss of independence by entering a public institution, emigration or immediate starvation.

There was, however, an important difference between the way in which Booth formulated his proposals for labour colonies and the formulations of Beveridge. For Booth, the rationale of the removal of the casual poor to colonies was that this would do away with the demoralising casual labour market, remove a source of social vice, and eliminate a competitive pressure upon the more respectable and employable poor.[37] Beveridge had added a further imperative – the unemployables were to be denied the right to reproduce. Procreation had become a central element in the way in which the genesis of the social problem was construed. In this shift we can see the signs of the reorganisation of the problem of degeneration in a manner amenable to a eugenic strategy. In this strategy, a conception of individual pathology would be linked with a statistical discourse on the distribution of human abilities in the population, a biological theory of the inheritance of abilities and their transmission across generations, a demonstration of the consequences of the reproductive levels of different social groups and a socio-political analysis of the consequences of the quality or efficiency of the population for the well-being and success of the nation.

In the closing decades of the nineteenth century, the problems of the great cities began to be posed in a different way. The deterioration of their inhabitants was not now seen as a consequence of the effects of conditions of life upon character – profligacy, idleness, intemperance and the absence of religious influences leading to demoralisation. Rather, these forms of anti-social behaviour were seen as the outcome of an inherited unfitness. The danger to the race was not therefore treatable by ameliorating conditions of life – this would only be treating the symptoms. The problem was a consequence of the fact that paupers, criminals and others of the lower moral type were breeding more rapidly than the strong and capable. As White put it:[38]

> Tainted constitutions, brains charged with subtle mischief, and languishing or extinct morality, transmit a terrible inheritance of evil to the next generation, there to taint once more a whole community. And those who multiply as ephemera are the squalid inhabitants of hovels subsisting on degraded and adulterated foods; and acquiring their joys from the gratification of lust, and the absorption in excess of drugged and poisonous forms of alcohol.

The problem, that is to say, was not simply one of demoralisation in towns, but a prospect of the degeneration of the race. And the solution that was suggested had as its central plank the prevention of those with such tainted constitutions from propagating their kind at all, by sterilisation and/or permanent segregation.

Whilst in the late 1880s the analysis and solution proposed by people like White was marginal and idiosyncratic, by the beginning of the twentieth century an extensive and forceful social strategy would be organised in these terms having at its heart the themes of differential reproduction, heredity and degeneracy.

Degeneracy and heredity

In the closing decades of the nineteenth century, medicine, anthropology, criminology and psychological medicine combined in the great project of mapping the domain of degeneracy.[39] In the language of degeneracy, the frankly moral judgments of vice, corruption and social threat were provided with a medicopsychological rationale. The moral categories of debauchery and excess had already found, in moral medicine, a condemnation more scientific than ethical – in terms of their deleterious consequences for an individual's sanity. Now, integrated with a theory of heredity and a concept of constitution, they posed a more extended danger – not merely to oneself, but to one's line of descent and, later, to one's nation itself.

Heredity operated in relation to mental pathology through the transmission of a 'constitution'. Constitution was an organic state which might be strong or weak. It could predispose an individual to certain ills, and this predisposition might or might not manifest itself depending upon the nature of the 'circumstances' in which individuals were reared and lived. By the mid-nineteenth century, the idea that mental pathology had a physiological or organic basis, an origin in a neuropathic constitution, intimately linked to the make-up of the brain and transmissible across generations was well established.[40] It was not that the inventories of causes of insanity disappeared. Rather, they were reworked into a new distribution, according to a division between *predisposing* and *exciting* causes. Inherited weaknesses, lesions or malfunctions in the brain could act as predisposing causes of insanity. Disorders of the blood, of the liver, intoxication and so forth could either directly cause insanity, through producing alterations in the brain, or could weaken the brain thus resulting in a predisposition. Moral depravity, indulgence, excess, intemperance or extremes of emotion could be predisposing causes if they were present in a parent at the time of conception or in the mother whilst the individual was *in utero* or suckling – in these cases they could have their effects through acting on the constitution of the growing child. Similarly bad management when the child was young might be a predisposing cause, by affecting the development of the brain or nervous system. And all the moral excesses familiar from earlier arguments could now be redeployed as *exciting* causes, which could provoke the onset of insanity. Thus although the notion of constitution was deployed in the texts of this period to contest theories of insanity as consisting of an exclusively *moral* disturbance, it nonetheless maintained the essential linkage between madness and immorality.

Discussions of the emergence of this constitutionalist medical psychology point to Gall and Spurzheim's phrenology in the period from about 1800 to 1820, promoted in England by George Combe, which conceived of mental faculties in terms of localised brain functions. They also indicate the rise of pathological anatomy and the use of post-mortem examinations of brains, tissues and blood vessels in those who died insane, and also the development of neurophysiology – especially the work of Carpenter.[41] But the conception of constitution as an organised and systematised nature within each individual which pre-dated and shaped experience was also bound up with a shift in the very object of a science of biology at the end of the eighteenth century. Living beings were now conceived of in terms of their systematic organisation, and it was this systematic relationship amongst organs and functions which was definitive of life and which was doomed to die. The view of living bodies as consisting in a dynamic internal organisation was necessary for the development of a conception of a constitution which could be normal or abnormal, and which had consequences which could be conveyed through heredity. For if organisms functioned according to a plan, and if each generation in its turn was fabricated according to the plan transmitted to it, was re-produced, then deficiencies, variations, malformations in this plan could lead to a variety of pathological consequences in the offspring.

Here too it is possible to locate the conventional acceptance within nineteenth-century biology of the action of the environment upon heredity – the inheritance of acquired characteristics. The plan of organisation could not adapt in and of itself; transformations in it were consequent upon the circumstances of organisms, which produced modifications which were then transmitted to future generations. As Jacob puts it, 'the plasticity of living structures and the flexibility of their mechanisms allow the organism, not to insert itself into the surrounding world, but on the contrary to insert this world gradually into its heredity.'[42]

This underpinned the theory of heredity which was conventional at the beginning of the nineteenth century, and which remained in essence unchallenged until the beginning of the twentieth century.[43] Acquired characteristics could be inherited, so that the events of an individual's life, inscribed upon his or her constitution, could be transmitted to his or her offspring. Heredity was an extended process, beginning with conception and ending only with weaning. Not only the constitution of the parents but also their condition at the moment of conception (inebriety, anxiety . . .) could have a crucial impact upon the child so conceived, as could events which occurred to the mother during pregnancy or whilst suckling the child. These were transmitted to the child via the blood of the mother, or through her milk, and again were permanently installed in the child's constitution despite being only temporarily present in the parent. What was inherited was not a specific condition or attribute but a predisposition, a tendency. Thus pathology was not passed down in the form of discrete or unitary qualities, but in the form of a 'diathesis' which, given the presence of certain exciting causes, could develop into one or other specific form of pathology. Until the last decade of the nineteenth century, and despite the theories of both Galton and Weismann, this form of explanation held sway. It was not until some twenty years after the publication of Weismann's arguments that the distinction between innate and acquired, so natural to us today, began to establish itself in theoretical, let alone popular, discourse.

The idea of organisation as the object of a science of biology was intimately linked to that of history. During the eighteenth century, and thus, of course, long before Darwin, time began to introduce itself into the living world. Firstly in the notion of cataclysm, notably developed by Buffon. Later, in the writings of Bonnet and Robinet, the conception of a single chain of order, of progression, a translation of all living things from the simple towards the complex. With Lamarck, however, it was organisation as a whole which became subject to progressive transformation and which had the capacity to transform itself. All living beings could now be linked into a single history describing their generation one from another. Time became one of the main operative factors in the living world but, for Lamarck, the mode of its operation was teleological – earlier meant simpler and simpler meant less perfect. Thus one had a continuum of beings from less to more perfect, and hence the possibility of living beings being more or less advanced along it – time had inscribed itself within the very structure of creatures. Variations in that structure could thus be represented as regressions down this continuum, variations destroying perfection, organisation and complexity. It was the combination of a notion of organisation, a theory of heredity and an axis of temporality which made a theory of degeneracy possible.[44]

It was first of all in France that such a theory was formulated, in the writings of Lucas, Moreau de Tours and, principally, Morel.[45] Morel defined degenerations as deviations from normal human type which were transmissible by heredity and which deteriorated progressively towards extinction. The causes of degeneracy were heterogeneous. According to Morel, degenerations could be caused by (a) intoxication (malaria, alcohol, opium, soil conducive to cretinism, epidemics, food poisoning), (b) the social milieu, (c) pathological temperament, (d) moral sickness, (e) inborn or acquired damage, (f) heredity. However, once acquired, and however acquired, the condition was hereditarily transmitted. What was transmitted was not a specific condition. Degeneracy theories unified all pathologies as deviations, and of all deviations as degeneracies – anxiety, alcoholism, idiocy, mania, melancholia were all forms of degeneracy. Further, it conceived of the individual as a unified organism, all parts of whose structure and functioning expressed the degeneracy. Thus degeneration was not confined to one particular behaviour or function; one could observe the degree of degeneracy alike in all aspects of the individual – head shape, facial features, body make-up, comportment, voice – all these both manifested degeneracy and were stigmata of degeneracy. Hence the presence of a degenerate constitution could be read on the surface of the body. The form in which degeneracy was expressed in any one generation was not constrained by its form in the preceding generation – mania in one generation could be cretinism in the next and so forth. But since degeneration was subject to the law of progressivity, it would tend, across generations, to the extinction of the degenerate line. The first generation in a degenerate family history might thus perhaps show simple nervousness, the second might show neurosis, the third psychosis, the fourth idiocy, with no fifth generation being conceived.

By the second half of the nineteenth century there was a firm scientific foundation for the conception of degeneracy that was deployed in social and political debate. It was backed by a set of accepted theoretical arguments and was linked to an established body of empirical evidence and clinical observation. The notion of degeneracy gave the issue of hereditary predispositions a new social pertinence. In the first half of the nineteenth century, the links between mental pathology and social pathology were contingent and residual. Burrows, for example, in 1828, accepted that a hereditary predisposition could manifest itself almost interchangeably in a range of pathologies, but did not suggest any systematic link between these pathologies and the social problems of pauperism, criminality or vice.[46] Bucknill and Tuke, thirty years later, accepted the notion of a heredity which might be manifested in intemperance or excited by it, but the immorality of the behaviour *per se* was pertinent only for its diagnostic or aetiological utility.[47] Similarly, Duncan and Millard discussed the question of pauper idiots, but without any suggestion that the one aspect was linked to the other, or that a congenital disposition to idiocy had any significance in relation to pauperism.[48]

But from about 1860 onwards, degeneracy began to provide the means of posing a whole range of questions concerning social and mental pathology. The spiral of urban deterioration, and the inter-relations of character and conditions of life, began to be conceived in terms of the ways in which the former was an effect of, and the latter had consequences for, a heritable *constitution*. For although degeneracy arguments maintained, indeed required, the view that acquired characteristics could be inherited, the priority of heredity over circumstances was absolute. Whilst writers disagreed over the inevitability with which an inherited degenerate constitution would express itself, and hence over the importance of careful early diagnosis and nurture of those suspected of carrying the taint, there was no doubt that the neuropathic constitution, once established, could not be overruled by environment, but only provoked or exacerbated to a greater or lesser extent. Heredity, the constitution which is inherited, now began to be seen as circumscribing the possible effects of circumstances or education – these could develop or not develop aspects of constitution, but could not produce results outside the boundaries set by heredity.

Further, degeneration itself owed its cumulative character to a number of features, two of which are especially significant. The first was the undoubted tendency of those with a neuropathic constitution to intermarry. Whilst authors tended to demonstrate this empirically, through the presentation of family histories, rather than to explain it theoretically, its consequences were very clear: that in each subsequent generation the degree of inherited taint was increased due to the contributions of degenerate heredity from both mother and father. This was a fact which was destined to have important social implications.

The second reason for the cumulative nature of degeneracy lay in the consequences of a degenerate or neuropathic constitution for the conduct of the neuropath's life, and the fact that the influence of life circumstances upon constitution was in one direction only. Since neuropaths would undoubtedly be led into various unsavoury and immoral forms of life, and since the influence of experience could only be to increase, never to reduce, the degree of hereditary taint, the inheritance of acquired characteristics would necessarily lead down the spiral path of degeneration. The moral faults of individuals, even when they produced no immediate damage to others – lone alcoholism or, in particular, masturbation – were no longer simply 'solitary vices' which merely influenced the moral status of the individual concerned. They had the gravest consequences for the remainder of his or her life and for the lives of future generations. Degeneracy was thus a principle which could operate both upon an individual's life history and across generations, and these two factors were reciprocally linked and mutually reinforcing. The translation of moral condemnation from the domain of ethics to that of science was thus not a distortion or corruption of such a theoretical discourse – it was constitutive of it.

The notion that the behaviour, speech, appearance and comportment of the body form a unified field of expression of a degenerate constitution was the condition for the reverse movement which would be of such importance within this form of explanation. Here, these visible elements became the identifiable stigmata in which degeneracy was marked clearly on the body of its victim, and which those versed in the language of the body could utilise in their diagnoses. Hence the significance of the appearance of the body, not only in the criminal anthropology of Lombroso, but also in all those illustrations of different degenerate types which were liberally and dolefully distributed through the textbooks of the day. The need for a psychological technology of individual differences would arise, in part, from a questioning of this possibility of reading internal states from outward appearances.

A whole range of anti-social behaviours, from vice and debauchery, through indigence and crime, to idiocy and insanity could now form the object of a unified system of explanation.[49] In France there was a general acceptance of degeneracy theories in medical psychology;[50] in England the position was more complex. However, hereditarian and organicist theories of mental pathology were dominant in the last decades of the nineteenth century, and the therapeutic optimism associated with moral treatment was overturned. Henry Maudsley, the most notable English proponent of the theory of degeneracy, limited the effects of environment to those of causing organic damage to the brain or nervous system, although allowing that these could sometimes occur at conception, during gestation, or in the early years when the system was delicate and susceptible. But in as many as three cases out of four, insanity was the product of an inherited constitutional predisposition, whose effects could not be escaped although they might be mitigated by the inculcation of correct moral habits and the avoidance of all those forms of excess which might occasion the onset of insanity.[51]

Degeneracy introduced the dimension of temporary into problems of mental and social pathology. Pathological constitutions were inherited, they might show themselves in any one of a number of disorders of body, mind or conduct and, for all the reasons discussed above, there was a cumulative worsening of the condition from generation to generation. But the crucial point was that the family history ended in sterility – *degeneracy was self-limiting*. Thus Maudsley argued that degeneracy 'will go on increasing from generation to generation and end finally in the extreme degeneration of idiocy. With the occurrence of idiocy there is happily the extinction of the degenerate variety, for with it come impotence and sterility.'[52] The theory of degeneracy, as it developed from Morel to Maudsley, appeared to ensure that no deleterious evolutionary consequences could flow from progressive deterioration – indeed the whole process could be conceived as a beneficial way of eliminating unhealthy variations. Thus whilst degeneration was cumulative along any particular line, its effects on the make up of the population as a whole were not a significant matter for discussion, for the consequence of the passage of generations was to prevent breeding from the degenerate variety.

At the end of the nineteenth century, there was a radical shift in the way in which the link between constitution, reproduction and inheritance was posed. This reversed the argument concerning breeding and degeneracy, claiming that those with pathological constitutions reproduced at a greater rate than others. Hence it also reversed the link between family histories and population characteristics – we see not the elimination of the degenerate variety but its proliferation. In the science of eugenics, first formulated by Francis Galton, a new set of connections were made between individual character and its hereditary determinants, the ills of modern existence and a set of proposals for government regulation of the population. The psychology of the individual was born in a new way of conceptualising the population and its variations, and a new way of evaluating the consequences of hereditary transmission across generations.

3
Heredity versus environment

In the earlier stages of civilisation natural selection and competition caused those who were strongest and most vigorous to leave the largest progeny behind them. It is to this cause, more than any other, that the progress of human life, as of all other forms of life, is largely due. . . . [But] there are increasing reasons for fearing, that while the progress of medical science and sanitation are saving from death a continually increasing number of the children of those who are feeble physically and mentally, those who are strong are tending to defer their marriages and in other ways to limit the number of children whom they leave behind. . . . Considering the causes that determine the supply of vigour, we must affirm with Mr. Galton that if the doctrine were to be acted on generally by the upper part of the nation including the great body of the more intelligent and capable artisans, but not the lowest classes, it would cause the race to decay.

Alfred Marshall, 1890[1]

The eugenic strategy in which a psychology of the individual, and a specifically psychological conception of individual pathology, took shape at the end of the nineteenth century entailed a new systematisation of the linkage between the capacities of individuals and the quality and fate of populations and a transformation in theories of degeneration. It was made possible by a reformulation of conceptions of population, variation and norm, which the writings of Francis Galton demonstrate most clearly.

Population and norm

> Eugenics is the science of improving stock, which is by no
> means confined to judicious mating, but which, especially in the
> case of man, takes cognisance of all influences that tend in
> however remote a degree to give the more suitable races or
> strains of blood a better chance of prevailing speedily over the
> less suitable than they otherwise would have had.
>
> Francis Galton, 1883[2]

Galton made no secret of the implications of his study of the
family trees of four hundred eminent men when his *Hereditary
Genius* was first published in 1869. By the time of its second
edition, in 1892, the programmatic aspirations of the text were
absolutely explicit: its object was to demonstrate that the standard
of the human race could be improved by political action which
encouraged those evolutionary developments leading to the good,
and discouraged those leading to the bad.[3] What Darwin revealed
of the blind forces that guided the evolution of man from the ape
need not be a sign of despair or resignation in the face of the
inexorable laws of nature – on the contrary, in recognising these
laws we could become their masters. Galton opened his *Inquiries
into Human Faculty and its Development* thus:[4]

> My general object has been to take note of the varied
> hereditary faculties of different men, and of the great
> differences in different families and races, to learn how far
> history may have shown the practicability of supplanting
> inefficient human stock by better strains, and to consider
> whether it might not be our duty to do so by such efforts as
> may be reasonable, thus exerting ourself to further the ends of
> evolution more rapidly and with less distress than if events
> were left to their own course.

The possibility of directing evolution by means of scientific
knowledge lay in Darwin's reformulation of the relations between
individual variation, inter-generational transmission and the
characteristics of populations. This linked the hereditary transmission of variable characteristics, the laws of variation within a
population and the effects of selective reproductive advantage. It
was this combination which gave a new political salience to the
question of individual differences, and allowed the reintegration of

existing conceptions of pathological individuals into a systematic account of the nature and importance of the distribution of varieties and degrees of pathology within the population. The Darwinian theory of evolution established the theoretical centrality of reproduction upon which eugenics was to depend for its politics. It allowed Galton to reformulate the hereditarian theory which underpinned degeneracy arguments. There was now no need to propose the inheritance of acquired characteristics in order to give a political pertinence to the inheritance of constitution. This is because, for Galton, what degenerated was not individuals or family lines but *the population as a whole*. Social danger was no longer conceived in terms of the progressive degeneration of a lineage. Such degeneration was idiosyncratic and variable; it led to the extinction of that line, and hence the elimination of the social danger it posed, without the necessity of administrative intervention. From Galton onwards it was rather the quality of the population as a whole which was threatened by the reproduction of those with defective constitutions. The individual degenerate now achieved his or her social and political significance from the point of view of the population of individuals of which they formed a part. This enabled Galton to argue for the threat posed by individuals, without being concerned with the effects of life history upon that which is passed to progeny, for the degeneration of a population could occur simply as a consequence of the inheritance of constitution and the differential reproductive rates correlated with different constitutions.

Eugenics operated with a conception of the population which was *statistical* in both its original and its modern senses. François Jacob has pointed out that Darwin had a statistical conception of population 'because variations only express the fluctuations of distributions inherent in every system; [and] because selection acts only by slowly altering population equilibria through the random interaction of individuals and their environment'.[5] Galton's arguments depended upon the possibility of analysing the evolution of populations in terms of the laws governing large numbers. Central terms of these analyses were those of population and norm. *Population* was a bounded field within which a multiplicity of individual elements were regulated according to a law which was neither biological nor cultural but mathematical. Thus Galton wrote 'The science of heredity is concerned with

Fraternities and large Populations rather than with individuals, and must treat them as units.'[6] The possibility of grasping the characteristics of such a population was provided by the concept of *norm*. Norm was that central point which, in virtue of the probability of deviations from it and their magnitude, allowed the statistical conceptualisation of populations in terms of the regular distribution of variations. The concept of the norm thus made possible the formulation of the law of frequency of error, of which Galton wrote:[7]

> I know of scarcely anything so apt to impress the imagination as the wonderful form of cosmic order expressed by the 'Law of Frequency of Error'. . . . The huger the mob and the greater the apparent anarchy, the more perfect its sway.

Population

> The most radical transformation of the biological attitude wrought by Darwin was to focus attention, not on the individual organisms, but on large populations.[8]

Both Darwin and Wallace attribute their conception of population to Malthus's 1798 *Essay on the Principle of Population*, yet it is well known that the implications which they drew from it radically transformed the Malthusian schema. The model which Malthus proposed depended upon an opposition between the growth of a population and the limits of the environment. The population was a unitary object located upon a geographical terrain which imposed environmental constraints as a conservative force – Malthus having written the *Essay* partly against Godwin and Condorcet and the philosophers of progress.[9] The *characteristics* of the population were not a central concern for Malthus; hence his weakness in Galton's eyes was precisely his failure to take account of the effects of population limitation upon variation and selection of characteristics across generations.[10] It is this question which became crucial in the writings of Darwin and Wallace. They introduced the conception of a systematic relationship between particular environmental limits and species characteristics. Hence speciation and change became possible, given only the possibility of variations which conferred selective reproductive advantage upon their bearers, and the conservation of these variations in the offspring through some unspecified mechanism of inheritance. Three points concerning this new conception of population are relevant for our analysis.

Firstly, the new notion of species. For Darwin, the term species was one 'arbitrarily given for the sake of convenience to a set of individuals closely resembling each other'.[11] In the classical morphology of Cuvier, species were a fixed type, defined according to a given and invariable set of characteristics. Within such a fixed classification, both the nature of, and the relations between, species were established once and for all; variations between individuals of the same species had no pertinence. After Darwin, species were constituted not in the resemblances of individuals to an invariable type, but in terms of the relations which existed between individuals within a population. A species, for Darwin, was a differentiated unity of interbreeding individuals. This population of individuals was no longer merely an expression, more or less perfect, of an essential type; its characteristics were nothing over and above the sum of its individual parts. The transformations which might occur in populations and species could thus be understood in terms of the same concepts as those used to characterise the population itself in its stability without invoking special processes or events. Differentiation was now merely the extended product of internal variability, fixed not *a priori* but in space and time. Within this mode of conceptualisation, therefore, Darwin had established a systematic relationship between population, variation and individualisation.

Secondly, a new pertinence was accorded to the constraints of environment in relation to these variations amongst individuals in a population. Variations conferred upon individuals' different degrees of 'fitness' for particular environmental conditions, and these had consequences in terms of the survival and reproductive abilities of those individuals:[12]

> as more individuals are produced than can possibly survive,
> there must in every case be a struggle for existence, either one
> individual with another of the same species, or with the
> individuals of another species, or with the physical conditions
> of life.

Populations were under constant pressure of competition for

survival and for reproduction – the survival of a species over time depended upon its ability to maintain an adequate rate of reproduction in the conditions which obtained, and those conditions included other species with which it was in competition. But, additionally, the characteristics of the species which did survive depended upon the differential reproductive success of its different members and the particular combination of variable characteristics which they manifested and passed to their offspring.

Two important axes were thus opened up for investigation. On the one hand, there were the effects of variation internal to a population upon the characteristics of the population as a whole in future generations. On the other hand, there were the consequences of the make-up of the populations upon its external relations with those other populations with which it came into competition. Population thus came to signify an organic unity of constituent individuals each of which contributed to the average characteristics of the whole, and the mean around which it varied. Population was not merely the sum of its parts but the effect of the differential nature and relations of its members. Not a type and its realisations but a unity of differentiated individuals.

Thirdly, a new significance was given to the individual within this conception of the population. Darwin asserted that 'individual differences are highly important for us, as they afford materials for natural selection to accumulate.'[13] The new biological attention focused upon the population, far from eliminating the question of the individual from the domain of evolutionary theory, precisely created the individual in its variability as a salient object for such a theory. The relationship between populations and individuals was an integral one – variation only happened in individuals, it had evolutionary effects only through populations: individual variation thus achieved its importance *from the point of view of the population*. Darwin's conception of normal and inevitable small variations between individuals entailed a notion of the grouping of such variations around a population average – it was the location of this average which was shifted by the differential reproductive advantages which variation might produce. The relation between individual variation and population averages allowed the possibility of an evolutionary schema being constructed in terms of population statistics; it was precisely upon this possibility that Galton's eugenic strategy would operate.

Norm

> The whole theory of evolution is based on the laws of large numbers.[14]

In his *Inquiries into Human Faculty* Galton began to construct the alliance between individual variation and population characteristics that provided the possibility for a rigorous systematisation of a theory of the distribution of human abilities:[15]

> The object of statistical science is to discover methods of condensing information concerning large groups of allied facts into brief and compendious expressions suitable for discussion. The possibility of doing this is based on the constancy and continuity with which objects of the same species vary.

If we were to be able to exercise control over the apparently random, yet evolutionarily crucial, processes of individual variation within a species, we had first to be able to grasp them, to conceptualise them in order to be able to operate upon them. Fortunately, since the time of Quetelet, it had been known that certain statistical propositions could bring variability within the grasp of scientific laws. And, Galton argued, the laws of chance applied to variability both outside and within the human sphere.[16] It is these laws which Galton proposed to develop and adapt to the purposes of analysis of evolution.

For Galton, the conception of species which Darwin developed shared the same properties as other species:[17]

> A species may be defined as a group of objects whose individual differences are wholly due to different combinations of the same set of minute causes, no one of which is so powerful to be able by itself to make any sensible difference in the result.

We see here, incidentally, that it was Galton's statistics rather than his biology or his desire to remain loyal to Darwin that produced his allegiance, and that of his followers, to biometrics rather than Mendelianism. Within any species, whilst variations for any individual may be random, the incidence of variation in a population is systematic, and may be plotted as a smooth curve – the ogive, or 'normal curve'. Thus chance becomes amenable to the formulation of a scientific law:[18]

We can lay down the ogive of any quality, physical or mental,
whenever we are capable of judging which of any two members
of the group we are engaged upon has the larger amount of
that quality. . . . There is no bodily or mental attribute of any
race of individuals that cannot be so dealt with, whether our
judgment in comparing them be guided by common-sense
observation or by actual measurement, which cannot be
gripped and consolidated into an ogive with a smooth outline,
and thence forward be treated in discussion as a single object.

If this thesis of continuity and regularity delivered up the
variability of population to the regularity of scientific knowledge,
it was the norm – the average amount of a quality – which
allowed the formulation of the laws of this variation, and hence
the organisation of all the features of human ability within a single
conceptual space. For the relationship between average and
deviation was the foundation of the theory of normal distribution
and the basis of the power of the normal curve:[19]

An average is but a solitary fact, whereas if a single other fact
be added to it, an entire Normal Scheme, which nearly
corresponds to the observed one, starts potentially into
existence.

It is this normal curve which would provide eugenic discourse
with one of the crucial theoretical conditions of possibility for its
strategy, and which would be central for the emergence of a
science of mental measurement. It was the norm which allowed
that 'gripping' of the population in thought which Galton desired,
and hence the formulation of a systematic relationship between
the four terms – population, norm, individual, deviation – which
regulated the theoretical field of eugenics. From its inception this
argument derived norms of psychological functioning not from an
investigation of its object – the human mind and its laws of
functioning – but from a question of differentiation – the measuring of degrees of variation. And variation, like normativity itself,
was conceived not in psychological but in statistical terms – or
rather, the terms of psychological analysis of variation in
populations were derived from statistical principles concerning the
laws of variation in large numbers. The psychology of the
individual was formed through this linkage betwen norms of
different orders, but, as we shall see, such a mode of conceptual-

isation inscribed the limits of such a psychology at the very heart of its theoretical system.

This conceptual structure enabled a reformulation of both the social and the psychological theories of degeneracy, within a strategy in which the question of individual constitution was linked to that of social worth and the consequences of differential reproduction. Not so much a new question, as a new way of posing the question of degeneracy.

Genealogy

If Galton could regard his statistical discoveries as having programmatic consequences, this was because they were immediately deployed within a field of social analysis whose organisation predated them, and with which we are already familiar: that of ability and nobility, of ancestry and lineage, of stock and constitution. In *Hereditary Genius* Galton sought to establish the variations in intellectual capacity in the population. Having considered briefly such varied evidence as the attainment of mathematical honours at Cambridge, the memory of Lord Macaulay and Séguin's experience with idiots, he concluded:[20]

> The range of powers between – I will not say the highest
> Caucasian and the lowest savage – but between the greatest
> and least of English intellects, is enormous. There is a
> continuity of natural ability reaching from one knows not what
> height and descending to one can hardly say what depth. I
> propose in this chapter to range men according to their natural
> abilities, putting them into classes separated by equal degrees of
> merit, and to show the relative number of individuals included
> in the several classes. Perhaps some person may be inclined to
> make an offhand guess that the number of men included in the
> several classes would be pretty equal. If he thinks so, I can
> assure him he is most egregiously mistaken.
>
>   The method I shall employ for discovering all this is an
> application of the very curious theoretical law of 'deviation
> from the average'.

Not *between* two populations, but within a single population there were huge differences in the degree to which individuals possessed intellectual ability – the majority falling into the classes near to the norm, fewer and fewer into the classes further from this average, both above it and below it. In other words, intellectual ability was distributed according to the laws of the normal scheme and could be analysed in terms of its statistical principles.[21] And in two further operations the possibility would be established for this 'fact' to be inserted at the very heart of contemporary debate on the 'social question' – first the rigorous formulation of the relation between ability and heredity, and the second the unification of ability as both the expression of a biological origin and the clearest index of social worth.

The principal task of *Hereditary Genius* was to show that the distribution and inheritance of intellectual ability followed the same laws as any other continuously varying ability – intellectual ability was transmitted and distributed according to the law of ancestral heredity. This law was Galton's formulation in mathematical terms of the Darwinian thesis of continuous variation and blending inheritance.[22] For Darwin and Galton, as we have seen, a population was a group of interbreeding individuals whose characteristics varied by small degrees; the character of any offspring was a result of the blending of the characters of its parents. Galton demonstrated, on the basis of these premises, that a child would receive one half of its nature from the parental generation, one quarter from the grandparents and so on, the contribution of each generation decreasing in geometric ratio. Continuous variation and blending of inheritance were, for Galton, necessary if the nature and effects of inheritance were to be graspable through statistics. And the law of ancestral heredity was to define the opposition between biometricians and Mendelians in the first decade of the twentieth century. Pearson, who mathematically refined the law, regarded it as one of equivalent status to those formulated by Newton:[23]

> If Darwinian evolution be natural selection combined with *heredity*, then the law must prove almost as epoch making to the biologist as the law of gravitation to the astronomer.

But despite Pearson's acrimonious opposition to the Mendelians, the law, for him, was purely mathematical – as a positivist Pearson refused to refer it to any ontological foundation. But Galton, despite some equivocation, did provide such an ontological status for the law, a grounding in a biological notion of 'stock'.

Galton had used the term 'stirp' for his earliest conception of a reproductively transmitted biological stock which was expressed in all the characteristics of the individual and which remained unaffected by environmental influences during the life of the organism. Darwin, in common with the hereditary theories we have already examined, did not rule out 'Lamarck' type explanations of the effects of use and disuse and on the inheritance of acquired characteristics, despite the fact that he accorded the major source of variation to the combinations effected during the process of reproduction. Indeed, as the evidence against the theory of natural selection mounted, Darwin attributed a greater role to such influences, and his particulate theory of pangenesis expressly allowed for them through the transmission of somatic information via particles to the germ cells.[24]

Galton also advocated a particulate form of inheritance, but argued that the particles were laid down in the ovum immediately after fertilisation, and were thus unaffected by circumstances that befell the organism during its life.[25] However in another respect Galton remained much closer to prevailing theories than Darwin. Where Darwin was concerned with the inheritance of discrete characteristics, Galton was concerned with the inheritance of stock – a term allied to the familiar notion of constitution. Stock – familiar to both breeders of horses and readers of Debretts – referred not to this or that characteristic, but to the general *quality* of a particular line of descent. Thus Galton, by forging a linkage between stock, ancestral heredity and the normal distribution of intellectual abilities, effected a kind of transformation of quality into quantity. In this transformation, the quantity of intellectual ability was both expression and index of the quality of all the faculties, both mental and physical, the surest sign of the state of constitution, indeed the measure of vital energy itself:[26]

> Energy is the capacity for labour. It is consistent with all the robust virtues. . . . It is the measure of fullness of life; the more energy, the more abundance of it; no energy at all is death; idiots are feeble and listless. . . . Energy is an attribute of the higher races, being favoured beyond all other qualities by natural selection. . . . In any scheme of eugenics, energy is the most important quality to favour; it is, as we have seen, the basis of living action, and it is eminently transmissible.

Thus good stock was allied with vigour, and became the principle object of both natural and artificial selection. And, for Galton, the wretched figures – crippled, blind, sick, paupers, lunatics, idiots, criminals – existing in such large proportions in the heart of our great cities were precisely those who manifested that weakness of vital energy which was the sure sign of a degenerate constitution.[27] Galton shared the earlier conception of degeneracy as a single constitutional essence, differentially expressed, transmissible across generations.[28] But this was placed within a rigorous conception of population, and, crucially, the role of reproduction was reformulated. What degenerated for Galton was not so much an individual or a line, but a population, in terms of the capacities of the individuals who made it up and their distribution around a norm. And what was thus the cause of alarm was the differential reproductive success of individuals with different capacities, different quality of stock. Eugenic politics would operate on the insight so lucidly expressed by Arnold White in 1886:[29]

> Criminals and pauperised classes with low cerebral
> development renew their race more rapidly than those of higher
> nervous natures. Statesmen stand idly by. . . . Dynasties of
> criminals and paupers hand down from generation to
> generation hereditary unfitness for the arts of progress and all
> that brings greatness to a nation, and engage themselves in a
> warring against all forms of moral order. . . .

Galton's Huxley Lecture to the Anthropological Institute, delivered in October 1901, will provide us with a model for the systematic relationship between notions of population, variation and norm, conceptions of human heredity and the problem of urban degeneracy which constituted the eugenic strategy.[30] Recall the way in which Charles Booth distributed the population into classes. Galton began his lecture by suggesting that this distribution, and the numbers in each class, followed precisely the pattern which would be predicted by the Normal Law of Frequency. He then demonstrated that by ordering these findings around the norm and applying the law of probable error, what he termed 'civic worth' could be seen to conform to the distribution expected of any other inherited trait. 'Civic worth' could thus be seen to be a further way in which a hered, table stock or constitution expressed itself, and so the inheritance of such a trait could be understood in terms of the theory of blending inheritance and the law of ancestral heredity. Once the situation was thus clarified, the appropriate conclusions became self-evident.

The improvement of human stock, in terms of civic worth, was possible, because the laws according to which it was distributed in the population and inherited across generations were understood. Conscious control must therefore be directed, first of all, to improving and encouraging the rate of breeding of the best stock, through the award of diplomas of civic worth entitling the holders to special privileges, through patronage by noble families, through provision of cheap houses and so forth. For 'The possibility of improving the race of a nation depends on the power of increasing the productivity of the best stock.'[31] But it was not only measures of this kind, 'positive eugenics', that were called for; so too was 'negative eugenics' to prevent the breeding of the lowest classes – Booth's classes A and B:[32]

> Many who are familiar with the habits of these people do not
> hesitate to say that it would be an economy and a great benefit
> to the country if all habitual criminals were resolutely
> segregated under merciful surveillance and peremptorily denied
> opportunities for producing offspring. It would abolish a
> source of suffering and misery to a future generation, and
> would cause no suffering in this.

The relation between population, variation and norm thus allowed Galton to link heredity and degeneracy in a rigorous statistical relationship, mapping a distribution formed through an alliance between economics and morality on to a distribution constructed according to the natural laws of large numbers. It is thus not surprising that Galton, in 1907, was able to deliver a lecture entitled 'Probability, the foundation of eugenics' in which the first half was devoted to a calculation of the degrees of mischief which were associated with classes of persons afflicted with specific degrees of degeneracy, in order to examine the justification for taking drastic action against their propagation; the second half to an exposition of the means of statistical computation of variability, medians, standard deviations, binomial series, indices of correlation and normal curves.[33] For the eugenicist strategy depended upon the use of the terms of population, norm, deviation and distribution, as a kind of relay between a theory of population statistics and a practice of population regulation. At one and the same time, eugenics elaborated a theory of population variation, a means of its calculation and a programme for the utilisation of this knowledge within a systematic technology of social administration. Thus Galton was able to conclude his Huxley Lecture with the confidence of a man who has grasped at last the key to a political arithmetic:[34]

> The faculties of future generations will be distributed according to the laws of heredity, whose statistical effects are no longer vague, for they are measured and expressed in formulae. We cannot doubt the existence of a great power ready to hand and capable of being directed with vast benefit as soon as we shall have learnt to understand and apply it.

Galton's eugenic programme was, of course, merely an ideal schema, and one that, to all accounts, was ill-received for some three decades after its initial formulation.[35] Despite its homology with the contemporary concern with urban degeneration, it might have remained merely an idiosyncratic diversion were it not for a displacement in the formation of the social question which was, for perhaps two decades, to bring to the fore the questions of efficiency and deficiency, to focus social concern upon the dangers posed to society by mental deficiency and to allow the formation of the discourse of individual psychology around the question of mental measurement.

Efficiency and deficiency

Social historians agree that eugenics took off as a political doctrine in the first decade of the twentieth century. Its terminology was utilised in the formulation of political arguments on a range of issues and from a variety of political positions; it was given an institutional form in the emergence of societies, journals and research laboratories; many leading politicians and intellectuals, especially radicals and socialists, were associated with eugenics in various capacities.[36] There has indeed in the secondary literature been a tendency to overestimate the degree of unity which this eugenic language implied, to succumb to the fascination of the rhetoric and the proliferation of the texts, and to find it difficult to explain the limited impact which the 'eugenics movement' had on the policies of government during this period. The tendency of much of this analysis has been to scrutinise the backgrounds of those involved, in order to reveal behind their beliefs and statements the cognitive interests which motivated them and the social interests which lay behind them.[37] Our concern is rather different – it is not with eugenics *per se* but with the social and theoretical conditions which made the eugenic strategy both possible and significant.

We have already seen that 'population' can become an object of political concern and governmental policy in a number of distinct ways, and with different consequences. In debates in the seventeenth and eighteenth centuries, the central point concerned the link between the size of the population and the wealth and power of the state.[38] In the seventeenth century, the principal theme was that the state should be concerned about the size of the population, and encourage growth in numbers which would inevitably increase its wealth. Thus Child wrote that 'whatever leads to the depopulating of a country leads to the impoverishment of it', and that 'most nations in the civilised parts of the world are more or less rich or poor according to the paucity or plenty of their people, and not the sterility or fruitfulness of their land.'[39] It was this link between population and wealth which placed demography at the heart of the political arithmetic of Graunt, Petty, Davenant and King.[40] In the eighteenth century the question began to be posed as to whether a limit existed beyond which further increases in the size of the population would create misery. Thus Turgot argued that a point was reached where 'the employer, since he always has his choice of a great number of working men, will choose that one who will work most cheaply,' with the result that 'the wages of the worker are limited to that which is necessary to procure his subsistence.'[41] And Malthus, as has been discussed, posed the question in a similar way when he formulated the principle of natural limits in terms of the contradiction between a geometrical increase in population size and an arithmetical increase in food supply.[42]

At the turn of the nineteenth and twentieth centuries, the problem of population was formulated in a new way. Where the old problematic of population had as its object the maintenance of a certain equilibrium in the relations between states, a link was now forged between population and a competitive struggle between states. And whilst the old problematic concerned population as a homogeneity, questions now concerned the variability of the population and its consequences. A different connection was constructed between external relations amongst states and the internal organisation of states. In the discourse of 'imperialism' this connection was construed in Darwinian language although the meaning of terms such as 'struggle for existence' and 'survival of the fittest' owed little to the theory of natural selection. Fitness was as a single dimension upon which nations and individuals might be ranked. The term in which fitness was conceived was *efficiency*.

A recent study of this period has argued that the term 'efficiency' structured the field of debate on diverse questions of government, industry, social organisation and individual welfare.[43] Efficiency should be seen not as a category of explanation imposed from outside, nor as a hidden principle governing many discourses, nor as a single concept utilised in many domains in a consistent manner. It functioned in rather a different way. It conferred a kind of regularity on the discourses of this period not because of the coherence of its meaning but precisely because of the variability which it permitted. Its ability to function metaphorically in a range of distinct formulations served as a principle of integration at the same time as its diverse significations permitted the organisation of controversy. In the present context what is pertinent to draw out is the sense in which efficiency can be seen as indexing a particular reformulation of concern with the population.

Those who advocated a policy of imperialism, from polemicists like White, through eugenicists like Pearson, to Fabians like Shaw and Tariff Reformers like Chamberlain, tended to write of the major form of international conflict in terms of a struggle between a number of great states.[44] This was a struggle for survival, a dynamic process of competition for scarce resources, in which the fittest would survive and the weakest would go to the wall.[45] In this type of argument a crucial relation was forged between success in the imperialist struggle abroad and continuing and expanding prosperity at home. In Lenin's analysis of the connection between imperialism and the corruption of sections of the working class, in the writings of the Austro-Marxists like Renner and Hilferding, in Chamberlain's speeches throughout England on the question of tariff reform, nations were seen to be engaged in an *external* struggle whose outcome was determined by their *internal* fitness.[46]

Internal fitness determined the outcome of external competition; internal fitness was a matter of efficiency. Efficiency of individuals, efficiency of business, efficiency of the armed forces, efficiency of administration and government, efficiency of the nation as a whole. If Britain had declined as a world power, this could now be understood in terms of the relative inefficiency of her industrial and social arrangements, and of her population, in relation to her competitors.[47] The débâcle of the British performance in the Boer War provided a prime example of the dependence of external success upon the internal efficiency of the nation. Arnold White's account was quite typical. 'Britain', he wrote, 'has received a warning to reorganise her education, her system of Imperial Defence and the administration of her public affairs.'[48] And in particular, for White as for many others, one fact stood out above the others from the events which produced this warning – the resulting revelations about the appalling physical status of the recruits:[49]

> In the Manchester district 11,000 men offered themselves for war service between the attack of hostilities in October 1899 and July 1900. Of this number 8,000 were found to be physically unfit to carry a rifle and stand the fatigue of discipline. Of the 3,000 who were accepted only 1,200 attained the moderate standard of the muscular power and chest measurement required by the military authorities. In other words, two out of every three men willing to bear arms in the Manchester district are virtually invalids.

Now this 'fact' had a range of possible significances depending upon the strategy within which it was deployed. For eugenicists, it was both the occasion for the insertion of eugenic arguments within a vociferous public debate, and the demonstration of the theses that they had long argued. It indicated not only the poor physical state of large numbers of the population, but everything else of which that state was an example and an index: the decline of national stock. And for eugenics, the origin of this decline had to be sought not in the environmental consequences of urban life, nor in the transmission of acquired conditions by inheritance, but in the relative frequency of reproduction itself. Hence the attention lavished upon the question of the birth-rate.

All the major European states suffered a decline in their birth-rate in the last half of the nineteenth century. Calculations based upon census data revealed that Britain's decline had not only been greater than that of any other nation except France, but its recovery had also been slower. With few exceptions, the debate over the decline did not hark back to the theme of the link between population size and wealth, but centred upon the distribution of this decline within the population, its effects upon the make up of that population and the consequences of these effects. For, as the evidence was organised to reveal, this decline in the birth-rate was not evenly distributed across the population: whilst the birth-rate of the lower classes was remaining stable, that of the middle classes was reducing rapidly.

The causes adduced for this phenomenon are of interest in their own right. They were not merely the rise of feminism and the movement for women's emancipation, which was causing women of the middle classes to abandon their proper role as childbearers and homemakers. Nor simply the desire of women to enter employment nor the willingness of the well-off to put selfish interests and standard of living above their patriotic duty to bear children. There was also a whole medical discourse upon the deleterious effects of education upon female fertility, especially at the time of puberty, or during menstruation, when it diverted sorely needed bodily energy to the mind and permanently reduced fecundity.[50]

However, more relevant for our purposes are the consequences which were argued to flow from such a differential reduction in birth-rate. The thesis that the transformation of a species was the consequence of differential reproductive advantage clearly could be applied to situations where this advantage accrued by other means than the natural selection of random variations. If those who limited their birth-rate were the well-off, the prudent, the thrifty, the educated, then it followed that the improvident, the poor, the ill-educated would effectively have a reproductive advantage. And if the characteristics of these two groups expressed the relative superiority or inferiority of an heritable stock, then the effect on the overall characteristics of the population was obvious. Indeed Galton had already drawn attention to precisely this point when discussing the effects which would follow if Malthus's exhortation to limit population by delaying the age of marriage were acted upon. For Galton this would only exacerbate the danger already faced by the higher civilisations – that they tend to multiply from the lower and not the higher specimens of the race.[51]

But while in 1883 Galton's arguments had appeared idiosyncratic and his concerns were unheeded, in the political debates two decades later their salience was clear, and the evidence for their truth was not difficult to obtain. Karl Pearson regularly drew attention to their pertinence in the opening years of the new century. In 1904 he wrote:[52]

We are ceasing as a nation to breed intelligence as we did fifty to a hundred years ago. The mentally better stock in the nation is not reproducing itself at the same rate as it did of old; the less able, and the less energetic are more fertile than the better stocks. No scheme of wider or more thorough education will bring up, in the scale of intelligence, hereditary weakness to the level of hereditary strength. The only remedy, if one be possible at all, is to alter the relative fertility of the good and bad stocks in the community.

The linkage between stock, fertility, energy and intelligence was here being discussed by Pearson in an article in *Biometrika*, the house journal of the biometricians, who now had an institutional base in the Department of Applied Mathematics at University College, London, of which Pearson was Professor. Aided by funds from the Worshipful Company of Drapers, the Biometric Laboratory was engaged in carrying out research which would put these reflections on the differential birth-rate on an unequivocally scientific basis.[53]

David Heron, Pearson's research assistant, working from the Biometric Laboratory and utilising the techniques of correlational analysis recently developed by Pearson, was able to use census data in order to determine the degree to which the reduced fertility of English wives was associated with social status or social problems as indicated by district of residence. Heron's results, though expected, were nonetheless alarming:[54]

As far as the present investigation goes it demonstrates I think conclusively that for the London districts there is a very close relationship between undesirable social status and a high birth rate. . . . Nor is the higher birth rate of the undesirable elements compensated by the higher death rate. . . . The relationship between inferior status and high birth rate has practically doubled during the last fifty years, and it is clear that in London at least the reduction in the size of families has begun at the wrong end of the social scale and is increasing in the wrong way. I have brought forward evidence enough to show that the birth rate of the abler and more capable stocks is increasing relatively to the mentally and physically feebler stocks.

Thus research confirmed what theory had predicted – the lowest 25 per cent of the adult stock was producing 50 per cent of the next generation.

But not only was tainted and degenerate stock given reproductive advantage by the limitation of fertility by the more advanced and developed sections of the population, this advantage was further consolidated by the suspension of natural selection within the population itself. The familiar critique of charity and philanthropy – that it encouraged precisely that state of pauperism that it wished to eliminate – was reformulated in the eugenic strategy. Medical developments, hygienist schemes of sanitary improvement, indiscriminate handing out of doles and so forth, had suspended natural selection within the population and allowed the flourishing of a mass of carriers of weakened and tainted stock in the heart of the great cities. Feeble constitutions made them easy prey for such diseases as tuberculosis, scrofula and phthisis; low levels of morality made them prone to promiscuity, inebriety and all forms of criminality; they were unable or unwilling to engage in productive employment or even to carry arms for their country. A drag on Britain's commercial efficiency in peacetime, a threat to her survival in war, they dragged down the average fitness of the British race and put her at a disadvantage in the international struggle for survival where the law of natural selection still held sway. If charity and philanthropy had so changed the ethical views of the British people that they could not tolerate a return to the primitive and natural forms which automatically eliminated the unfit, then this process must be taken under conscious and rational control. The pauper class must be prevented from reproducing their kind, by segregation or sterilisation; the good stock must be encouraged to breed. Only thus could the wholesale decline of the British race be prevented.[55]

Thus the spiral of urban degeneracy was redrawn in hereditary terms and the concept of unemployability re-organised around a notion of degenerate stock. This did not transform the crucial point of intervention, which remained between the employable and the unemployable. Nor did it transform the objective of intervention, which remained that of attaching the improvable to the social order and segregating the residuum. But what was crucial was the unravelling of the confused play of causes and effects which had characterised the nineteenth-century writings on degeneracy. In the earlier discussions, as we have seen, degenerate character functioned as both cause and effect of the occupation of a particular milieu. Conditions of living were immediately ethical both in their nature and in their consequences, and there was thus no contradiction between the formulation of proposals for reform of milieu and the advocacy of detention colonies for unemployables. The modern opposition between hereditarianists and environmentalists cannot be utilised as a grid for the analysis of such strategies. But what one can see in the formalisation and spread of eugenics is the crystallisation of the strategic differentiation and contestation between those who deployed a form of explanation based upon heredity, and advocated a strategy of reproductive control based upon it, and those who, freed from the theme of the inheritance of acquired characteristics, produced arguments, explanations, and strategies of social reform, which centred upon the *environment*, conceived in something like its modern form.

The eugenic strategy played a triple role in the questions which concern the present study. *Firstly*, as we shall see in the next chapter, it provided the conditions which allowed the question of mental deficiency, of feeble-mindedness, to take the form it did, and to offer to psychological discourse a particular object around which it would begin to regularise and institutionalise itself as a practice. *Secondly* it provided the forms of explanation within which the authors and agents who were the pioneers of individual psychology operated. Karl Pearson, Charles Spearman, Cyril Burt were all eugenicists, as were such leaders in the theory and practice concerning the mentally deficient as Alfred Tredgold and Ellen Pinsent. But it would be a mistake to regard this as an outcome of individual biographies, of prejudices or intentions or of class or sectional interests. It was rather the outcome of the mode of conceptualisation entailed within eugenics, which allowed the posing of a problem of mental efficiency and deficiency in a way which made individual psychology possible.

And *thirdly*, the eugenic strategy was one of the protagonists in the struggles over shape, direction, objectives and mechanisms of social policy, within which the discourse and practice of individual psychology would be installed. But it is important to recognise that however prolific the eugenic texts, however intriguing their political frankness, the events which followed were no realisation of the eugenic strategy. Eugenics established the field of problems concerning the hereditary transmission of stock and human abilities as the domain for a psychology of the individual. At the same time it freed the domain 'environment' – its nature, effects and reform – for elaboration within an opposing strategy. This was a strategy of social hygiene which found its principal spokesmen in the doctors, and which utilised as evidence the results of a tradition of social investigation concerning the interaction of environment and health.

Rowntree's survey *Poverty* had argued that the condition of the Boer War recruits at York, Leeds and Sheffield was the effect of the falling of their living standards below the minimum necessary to maintain physical efficiency.[56] Rowntree's early texts were just as 'moralistic' as Booth's, although this 'moralism' had a different point of insertion.[57] For example, in the estimation of total poverty based on house-to-house visits, households were considered in poverty where the investigator was informed by neighbours that the father or mother was a heavy drinker, or where the appearance of the children or the home concurred with the investigator's conception of what a poor home looked like.[58] And Rowntree's use of the language of efficiency allowed the text regularly to link problems concerning physical fitness with all those other social problems of 'inefficiency'. Indeed, the point is that the social hygienist argument could be deployed in relation to the very same problems as the eugenicist argument. Thus Rowntree argued in 1914 for the centrality of casual labour in the process of racial decline: the production of a class of incompetents who drag down wages, depress the standard of life and must be eliminated from the industrial field. And Rowntree concurred with eugenicists, and with the proposals of Booth and Beveridge, that segregation in labour colonies was the only solution for adult unemployables.[59] But the problem of the production of unemployables was set up differently. Unemployables could be made from the evil influence of drink, gambling and so forth on those who had a fair start in life. They were also produced from the hopelessness and lack of respect engendered by the effects of an unwholesome environment upon children, or from inadequate nutrition, which led to ill-health and low physical efficiency. Thus the strategy proposed was one of preventive medical scrutiny and environmental reform.

It is hardly surprising, then, that the most enthusiastic spokesmen for this medicalising strategy should have been the doctors. In a leading article of 1903 the *British Medical Journal* demanded an enquiry into the physical deterioration of the population. Referring to Booth as well as to Rowntree, they argued that if the stunting effects of work upon children were combined with lack of sunshine, outdoor exercise and fresh air, and if family earnings were insufficient for the maintenance of physical efficiency, it was 'easily conceivable that the British race will deteriorate'.[60] While the eugenicist strategy proposed segregation and sterilisation of those recalcitrant elements destined by their inherited constitution to pose a threat to a civilised and efficient social order, this medical strategy gave these operations only a limited tactical role. Prevention, in this strategy, took a different form. It depended upon environmental reform coupled with hygienic and medical education of parents, and the education and medical inspection of children. Appropriate norms of child rearing and nutritional standards were to be diffused into the home through an alliance between medicine and mothers, utilising the school as the place where universal and compulsory medical screening, diagnosis and determination of appropriate forms of treatment could occur.

The report of the Interdepartmental Committee on Physical Deterioration, set up under pressure to investigate this question of deterioration and its prevention, eschewed the eugenicist strategy and adopted instead this neo-hygienist model. Unfitness, it discovered, was not due to degenerate stock but to environmental conditions, lack of income, hygiene and education and hence of proper nourishment. Eliminate these and unfitness too would disappear:[61]

There is . . . every reason to anticipate RAPID amelioration of physique so soon as improvement occurs in external conditions, particularly as regards food, clothing, over-crowding, cleanliness, drunkenness and the spread of common practical knowledge of home management.

This strategy involved the breaking down of the opaque masses of the poor into visible units, and action upon the efficiency of the population at the level of the household through its transformation into a technical machine for the rearing of healthy children. Such children would be clean, adequately clothed, fed according to medical norms and taught to eschew habits – excessive consumption of alcohol, sexual excess and promiscuity and so forth – which were now regarded as being not only morally undesirable but also damaging to health and constitution. The objective: to produce a population simultaneously physically, morally and mentally efficient. The mechanism: the reform of individuals by means of the link between the home and the school and the relay of the child. The hitherto inaccessible corners of social life in the cities were to be opened up to sight and to reform through the institution of the school and the agency of the child.

Universal and compulsory education had the function both of revealing and of helping to resolve the problems of the appalling standards of physical and moral health of the population. Revealing it because, for the first time, all the children of the entire population were brought into contact with those who could recognise lack of physical and moral well-being when they saw it, and who saw it with alarming frequency. But also helping solve it because, through the school, it could be diagnosed and remedial measures put into operation.[62] As we shall see in a later chapter, this is precisely the point where the problem formed which was the occasion for the development of a technology of mental measurement and a psychological apparatus to administer it. And it was the opposition between the neo-hygienist strategy and the eugenic strategy which defined the first struggle within which individual psychology was engaged.

The eugenic and the neo-hygienist strategy appear to be in opposition. The former proposed segregation, the latter socialisation, the attachment back to the social order of those groupings who were marginal to society because they had escaped its norms. Eugenics operated in terms of a rigid policing of the boundary between those in society and those who threatened it; medicine operated by attempting to integrate the disaffected through education and the inculcation of norms. But this opposition was by no means an absolute one: not only could these strategies be combined into a single schema of administration, but such a schema illustrates exactly the key point at which an individual psychology was to try to establish itself. For what became central were techniques of individuation and assessment which would enable a rational distribution of individuals amongst a variety of social institutions and practices specialised to deal with them according to their personal characteristics, problems and difficulties in order to produce the most efficient and productive population.

Nothing illustrates the ideal form of this combination of eugenics and neo-hygienist environmentalism more clearly than the programmes of the Fabians, in particular Sidney and Beatrice Webb. When Sidney Webb was asked to lecture to the Eugenics Society on the Minority Report which was submitted by the Royal Commission on the Poor Laws and the Relief of Distress in 1909, he outlined its policy in six points:[63]

(1) Deliberately altering the social environment so as to render impossible (or at least more difficult) the present prolific life below the National Minimum, or the continuance at large of persons who are either unable or unwilling to come up to the National Minimum Standard of Life; (2) 'Searching out' every person in default irrespective of his destitution or his application for relief; (3) Medical and other inspection of all infants, school children, sick or mentally defective persons, and all who otherwise need public help, so as to discover the unfit, as well as to remedy their defects; (4) Segregation, permanent or temporary, of many defective persons now at large; (5) Enforcement of the responsibilities of parenthood at a high standard, and hence discouragement of marriage among those unable or unwilling to fulfil them; and (6) Taking care that no one sincerely desirous of fulfilling his social responsibilities shall, by lack of opportunity, be prevented from doing so.

Whilst Webb assured his audience that the Report was constructed 'on strictly eugenic principles', what it demonstrates rather is a specific and delimited utilisation of a eugenic strategy. What is entailed is a rigorous discrimination between the socialisable and the residuum, the former being subjected to a regime of environmental improvement, medicalised scrutiny and education; the latter being subject to segregatory exclusion.

The fulcrum of this schema was the social apparatus which was to provide the technical means for establishing this rational distribution of individuals. It is on this note that the Minority

Report began.[64] It condemned the Poor Laws for their use of the General Mixed Workhouse, with its promiscuous intermingling of the sick, the paupers, the feeble-minded, such that any scientific treatment of the inmates was impossible. While eugenicists saw in the inhabitants of the workhouse only the different manifestations of a single degeneracy of stock, the central operation in the scheme which the Minority Report proposed was discrimination and classification. Firstly and most crucially, the differentiation between the able-bodied and the non able-bodied. Each non able-bodied pauper was to be inspected, classified, distributed to the appropriate authority for specialised treatment: pauper children to the new Local Authorities, lunatics to the Asylum Committees, the sick to Health Committees, the feeble-minded to a new committee which would ensure their segregation in conditions where breeding was not possible. The Report accepted that this strategy entailed the creation of a group of public officials with sweeping powers of detention over those who fell below the minimum standards of mental and physical fitness recognised by society: this was the necessary price of protection for the community, and the decisions were, of course, to be taken on purely scientific grounds.

Yet more radical and innovative was the proposal to extend these techniques to 'the prevention and treatment of Able-bodied Destitution and Distress from Unemployment' – new objects for social policy for whom no technique had yet been established.[65] The technical device adopted by the Minority Report was the Labour Exchange. Drawing on Beveridge's proposals, it advocated the utilisation of this mechanism for the rationalisation of the labour market and the elimination of futile drifting and wastage in periods between work.[66] Coupled with decasualisation, the Labour Exchange would transform the market for employment into one whose workings were ordered and visible. But it would not only enable those genuinely seeking work to find it; more importantly it enabled those not genuinely seeking work to be identified:[67]

So long as the workman in search of a job has to wander, it is impossible to distinguish between him and the Professional Vagrant. . . . With a National Labour Exchange organised in all towns there will cease to be any excuse for wandering in search of work. . . . If this were done it would be possible to make all the minor offences of Vagrancy . . . occasions for *instant and invariable commitment* by the Justices to one or other of the reformatory detention colonies which must form an integral part of the system of provision.

The Report here took up the theme of internal colonies, deployed in a variety of strategies during this period, not simply for compulsory detention and reformation but also for the solution to urban poverty and overcrowding and the revitalisation of the economy through the bringing into cultivation of abandoned or under-utilised agricultural land.[68] But for present purposes, this aspect is of less importance than another.

Labour exchanges were significant not only because they allowed labour to be exchanged but also because, like the schools in relation to children, they provided a site for the production of knowledge, the extraction of information and the application of diagnosis and treatment. In relation to unemployment, they allowed the various forms of lack of employment to be analysed and documented, causes sought and treatments deployed. But before the treatment must come the diagnosis. Unemployment may operate on the population as a whole and result from a generalised condition of the market, but it nonetheless operated by selecting out individuals:[69]

> The National Authority dealing with the Able-bodied requires, therefore, what we might almost term a Human Sorting House, where each man's faculties would be tested to see what could be made of him; and a series of Training Establishments, to one or other of which the heterogeneous residuum of Unemployed would be assigned.

A concern for the well-being of the population as a whole now implies detailed attention to the characteristics of the individuals who make it up. Individualise, discriminate, test, train, reform according to appropriate social norms and release the previously unemployed back into the community. These individuals would now be trained to the highest levels of physical and mental efficiency to which they could be raised, and would have become accustomed to the salutary discipline imposed by a regime which would be the double of employment but rather more severe and hence still in keeping with the principle of less eligibility.

In the strategy put forward in the Minority Report, social intervention was discontinuous, prohibitory and *ex post facto*; it was the *penalty* for neglecting one's obligations to society:[70]

So long as he commits no crime, and neglects none of his social obligations – so long as he does not fail to get lodging, food and clothing for himself and his family – so long as his children are not found lacking medical attendance when ill, or underfed at school – so long, indeed, as neither he nor his family ask nor require any form of Public Assistance, he will be free to live as he likes. But directly any of these things happen, it will be a condition that the husband and father, if certified as Able-bodied, shall be in attendance at the Training Establishment to which he is assigned. If he is recalcitrant, he will be judicially committed to a Detention Colony.

The Minority Report demonstrates the productive possibilities of a combination of eugenicist and neo-hygienist strategies, and the key role within such a combination which was accorded to the individualisation, diagnosis and classification of those who came into contact with the agencies of the state. But as is well known, the scheme of social legislation undertaken by the Liberal Governments of 1906 and 1914 implemented neither the proposals of the Minority nor of the Majority Report of the Royal Commission on the Poor Laws. In the insurance based strategies for social regulation which began to be formulated during this period, socialisation was not something to be enforced as a penalty for resisting social norms, something operative *ex post facto* and relying on individualisation and classification. On the contrary, insurance was, in its ideal form, general, universal, compulsory and preventive. It entailed a radical restructuring of the relations between government and population, opening a direct contractual relation between each and every individual and the state, a relation of mutual obligation in which both parties had their rights and their duties, and which, though technical in its form, was moral in its intentions and consequences. But in respect of one particular class of 'unemployables', the Webb's schema proved no dead letter. This was in relation to a category of degenerates who came to occupy a very special place within the social and political arguments of the early twentieth century, and who came to be termed the feeble-minded. It was these feeble-minded persons – their diagnosis, classification, administration and treatment – who provided individual psychology with its first objects and targets.

4
The psychology of the individual

The psychology of education, of industry, and of war, the study of the criminal, the defective and the insane, all depend for their development upon a sound analysis of individual differences; and the investigation of the more practical problems has already begun to pay back its debt, by furnishing fresh data of the utmost value to the mother science. And so at last we have seen the birth of the youngest member in the list of sciences – the psychology of the individual. . . . It aims at almost mathematical precision, and proposes nothing less than the measurement of mental powers.

Cyril Burt, 1927[1]

When Cyril Burt became 'the first official psychologist in the world' in 1913, his principal task was the examination of elementary school children who had been nominated for admission to schools for the mentally defective.[2] It was in relation to the assessment of the mental powers of individuals, in particular the ascertainment of the degrees of mental defectiveness or feeble-mindedness which individuals manifested, that psychology made its first inroads into the processes of administration and began to establish itself as a functioning social practice. And the psychology that established itself in this way characterised itself as the psychology of the individual.

Speaking in Edinburgh in 1927, on the subject of the measurement of mental capacities, Cyril Burt began by reflecting on the conditions of emergence of the scientific psychology of which he was a spokesman. He identified two major transformations – that in the nineteenth century wherein psychology changed its *method* to that of systematic observation and research, and that in the twentieth century wherein psychology changed its *subject* from man-in-general to a concern with individual differences.[3] For Burt, the scientific psychology of the twentieth century constituted itself around the question of the individual and its differentiation. It was on this subject that Alfred Binet and his pupil, Victor Henri, elaborated in their programmatic text of 1896, '*La psychologie individuelle*':[4]

> The aim of individual psychology is to study different psychic processes in man and, in studying them, to pay attention to the individual differences in them. . . . Individual psychology . . . studies the properties of psychic processes that vary from individual to individual – it has to determine the various properties and then study how much and in what respect they vary with the individual.

The psychology of the individual, for Binet, thus formed itself around the twin operations of *measurement* and *differentiation* – the psychological individual was specifiable only to the extent that it was constituted as both measurable and differentiable:[5]

> We must search with the present knowledge and methods at hand for a series of tests to apply to an individual in order to distinguish him from others and to enable us to deduce general conclusions relative to certain of his habits and faculties. . . . There are, it seems, four principal routes to be pursued: the study of races, the study of children, the study of patients and the study of criminals.

Perhaps it was because the mental defective was such an apt combination of these four routes in one – part race, part child, part patient, part criminal – that it would be around a question of mental defect that the individual psychology of the first decades of the twentieth century would begin to organise itself. As a knowledge, as a technique and as a complex of agents and agencies, the first objective of the psychology of the individual was to be the mental defective, or rather, the 'feeble-minded'.

The discovery of the feeble-minded

Of the gravity of the present state of things there is no doubt

... there are numbers of mentally defective persons whose training is neglected, over whom no sufficient control is exercised, and whose wayward and irresponsible lives are productive of crime and misery, of much injury and mischief to themselves and to others, and of much continuous expenditure wasteful to the community and to individual families.

Royal Commission on the Care and
Control of the Feeble-minded, 1908[6]

It is tempting to regard the public debate over the feeble-minded, the setting up of the Royal Commission on the Care and Control of the Feeble-Minded consequent upon it, and the passage of the Mental Deficiency Act 1913, as the one success of the eugenicist strategy. The feeble-minded were, of course, fundamental targets of eugenics – not merely one category of problems amongst others, but having a matrix role in establishing the relations between all the different types of social problem. From Galton onwards, variations in human intellectual powers were necessarily linked with variations in industriousness, moral and civic worth and so forth. An individual's intellect was an index of the quantity of heritable vital energy possessed, of the general quality of stock.

For the eugenicists in the debates at the turn of the century, mental defectives progressively became the archetypal representatives of the deterioration of the race. In them were conjoined all those behaviours in which degenerate stock might manifest itself: immorality, criminality, indigence, inebriety, vagrancy, unemployability and, crucially, prostitution and promiscuity. Mental deficiency was well known to run in families, and hence here at least it was beyond dispute that degeneracy was transmitted through heredity. The mental defective was unsocialisable, congenitally incapable of receiving the moralising influences of civilised life, and hence the fact of defectiveness could explain all those behaviours which constituted degeneracy. And, crucially, the reproductive activities of the mentally defective posed a major threat. For the defective was impervious to the imprecations of morality and the curb on promiscuous sexuality which conscience and responsibility produced. And the old link between idiocy, animality and profligate sexual couplings took on a new significance when redeployed in a discourse convinced of the malign consequences of differential fertility. The mental defective, indiscriminately propagating degenerate stock and incapable of voluntary limitation of reproductive functions was a justification for the eugenic proposals of compulsory permanent segregation and/or sterilisation.[7]

It is certainly the case that these eugenic arguments had a place and a function in the events which we are about to discuss, but the terms of the Commission's discussion and recommendations, and the Act itself, demonstrate that these were no simple actualisation of the eugenic programme. It would be misleading to conceive of what was involved here in terms of a single campaign which obtained a hold on the real through its insertion into a 'moral panic' concerning racial degeneracy, or as the success of the 'moral entrepreneurship' of the eugenicists.[8] This would make it impossible to understand the terrain upon which the early psychological discussions of the measurement of mental ability operated, the configuration into which the first test of intelligence was inserted, and the fact that the key professional agents involved were neither psychologists nor eugenicists but doctors.

Eugenics constituted mental defectives as a *threat*, both immediate in terms of the social problems with which they were associated, and long term, in relation to the decline of the quality of the population resulting from their high rate of reproduction. But the mental defective had already entered social and political arguments in at least three other ways – as a *challenge* to philanthropy and science, as a *burden* upon the nation and those producing its wealth, and as an *obstacle* to the smooth operation of a universal system of education.

No general problem of idiocy existed before the nineteenth century.[9] Different practices and different discourses varied in the significance accorded to the term 'idiot', and in the status and consequences of idiocy. Legislation very early made a distinction between the idiot, or natural fool, and the lunatic, with regard to property rights over their estates. Thus in 1325 the King's prerogative was affirmed in the statute *De praerogativa regis* as:[10]

1 To protect the lands of idiots and take the profits of them and provide for their necessities, and to render the lands on death to their rightful heirs; and

2 To provide for the safe keeping of the lands of lunatics so that the lands may be restored to them on recovery or to their representatives on their death.

But while this distinction between lunatics as curable, potentially able to regain their normal faculties, and idiots as incurable, bound to suffer for life, crosscut many arguments, the law was only concerned with such questions to the extent that they involved rights over property. In theological discussions the significance accorded to idiocy was very different. Were fools equal to others in the sight of God? Were they closer to God because through them the truth could clearly shine? Were they a punishment inflicted upon families for their wrongdoing? Were they the result of sin, or sexual intercourse with the devil? Were they a test by God of man's compassion (as God is to man, so man is to fool)? For those involved with administering the Poor Law and other social institutions, from the eighteenth century onwards, idiots were merely one element amongst those filling the poor houses, work houses, gaols and lunatic asylums on account of their inability or unwillingness to enter productive employment or abide by the requirements of the law. Which of these institutions idiots ended up in depended upon the contingent events which might bring them into contact with parish or other authorities. As far as medicine was concerned, the incurability of idiocy made it unfavourable and uninteresting material both for eighteenth-century medical practice and for the emerging moral treatment of the nineteenth century. Although there were debates over aetiology or over diagnosis, once the classification of idiocy had been established this was equivalent to an affirmation of intractability to medicine.

When in the mid-nineteenth century idiots became a possible and distinct object for reformatory education, it was, as we have seen, within a philanthropic strategy which sought to rescue and improve a previously neglected class of unfortunates. This new target for philanthropy did not come about through disputing the medical judgment concerning the *incurability* of the idiot. As we have seen, Itard set out to train the 'Wild Boy of Aveyron' with the conviction that he was *not* an idiot, and that his condition was a consequence of his life outside human society. But Séguin believed that the Wild Boy *had* been an idiot, and took the results of Itard's labours to show that idiots, whilst not being curable, were nonetheless improvable, trainable, educable. The first asylum in England specifically for idiots was founded in 1847 in Highgate, London. Its brochure proclaimed the discovery that had provided its inspiration: 'We have laboured under the appalling conviction that idiocy is without remedy, and therefore we have left it without help. It may now be proclaimed, not as opinion but as a fact, a delightful fact, that THE IDIOT MAY BE EDUCATED.'[11]

It was as a new object for philanthropy that the idiot first became a discrete and specific target for social reform in England. For Séguin's philanthropic discovery was not isolated; the conditions which made it possible and allowed for its social deployment also obtained elsewhere. Within a few years of his work Saegert in Germany and Guggenbühl in Switzerland, apparently independently, discovered that idiots were educable. And in America, Sidney Howe led a campaign for the public education of idiots from the 1840s onwards.[12] Reports of the work of Séguin are said to have provided the inspiration for the first English asylum in Highgate. In the decade which followed, a number of similar institutions for the education of idiots opened in England. From about four hundred inmates of idiot asylums in England in 1864, the number rather more than doubled in the next decade. Texts of the period extol the order, calm, obedience, diligence and cheerfulness which characterised these institutions, their improving effects upon bodily and mental discipline, the very fulfilment of Séguin's programme of physiological education.[13]

But only some 3 per cent of the estimated 29,542 idiot inmates of institutions in 1881 were in such asylums.[14] The remainder were still intermingled with criminals, lunatics, indigents and others in workhouses, lunatic asylums and prisons. For these specialised idiot asylums were directed towards the improvable idiot, they charged for their inmates, and they explicitly excluded paupers. It was these pauper idiots who were to be the focus of a second discourse on idiocy which emerged towards the end of the nineteenth century, for which the idiot was not so much a challenge for a scientific and philanthropic pedagogy, as a burden on the nation.[15]

It was the Charity Organisation Society which was the locus for the organisation and promotion of the need for State action to counter the burden of the idiot. Despite its general strategy of individualised case-work methods linked to the moral reformation of the poor and hence the suppression of mendicancy, the Society argued that the case of the idiot warranted action by the State in respect to a whole class of persons who were presently exacerbating social problems in a number of different ways.

Firstly, idiots were a large and increasing drain on the poor rates. The Lunatic Asylums Act of 1853 required that the Justices of each county provide an asylum 'for the pauper lunatics thereof', where the word 'lunatic' included every person of unsound mind and 'every person being an idiot'. The Act did not prevent provision for idiots in separate institutions, but it was only in London that such separate provision was made.[16] When the Charity Organisation Society's Special Committee on the Education and Care of Idiots, Imbeciles and Harmless Lunatics reported in 1877, it estimated that there were 49,041 individuals in these categories.[17] Basing its figures on census returns, it reckoned that 35,963 of these in England and Wales were chargeable to the poor rates, but only a very small proportion of these, around 10 per cent, were in receipt of specialised treatment. The bulk of the remainder were promiscuously intermingled in the public workhouses, in lunatic asylums and in prisons, a burden on the rates, yet receiving nothing which might improve them as a consequence of this financial obligation. But whilst only a small proportion of these might be made self-supporting, a further large proportion might be trained to do some useful work, and 'the habits of the remainder can be improved so as to make their lives happier to themselves and less burdensome to others'.[18]

The Report urged special treatment for idiots, imbeciles and harmless lunatics and the application to them of the special means of training based upon education of the senses. However what motivated the Charity Organisation Society was not that philanthropy which had caused Séguin some forty years earlier to single out the similarly intermingled improvable idiots for specialised reformatory treatment. It was motivated by the desire for *economy*. The idiot was an economic burden in four ways. Firstly, the present cost to the rates was in no way justified by the reformatory effects of the institutionalisation which was provided; indeed institutionalisation exacerbated the dependence of the idiot rather than ameliorating it. Secondly, the present situation ran counter to the principles of political economy, for idiots so treated represented a waste of useful labour and a drain on economic resources, whereas, under appropriate management, they could not only provide for their own support, but also contribute to industry and agriculture. This would have the additional advantage of allowing the idiot to benefit mentally and morally from the industrial principle. Thirdly, those idiots at present outside institutions were continually open to ill-use and exploitation by corrupt and criminal elements, further exacerbating the demoralising milieu which was the very source of the social problem which so much money and effort was being expended to eradicate. And fourthly, idiots placed an entail upon their families, disadvantaging them, an extra burden in their struggle for existence which might easily force them down towards mendicancy and the workhouse.[19]

Indeed these arguments might appear to have been politically successful. The Idiots Act of 1866 passed uncontroversially through parliament. It distinguished idiots and imbeciles from lunatics, and it laid down conditions for their admission to and discharge from asylums, and for their registration and inspection. But to take this for a success would be to fall into the trap of confusing the passage of a law with the construction of an effective apparatus. Not only was very little of the separate provision allowed for in the Act ever established, but the Lunacy Act of 1890, which was to consolidate the various enactments with regard to lunacy over the last half of the nineteenth century, failed to make any such distinction, merely saying, in Section 341, ' "Lunatic" means an idiot or person of unsound mind.'[20]

The issue of mental defect would have to be reformulated before it could move to the centre of the debate over the social question. This reformulation revolved around the category not of idiocy or imbecility, but of *feeble-mindedness*. The idiot, from Pinel through Esquirol and Séguin to the Charity Organisation Society, was *visible*. The mark of idiocy was impressed upon the surfaces of the body, in physical signs and external stigma. Idiots might pose a problem of economy, a problem of order, a problem of philanthropy, pedagogy or treatment but they did not pose a problem of detection except in a few, rare, doubtful cases.[21] As the category of feeble-mindedness began to solidify, a transitional state was introduced between the normal and the pathological. The defective mind began to lose its immediate links with the defective body; the surface of the body gradually began to lose its ability adequately to represent its truth and inner nature. Idiocy was no longer readable on sight, through the interpretation of visible bodily signs. In the category of feeble-mindedness, idiocy was progressively hidden from view, *hidden in order to be discovered*. It was the consequence of this shift, rather than a simple 'eugenic panic', which provided the conditions for the

widespread social concern which led to the Royal Commission on
the Feeble-Minded and the Mental Deficiency Act 1913. And it
was this too which provided the pertinence for a technique of
measurement of intellectual powers, and for a psychology of
individual differences.

The place of the idiot in the discourse of degeneracy has already
been alluded to. The medical texts of the second half of the
nineteenth century analysed idiocy in these terms. Willis had
already suggested, in the seventeenth century, that parental
intemperance, indigence or vice might lead to the production of
idiot children.[22] Howe's influential text *On the Causes of Idiocy*,
published in 1848, similarly argued that idiot children were
produced as a result of intemperance, masturbation, ill-health,
fright and so forth in the parents, in combination with a general
inherited disposition to idiocy.[23] And Ireland, a Superintendent of
a Scottish idiot asylum, repeated the familiar configuration of
inherited predisposition, itself perhaps acquired as a result of
unhealthy or vicious influences, manifesting itself in the appearance of insanity, imbecility or epilepsy among family members.[24]
Ireland, in 1877, paraded before his readers the figures of the ten
types of idiocy, marked by their syphilitic teeth, misshapen
palates, malformed or incorrectly proportioned heads, irregular
limbs – each combination of stigmata expressing some particular
organic defect, usually a brain lesion. But Ireland already felt the
need to justify this analysis and approach to diagnosis against
another, which tried to base itself not upon brain lesions and
stigmata but a belief that the deficit was confined almost entirely
to the mind, a 'want or hebetude of intellect'.[25]

What was involved in the formation of the category of feeble-
mindedness was first of all a different mode of connection
amongst the elements which went to make up idiocy as a
functional social reality. In the category of the feeble-minded there
was a connection, not between brain lesions and visible stigmata,
but between a disordered or defective mind and undesirable
behaviours. And this problem of undesirable behaviours emerged
most forcefully not in the prisons, the asylums or the workhouses
– though it had consequences for all of these – but in the schools.

Of course, questions of education had been bound up with
general social programmatics of reform and moralisation since at
least the late eighteenth century.[26] But the institution in the 1870s
of a system of universal education which was both free and
compulsory created a generalised field for the inspection and

evaluation of conducts, capacities and behaviours. It created a site within which that evaluation could occur, a common standard of evaluation, a set of norms and expectations tied to the functioning of the techniques of pedagogy in the schools, and a group of agents whose daily activities depended upon the ability of individual children to display appropriate capacities and conducts. The technology of education required certain attributes in those who were to be its subjects, and the schools were filled with crowds of children who, for a whole variety of reasons, could not support the interpellation which was addressed to them. It was, first of all, a problem of the senses. The blind, the deaf, the dumb – those figures who had already occupied such a privileged place in sensationalist philosophy – now presented a problem of a different order, for their physical disabilities made them unable to receive the sensory input upon which pedagogy relied.[27] But there were also rapidly found to be children who, while apparently fully provided with their complement of senses, appeared unable to learn the lessons of the school.[28] The Royal Commission on the Elementary Education Acts requested the Royal Commission on the Blind, Deaf and Dumb to consider the treatment of these children in detail, and it was to this class of children that their Report of 1889 referred as 'educational imbeciles', or, more simply, the feeble-minded.[29]

The term 'feeble-minded' gradually came, in England, to designate those who, whilst not committable to an asylum under the various lunacy laws, were nonetheless sufficiently weak-minded to be incapable of receiving the benefits of socialisation in general, and education in particular.[30] Thus the Defective and Epileptic Children Committee of the Education Department reported in 1898 that:[31]

> From the normal child down to the lowest idiot, there are degrees of deficiency of mental power; and it is only a difference of degree which distinguishes the feeble-minded children referred to in our enquiry, on the one side from the backward children who are found in every school and, on the other side, from the children who are too deficient to receive proper benefit from any teaching which the School Authorities can give. . . . Though the difference in mental powers is one of degree only, the difference of treatment which is required is such as to make these children, for practical purposes, a distinct class.

This Committee adopted the term 'feeble-minded' from the Royal Commission on the Blind, Deaf and Dumb and from the Poor Law Schools Committee, which had expressed its concern in 1896 that so many of its children were of the feeble-minded class.[32] Gradually a link was established between feeble-mindedness and pauperism, though not, in the first instance, in terms of arguments about progressive degeneration or eugenics. Rather, the problem was the excessive number of children in the pauper class who required special educational provision, the cost of this provision, the consequences of not providing it, and the means of establishing who needed it.

The estimation of numbers seemed at first to present no problems, at least not to the trained eye. The Charity Organisation Society, aided by funds from the British Association and the British Medical Association, set up a committee in 1890 to arrange a series of school inspections with a view to discovering what proportion of pupils in different areas suffered from physical, mental and moral defects.[33] Dr Francis Warner, who carried out the investigations, was Professor of Anatomy and Physiology in the Royal College of Surgeons. He had published his 'Method of examining children in schools as to their development and brain condition' in the *British Medical Journal* of 1888.[34] This was a technique of reading from physical stigmata and bodily comportment back to underlying pathologies of the brain. Children exhibited themselves to the doctor, who observed '(a) the form, proportion and texture of the visible parts of the body; and (b) the signs of action in the central nervous system, as seen in the muscles producing movements or attitudes or balances of nerve-muscular accuracy'.[35] This was a procedure which Warner considered to be both practicable in terms of time and reliable in terms of scientific accuracy. On the basis of this method, Warner considered that some 15 per cent of the 50,000 schoolchildren whom he surveyed were defective in some respect – dull, defective in nutrition or with nervous defects – and about 1 per cent were feeble-minded.[36]

And the weight of numbers was demonstrated in a more practically compelling sense. For large numbers of children accumulated in the 'Standard O' classes, apparently incapable of reaching the standards laid down in the Board of Education's code. The London School Board had begun to group such children in special schools in 1891, following the advice of the Royal Commission on the Blind, Deaf and Dumb. When legislation authorised special grants for provision for blind and deaf children in 1893, they urgently requested larger grants for these feeble-minded children as well, in the light of the increasing cost of such schools.[37]

There could be no doubt that here was a class of persons who were not legally committable to asylums yet were a constant drain on the resources of the school boards, the poor law authorities and the State. A group which did not constitute the same sort of burden as the idiot and the imbecile, for they were able, to some extent, to mingle with normal society. Yet precisely this exacerbated the problem because, though this was not immediately obvious, their moral senses had not been awakened either by parental, religious or educational influences, and hence they were in constant danger of exploitation by others and lived a life of considerable unhappiness to themselves. Three questions were constantly posed within the growing debate on the feeble-minded in the last decade of the nineteenth century. How were these feeble-minded children to be detected; how could they be socialised to awaken their moral sensibilities and to make them resistant to the temptations of vice and crime; what was to become of them when they were no longer of school age?

The Defective and Epileptic Children Committee of the Education Department was particularly concerned with deciding the means of identification of this class of children and the appropriate agents to utilise these means. The witnesses to the Committee were principally doctors and the criteria which they advocated were constructed in terms of the familiar combinations of physical stigmata. The Committee agreed with Warner, Beach, Shuttleworth and Harris that, like idiocy and imbecility, feeble-mindedness was inscribed upon the surface of the body:[38]

> Feeble-minded children are, in the great majority of cases, marked by physical defect or defects discernable to the trained observer. . . . The most conspicuous of such defects are irregularity in general bodily conformation, malformation of the head, the palate, tongue, lips, teeth and ears, defective power of motion or control in almost any of the different forms of muscular action, as shown in balance, attitude and movement, and defects in some one or more of the sensory functions, besides the ordinary varieties of deformity and ill health.

Yet the knowledge required for such a reading was becoming increasingly esoteric. Signs were becoming deceptive to the untrained eye, significant only in their combinations and when supplemented by life histories and information about family background, even requiring on occasions examination of the intellectual powers of the child directly by means of assessing their performance on a task involving reading or numbers. So specialised had this knowledge become that Beach estimated that there were no more than six doctors in England capable of discriminating between feeble-mindedness and imbecility,[39] and even amongst the witnesses to the Committee there was no agreement on criteria. Whilst the Committee recommended legislation, the Permanent Secretary had to admit, during the drafting of the Bill, that none of the Committee's witnesses had been able to 'offer any verbal definition of that degree of want of intelligence which was to constitute a defective child'.[40]

The Committee had to reconcile an impossible contradiction. They were required by their terms of reference to advise on the means of discriminating between idiots, imbeciles, feeble-minded and normal children. The only professional agents with a claim to competence were doctors. Teachers had no claims to rival medicine as the adjudicative instance; psychology did not yet exist as a body of agents with a claim to social expertise. Yet the discovery of feeble-mindedness owed nothing to medicine. The problem emerged in the practices of the school and the classroom, which required certain definite norms of conduct including the capacities to obey the disciplinary demands of pedagogy and to fulfil the expectations as to the tasks of learning which that pedagogy prescribed. In the case of feeble-minded children, then, it was education which had produced the problem and necessitated the solution: the construction of a specialised apparatus for their training and hence a specialised set of knowledges and techniques for the diagnosis and allocation of feeble-minded individuals. Hence the Committee was forced to adopt educational criteria. Normal children were those capable of benefiting from normal schools; feeble-minded children were those capable of benefiting from special schools, idiots and imbeciles were those incapable of benefiting from schools at all. It was these criteria which were embodied in the permissive Elementary Education (Defective and Epileptic Children) Act of 1899, which gave local authorities the power to create special schools and classes for those children, who, not being either imbeciles or merely backward or dull, were 'by reason of mental defect, incapable of receiving proper benefit from the instruction in ordinary schools'.[41] Educational criteria and medical agents: this set the scene for a problem which would take over a decade to solve, and established the terrain for a lengthy battle between doctors and psychologists which is not yet fully resolved.

Ascertaining the problem

By 1903, special schools for the feeble-minded had been established in London and fifty other authorities and, as the act of discrimination became more frequent, the means of discrimination became more crucial and more problematic. Gradually the pertinence of classification by means of visible signs began to be called into doubt as the relation between such signs and the behaviours which were the pedagogic and disciplinary occasion for diagnosis became more obscure. For the teachers and educators, who were given the task of nominating children for examination by medical officers, were unversed in the esoteric reading of stigmata. They were concerned with the category of feeble-mindedness only as a means of explaining a diverse range of obstructive or undesirable behaviours as consequences of an intelligible and unified cause. Teachers very early on began to develop their own techniques, based upon criteria directly relating to the exigencies of pedagogy, and straightforwardly in terms of behaviours and competences.[42] School medical officers were faced with the problem of reconciling their diagnostic privilege, which they owed to their status as medically qualified agents, with their institutional role. This concerned a problem where clinical judgment was to function as an assessment not of organic malfunction but of school conduct. They similarly began to utilise a range of means of evaluation in which externally visible physical signs played only a subsidiary part.[43]

Feeble-mindedness thus gradually came to be constructed in terms of a direct link between mental powers and behaviours, a link in which the body was no longer able to have a pivotal role as the surface upon which interpretation was to be exercised. It was in an almost identical situation, in France, that Alfred Binet was called upon to advise upon modes of ascertainment of mentally defective children. A psychological notion of intelligence and the means of assessing it would have the possibility of fulfilling the institutional and administrative role which preceded it and which established the parameters within which it could operate. But before considering Binet's discovery, it is necessary to say a little more about the conjuncture into which his test was inserted in England.

In the debate we have just been examining, it was only at this point, after the formation of the problem of the feeble-minded within quite different strategic configurations, that the eugenicist arguments could come into play. With the discovery of the feeble-minded, with the link between feeble-mindedness and pauperism, with the emergence of a conception of human powers as varying along a continuum, this class gradually became the ideal object which regulated eugenic discourse. And in this discourse the feeble-minded were not a challenge to philanthropy, an economic burden, or an obstacle to the smooth operation of socialising education, but the evidence and the motive force in a hereditary cycle of urban degeneration and national deterioration, through the means of differential rates of reproduction.

The National Association for the Care of the Feeble-Minded, established in 1896, was the key organising locus for this strategy; Mary Dendy and Ellen Pinsent its two stalwarts. They redeployed the familiar pleas for the limitation of the reproduction of degenerates – whether by sterilisation or by permanent segregation.[44] In 1903 Pinsent proposed, in the *Lancet*, a 'thorough and complete scheme of State intervention' for the feeble-minded.[45] The evidence of the schools was re-utilised in this more general strategy. Having once discovered the numbers of such children and developed institutional provision for them, were they to be released into society at the end of compulsory schooling? Surely what was required were 'permanent industrial colonies or permanent custodial homes to which children who were unfit to face life on their own responsibility could be transferred' after leaving school, for in this way 'they would never be allowed the liberty which they can only misuse to their own degradation and to the degradation of the society in which they live.' And if this entailed an exceptional degree of State restriction upon personal liberty, it was only doing sooner what would otherwise be done later when they ended up in the gaols or the workhouse.[46]

The setting up of the Royal Commission on the Care and

Control of the Feeble-Minded in 1904 seemed to have had less to do with any eugenic concern about the degeneration of the race than with economic considerations. But after its Report was published in 1908, the National Association, in conjunction with the Eugenics Education Society, founded in 1907, engaged in a large-scale exercise of propaganda. A flood of books and pamphlets was produced by eugenicists on the threat of the feeble-. minded and a joint committee of the two organisations was established, headed by the Archbishops of Canterbury and York, and including many bishops, clergy, doctors and members of the aristocracy, to campaign for the passage of the Mental Deficiency Bill which would translate the recommendations of the Royal Commission into legislation.[47] Immediate action was necessary:[48]

> BECAUSE at the date of the Report of the Royal Commission, there were 270,000 mentally defective people in England and Wales, of whom 149,000 are uncertified. There is for them no recognised and generally no possible means of control, although they are totally incapable of managing themselves or their affairs. . . . BECAUSE in consequence of the neglect to recognise and treat their condition, the mentally defective become criminals and are sent to prison; they become drunkards and fill the reformatories; they become paupers and pass into the workhouses. BECAUSE they are frequently producing children, many of whom inherit their mental defect, and nearly all of whom become the paupers, criminals and unemployables of the next generation.

And in 1908 Alfred Tredgold published the first edition of what was probably the first theoretical text on mental deficiency from within this new configuration. His *Mental Deficiency (Amentia)* was to become the standard text on the subject, going through eleven editions, the most recent being published in 1970.[49] Tredgold was a member of the Royal Commission, Consulting Physician to the National Association for the Care of the Feeble-Minded, later Member of the Board of Education Mental Deficiency Committee and the Ministry of Health Committee on Sterilisation (the Brock Committee) of 1932-3. Summarising the recommendations of the Royal Commission in 1910 he wrote:[50]

> The whole tendency of recent enquiries is to show that the feeble-minded are not an isolated class, but they are merely one

phase and manifestation of a deeply ingrained degeneracy. They are kith and kin of the epileptic, the insane and mentally unstable, the criminal, the chronic pauper and the unemployable classes, and I am convinced that the great majority of the dependent classes existing today owe their lack of moral, mental and physical fibre to the fact that they are blood relations of the feeble-minded and are tainted with their degeneracy.

Opponents of the Bill argued that the State was not justified in exercising administrative control over the feeble-minded: individual restriction could be justified not on the grounds of what a person was but only on the grounds of what they had done. Only when crimes had been committed, and through the action of the judicial instance subject to the safeguards of due process, had the State the right to deprive someone of their liberty.[51] Certainly the Report, and the 1913 Mental Deficiency Act which followed, departed fundamentally from such an ideal. Not what one does, but *who one is* and what one *might* do or what *might* be done to one, or what one's progeny *might* do because of this hidden nature – this was what was adjudicated upon. And this adjudication was done prophylactically, outside the legal process although sanctioned by it. It was carried out by agents other than the judiciary, subject to none of the procedures of due process. What was significant about the mechanisms set in place was not that they were the realisation of a eugenic strategy, but that they effected this shift in the object, grounds, limits and mechanics of adjudication.

Indeed the Report and the Act did not constitute a eugenic schema. Rather there was a stabilisation of the various strategies concerning the feeble-minded into complementary axes of a single programme. Within this programme, and the technology to which it gave rise, the feeble-minded became simultaneously the object of a theoretical knowledge and the target of an administrative apparatus. This object/target was not the drooling idiot with syphilitic teeth and degenerate ears, but a problem both more direct – concerning the details of behaviours in relation to the norms of pedagogy – and more remote – having its origin in an invisible pathology of intellect.

Life was a struggle in which the feeble-minded sank to the bottom. They filled our prisons, clogged our schools, burdened our Poor Law Institutions, occupied our homes for inebriates. And what was worse, they accumulated in our slums out of contact with any institution of the State and open to exploitation by others. Thus these defectives were a burden economically, a concern morally and a threat socially. It was not only that they constituted a problem for society, but also that the defective himself, deprived of the benefits of socialisation and moralisation, lived a life of misery and degradation, unable to aid himself and cruelly used by others. The obligatory opening of a contract between the State and the defective could thus be presented as a benefit to both parties; segregation would increase the happiness of the defective himself.[52] The Commission managed without difficulty to articulate the hereditary transmission of defect and the necessity of preventing procreation with the benefits of training both for the defective and for society, and the need for economy. After reviewing the arguments for hereditary and environmental causation it concluded:[53]

(1) That both on grounds of fact and of theory there is the highest degree of probability that 'feeble-mindedness' is usually spontaneous in origin – that is not due to influences acting on the parent – and tends strongly to be inherited.
(2) That, especially in view of the evidence concerning fertility, the prevention of mentally defective persons from becoming parents would tend largely to diminish the number of such persons in the population.
(3) That the evidence for these conclusions strongly supports measures, which on other grounds are of primary importance, for placing mentally defective persons, men and women, in institutions where they will be employed and detained, and in this way, and in other ways, kept under effective supervision so long as may be necessary.

Even though the behaviours characteristic of feeble-mindedness were most common amongst those brought up in the slums, this did not militate against the hereditarian hypothesis. The Commission appeared to accept Tredgold's position, as, for example, he expressed it in his book:[54]

My own enquiries have convinced me that in the great majority of these slum cases there is a pronounced morbid inheritance, and that their environment is not the cause, but the *result* of that heredity. The neuropath is one who is at an economic disadvantage in the struggle for existence. He frequently finds it difficult to hold his place, and he is often possessed of careless, improvident, and intemperate propensities, which cause him to fritter away the money he does earn. He is on the down grade. No wonder, then, that he drifts to the slums.

Feeble-mindedness had become a question of a hereditarily transmitted attribute, to be controlled by measures of regulated segregation which would alleviate the problem in the short run by removing defectives from the social milieu in which they might cause danger, and curb it in the long term through the limitation on fertility which it imposed.

A new object for social regulation had been formed: 'the mental condition of these persons, and neither their poverty nor their crime, is the real ground of their claim to help from the State.'[55] The conducts in which feeble-mindedness was evident were grounds for intervention not so much on their own account but only insofar as they were indices of a transmissible, multipliable defect. It was this origin of behaviours that the strategy concerned. Not poverty (which had itself only recently become a ground for legitimate governmental action) nor crime (which had long been so) but *mental condition* had become a new object of judgment and of legitimate and compulsory social action. Feeble-mindedness was a psychological state which was knowable only on the basis of the social behaviours which it induced. As Tredgold put it in his book:[56]

> the condition is a psychological one, although the criterion is social, and we may accordingly define amentia as a state of restricted potentiality for, or arrest of, cerebral development, in consequence of which the person affected is incapable at maturity of so adapting himself to his environment or to the requirements of the community as to maintain existence independent of external support.

Breaching social norms was now a failure of adaptation consequent upon a mental condition. As the Report put it, feeble-minded criminals, inebriates, paupers, children of school age 'are not so much prisoners, or inebriates, or paupers, or school children as persons who are mentally deficient.'[57]

How was one to deal with individuals as persons who were mentally deficient? What was necessary first of all was a definition and classification of the degrees of deficiency. The Commission proposed to divide persons of unsound mind into nine classes 'subject to be dealt with', within which mental defectives were distributed among four. Idiots, imbeciles and feeble-minded were classified according to a rising scale of social competence; 'moral imbeciles' were a discrepant class – persons who from an early age displayed some mental defect, coupled with strong vicious or criminal propensities on which punishment has little or no deterrent effect. Despite the heated debate over definitions which accompanied the passage of the 1913 Act, this schema, though limited to the four classes of defectives, was realised in a way denied to the programme put forward by the Webbs. Like the Minority Report of the Royal Commission on the Poor Laws, which warmly endorsed these proposals, classification and distribution were to provide the keys for the re-establishment of a regulated and orderly social regime, and scientific social administration was to operate through the affixing of unambiguous labels to previously floating groups of persons, thus allowing their appropriate location within a range of specialised forms of social provision:[58]

> We desire to promote the establishment of such institutions as are necessary for the classes which the different words of our classification represent; and we would prevent the sending of patients who, though differing in the extent of their defectiveness, are called by one name, to institutions unsuitable for them, as much as we would avoid the sending of such patients to suitable institutions under unsuitable names . . . in consequence of a change of this kind, consistent alike with better nomenclature and more exact certification, institutions and homes might to a larger extent be specialised; and asylums might become hospitals to a much greater extent than they are at present, thereby fulfilling an infinitely greater service to science and to administration.

Science and administration: the symbiosis which would characterise the psychology of the individual throughout its history. When administration becomes dependent upon classification, the question of diagnosis, of ascertainment, becomes the fulcrum of the whole system. Ascertainment depended upon a knowledge and technique to enable individuals to be properly evaluated, and a class of agents and system of administration to carry out the job. This complex of agents, agencies, apparatuses and techniques which the Report's proposals entailed, was, in its ideal form, to spread out from a central point to the farthest reaches of the social body, bringing each individual into contact with the authorities, and simultaneously instituting a judgment as to their true nature. The 1913 Mental Deficiency Act called into being just such a complex and hierarchical structure of detection, ascertainment, supervision, distribution and institutional confinement which had the mental defective as its subject. A special mental deficiency committee in each local authority area was to provide for the ascertainment of persons subject to be dealt with under the Act, was to provide suitable institutions, was to maintain the defectives it placed therein, to provide for the conveyancing of defectives to and from such institutions, and was to appoint officers to supervise the care of defectives in the community. This whole structure was to be under the watchful eye of a central body named (in terms which would gladden the heart of a radical sociologist) the Board of Control.[59]

As far as adults were concerned, the reaction of local authorities continually failed to live up to the desires of the Board. New institutions were slow to be built; the war intervened to direct energies and resources elsewhere; many local authorities failed to take their duties sufficiently seriously. According to Jones, by 1920, only 10,129 defectives had been ascertained, whilst the Board considered the true figure to be in the region of 3.55 per thousand of the population. By 1927, the number of defectives ascertained had risen to over 60,000; however, despite the urgency and necessity of immediate and permanent institutional-isation, many of these were being supervised in the community, and only 5,301 places in institutional accommodation were being provided by local authorities.[60]

But whilst for adults the problem of the mental defectives could be avoided at the administrative level, for children the case was rather different. For adults, ascertainment required the construc-tion of a new and specialised apparatus; but children, since the 1870s, had been brought into daily contact with the authorities. And the place of this daily meeting was, of course, the school. The Elementary Education (Defective and Epileptic Children) Act of 1914 replaced the permissive Act of 1899 with one which imposed a set of duties on local education authorities, introducing into the school system a copy of the structure of detection, ascertainment, supervision, distribution and institutionalisation laid out in the

Mental Deficiency Act of 1914. The question of the means available for ascertainment had now become an urgent one. As Tredgold remarked in a new chapter on Mental Tests and Case Taking, which he introduced into the 1914 edition of his book:[61]

> the diagnosis of mental defect will come to occupy a very important place in medical practice . . . the legal position of the mentally defective now renders it extremely advisable that such examination should be systematic and carefully recorded . . . [although mental tests are still in their infancy] there can be no doubt that the science is one which has a great future before it in the elucidation of the problem of mental development and the practical work of education . . . they will be the means of carrying us from that imperfect knowledge of the defective mind with which we have hitherto been compelled to be satisfied to a more precise and scientific knowledge of the subject.

A technique of mental measurement had become necessary.

5
The measure of intelligence

The most sensational charge of scientific fraud this century is being levelled against the late Sir Cyril Burt, father of British educational psychology. Leading scientists are convinced that Burt published false data and invented crucial facts to support his controversial theory that intelligence is largely inherited. . . . Of course, the accusations do not totally invalidate Burt's theory, but they destroy the evidence with which he supported it.

Sunday Times, 1976[1]

Few elements of psychological technology have attracted as much critical attention as the intelligence test and the concept of IQ with which it is associated. Recently, criticism has come to focus upon the issue of scientific fraud – Sir Cyril Burt's invention and adjustment of the data concerning the IQ scores of twins and other kin which purported to demonstrate the heritability of intelligence. This controversy has thrown into question Burt's other achievements, especially the general claim that intelligence is largely innate and genetically determined.[2] It is a nice paradox that Burt – who did so much to establish the truth claims of psychology in England, to construct the bases of contemporary psychological techniques and to introduce these into social and educational policies and programmes – should be guilty of deceit. But while Burt may be discredited, the theories and practices of the psychology of the individual are not. Despite the repeated sociological, psychological, genetic and epistemological critiques of the validity of measuring a heritable intelligence quotient with standardised tests, psychometrics constantly extends its remit in education, psychiatry, industry, the criminal justice system, the prison and the army.[3] And the procedures which it employs – assumptions of normal distribution of data, standardisation, advanced statistical techniques of correlation and factor analyses and so forth – are precisely those pioneered by Burt and his collaborators. Burt may have adjusted his data to fit his theories – but we should not simply focus upon the adjustment but upon the knowledge which it sought to support. Not simply on the answers which Burt purported to provide, but on the questions which he asked. What made it possible for Burt to pose the problem of the measurement, distribution and inheritance of intelligence in the way in which he did? And how was it that the claims which he made were accepted by so many eminent scientists without demur?

Perhaps we may understand something of the tenacity of testing by going beyond a demonstration of the falsity of measuring a heritable intelligence quotient with standardised tests, to examine how it was that such an enterprise managed to propound and establish its claims to truth.

Measurement and discrimination

> the object of the quantitative experiment is to measure. . . .
> What we do is to carry out a long series of observations under
> the simplest and most general introspective conditions. Then
> we gather up the results of these observations in mathematical
> shorthand, and express them numerically by a single value. The
> questions asked of consciousness are, in the last analysis, two
> only: 'Present or absent?' and 'Same or different?'
> Edward Titchener, 1901-5[4]

From Gustav Fechner's psychophysics to Edward Titchener's textbook of experimental psychology, psychological measurement operated upon the model of the experiment. It concerned a space bounded by the stimulus, the sensation and the reaction; its object was the formulation of the general laws of experience. To be adequate to the task it was now set, measurement would have to leave the closed space of the body and the artificial territory of the laboratory. It would have to relinquish the quest for indexical measures in search of distributional rankings. It would have to concern itself not with the laws of the relation between body and soul but with the classifications of the behaviours and abilities of individuals with respect to social norms. And it would have as its object not the formulation of general laws of consciousness, of that which is common to all humans, but differences amongst individuals within a population. Only then would a psychology of measurement be able to establish itself in the space which had opened up for it in the apparatus of social administration.

Gustav Fechner published the *Elemente der Psychophysik* in Leipzig in 1860.[5] Psychophysics was formed at the intersection of two sorts of questions. Firstly, what was the relationship between matter and mind, between body and soul? And secondly, if every science must proceed by establishing the laws which express quantitative relations between objects, was mind adequate to a scientific knowledge, could the soul be measured? Psychophysics operated within this space, and its laws and measurements thus concerned a domain *internal* to the subjects it studied. It was to be, in Fechner's words, 'the exact theory of the functionally dependent relations of body and soul, or, more generally, of the material and the mental, of the physical and the physiological worlds.'[6] The quantitative relations which psychophysics sought to determine were thus those between the stimulus and the sensation, and the laws which concerned it were the general laws governing this relation.

This too was the space in which Wundt's analysis of the elements of consciousness operated, and which the measurements he carried out in his psychological laboratory at Leipzig concerned. Break down experience into its constituent elements through introspection; relate these elements to the measured stimuli that evoke them under stated conditions; measure the quantitative relation between stimulus and experience; develop the general laws of these relations and of the combination of the elements into complex unities. Hence Wundt measured the senses, especially those of vision and hearing. He measured reaction time: the period spanning the stimulation of the sense, its presence in consciousness (perception), its identification, appropriation and synthesis by the subject (apperception) and the reaction (an act of will). He measured the smallest noticeable difference between stimuli. And he measured associations between words. But all his measurements and analyses operated within this space bounded by the stimulus, the experience and the reaction. Thus Wundt was forced to make an absolute separation between the sphere of objects, problems and concepts proper to experimental psychology and those proper to the social field, which must be the concern of the quite discrete knowledge of *Volkpsychologie*.[7]

It was not, of course, that the question of individual differences was not thinkable in these terms. Indeed Galton himself had made observations on differences in sensitivity and discriminatory ability and tried to relate these to differences in intellectual ability, his trials confirming:[8]

> the reasonable expectation that it would on the whole be highest among the intellectually ablest. . . . The discriminative faculty of idiots is curiously low; they hardly distinguish between hot and cold and their sense of pain is so obtuse that some of the more idiotic seem hardly to know what it is.

And both Galton and James Sully, from the mid 1880s onwards, had urged that large-scale surveys be carried out on physical, sensory and mental differences, especially in children, and had suggested that such surveys might provide information of use to education. According to Keir, Galton and Sully wished to obtain more accurate information about the average or normal characteristics of children at successive stages of life; about the approximate number of cases needing special attention, special treatment, or special types of school; and about changes in mental and educational level from year to year or from one generation to the next.[9] Some of the ways in which evidence from such surveys was deployed in relation to mental deficiency have already been discussed. But as important was the development of detailed knowledge about individual children, and the development of methods of assessment of their abilities and qualities.

The British Child Study Association was established by Sully in 1893 with the support of teachers and educationalists. It urged the importance of making 'a scientific study of individual children by psychological, sociological and anthropometric methods', in particular, it promoted the development of methods for the 'direct assessment' of intellectual, emotional and moral qualities, instead of relying on indirect inferences from physical characteristics, and the study of 'the normal as well as the abnormal, paying special attention to the investigation of the commoner causes of minor deviations among normal children, as well as to the diagnosis of the rarer abnormal or pathological types.'[10]

In 1884 Galton opened an 'anthropometric laboratory' as part of the International Health Exhibition.[11] Parents were charged a nominal fee for their children to have their 'powers' measured and recorded on an individual case history sheet. This was a sort of contractual arrangement, made directly between scientist and parents, in which the latter, in return for allowing their progeny to become objects of scientific knowledge, obtained information as to their abilities or warnings as to faults which might be put right. But this direct exchange was to be short lived.

In 1896, three years after his appointment as Professor of Mind and Logic at University College, London, Sully opened what was the first exclusively *psychological* laboratory in England. He had William McDougall first as his assistant, then as Director of the Laboratory from 1899 to 1907, when McDougall resigned to allow Spearman to take up this position. Galton and Sully both saw this laboratory as a prototype of a form of institution which could be set up throughout the country. This institution was to operate in connection with the schools; hence its difference from the direct relationship with parents which Galton's first laboratory offered. Parents were now party to the relationship only in so far as they were mediated through the school and the child. Teachers were to bring to the laboratory their problem children, those pupils who were proving 'difficult', and there they would be examined and experimented upon by the laboratory's psychologists. Scientific knowledge and pedagogic techniques were welded together once more. In a sense, all those subjects of investigation in the psychological laboratory were little wild children, Victor's siblings. Like Victor, they were caught up in a process which simultaneously sought to extract knowledge from them – to make them answer up as to the nature of their mental processes – and to make them the objects of reform – in that this knowledge was to be turned to account in technical operations to change, develop or reconstruct these processes. The happenings in the laboratory were observed by students of psychology or education, so children made their own contribution to the furtherance of pedagogy, even if not their own. But in return, teachers received a report on the mental and physical characteristics of the child with suggestions as to treatment which might be appropriate for the reformation of undesirable aspects.[12]

Despite the possibilities offered by the school-child-psychologist relation, psychological methods of assessment were unable to leave the laboratory before being radically transformed. For the psychology of individual differences to be able to affix itself to the institutional demand for the assessment of individuals, a shift would have to occur away from the rationale which guided psychophysics, a shift of both the object and the form of calculation. The move was, first of all, from the investigatory rationale of the experiment to the adjudicatory rationale of the *test*. The term 'test' was first introduced into psychological discourse rather unassumingly in a paper written by James Cattell and published in *Mind* in 1890. He still employed it in the context of the laboratory:[13]

> Psychology cannot attain the certainty and exactness of the physical sciences, unless it rests on a foundation of experiment and measurement. A step in this direction could be made by applying a series of mental tests and measurements to a large number of individuals. The results would be of considerable scientific value in discovering the consistency of mental processes, their interdependence, and their variation under differing conditions.

So the idea was that you measured individual attributes on a range of different tests, and you measured a lot of different individuals, and thus you could not only establish individual differences but also see how these were ranged in the population, *and* how any individual fitted within that range. We can see how the object of the application of measurement has changed from psychophysics. Measurement does not examine the capacities of a number of individuals with a view to establishing some general law true for all, but focuses upon the particular combination of functions in each specific individual in relation to their distribution and variation across the population, with a view to establishing the parameters of individual differences. At this point we are close to the modern notion of a psychological test, but there is still some distance to go.

Whilst the technique of the experiment focused upon the individual only to the extent that he could supply data which would allow the formulation of general laws, in the practice of the test, measurements were made of individuals with a view to pronouncing a judgment upon them in comparison to some other individual or the general population of individuals. The displacement of the object of measurement marked by the emergence of the test allowed two complementary alliances to be formed. Firstly, an alliance with statistical techniques which allowed the mathematical analysis of variations between individuals in a population. Secondly, an alliance with technical operations of classification and distribution of individuals on the basis of their relations with other individuals in the population. But it was the demands of administration rather than the hesitancies of science which forced the combination of these two alliances, and hence revealed the true utility of the test. This came about because of two challenges which were posed to the psychological conception of intelligence and its measurement. On the one hand, a challenge which consisted in the nomination of medicine as the adjudicative instance in the assessment of the feeble-minded. And on the other hand, a challenge contained in the development and utilisation of the Binet test as the means for this assessment.

If individual psychology in England was initially unable to fulfil its task as the knowledge competent to pronounce on questions of intellectual ability, this was, paradoxically, at least partly because of the eugenic strategy in which it was caught up for its first two decades. Why was this an obstacle? It was an obstacle because individual psychology sought to adjust its techniques of measurement not simply to the externally variable conducts and abilities of individuals assessed, but also to some common, underlying, heritable and hence biological substrate of these behaviours and abilities. With admirable rigour, it continually sought to reconcile the exigencies of social judgments of abilities with the faculties of the sensory apparatus as measured by the technical devices of psychophysics. Hence the schema of tests which Cattell proposed differed but little from those utilised by Galton in his anthropometric laboratory. They ranged from bodily measures such as dynamometer pressure, through such classical psychophysiological measures as least noticeable weight difference, to 'purely mental measures' such as the number of letters remembered at one hearing.[14] This was still a long way from the 'direct' measures of assessment desired by the British Child Study Association, or, rather, it was caught in a particular conception of what a 'direct' measure must look like.

Between the senses, which it was possible and legitimate to measure, and behaviours, upon which it was necessary to adjudicate, only statistical devices exist to commensurate the incommensurable. When Cattell's paper was published in 1890, it was followed by some remarks by Francis Galton. Galton expressed great interest in Cattell's proposals, but considered that they would only achieve their goal of differentiating individuals if the measures made by Cattell were correlated with 'an independent estimate of the man's powers', for example 'mobile, eager, energetic, well shaped. . .'.[15] It was towards the problem posed by these remarks that Spearman's famous paper of 1904 on ' "General intelligence" objectively determined and measured' was directed. Spearman recognised that all previous attempts at psychological measurement had failed in that they had been unable to show any relationship between the measures they obtained and the abilities of individuals in their ordinary life. Indeed, they had even failed to demonstrate any relationship between the values on the different measures used for any one individual. And these criticisms applied not only to measurements of simple sensory properties, but also to Binet's attempts to measure complex mental functions.[16] Spearman's well-known solution, using complex correlational techniques, was to propose a two-factor theory of intelligence, comprising a central and fundamental function of general intelligence, which acted in common with specific intelligences to produce the abilities which individuals demonstrated in particular tasks.

Spearman obtained measures of his samples of Harrovian schoolboys with regard to their discriminatory abilities on weight, sound and vision, and employed a development of the statistical methods of Bravais, Galton and Pearson in order to correlate these measures with independently obtained rankings of these children in order of intelligence. This enabled him to forge statistically the link between these sensory abilities and the pertinent behaviours, in the manner that has been utilised throughout the whole subsequent history of psychological tests of intelligence. The interdependent rankings of intelligence were obtained from the order in which the children were placed by their school results, by their teacher, by a fellow schoolboy and by the Rector's wife (who, Spearman regretted, could only provide an incomplete list). The circularity of this procedure, its assumption of the forms of differentiation and of a unilinear distribution of individuals in the population according to mental powers which it claimed to demonstrate – all these are by now familiar criticisms. What concerns us here are the consequences which followed from the fact that Spearman considered his statistical manoeuvres to have demonstrated that 'the common and essential element in the Intelligence wholly coincides with the common and essential element in the sensory functions.'[17]

Two things had happened here which allowed this discourse on intelligence to be situated within a eugenicist strategy. Firstly, the measurement of intelligence had become a question of differentiating between individuals in terms of the position which they occupied in a linear series. This linear series was a measure of some characteristic which could be regarded as having a continuous distribution with a pattern which followed the normal curve. Intelligence thus unified could be treated according to the statistics of large populations, in which individual scores received their pertinence from the perspective of the population and their relation to its norms. And second, intelligence could be conceived in terms of the links between the outward and visible effects (behaviours, performances) and an internal and biological cause (sensory functions). It was thus entirely consistent that Burt's attempt to extend and develop Spearman's work, in his investigation of the intelligence of Oxford schoolchildren from schools of differing qualities should have been undertaken at the instigation of William McDougall, who could then celebrate the results a few years later in a paper entitled 'Psychology in the service of eugenics': 'we have discovered a measurable factor which is involved in, and is an important factor or condition of proficiency in, many mental operations; a factor which is possessed in very different degrees by different individuals.'[18]

McDougall chaired a sub-committee of the Anthropological Section of the British Association which was set up to consider the gathering of psychological measurements as a part of a scheme for a comprehensive survey of the population which had been proposed in 1905.[19] The drive to measure was undoubtedly produced within the debates over physical and psychological deterioration which have already been discussed. This was true also of the recommendation made by the Board of Education in 1907 for 'anthropometric observation of children in schools' which, according to Hearnshaw, greatly facilitated Burt, Flugel and English – whom McDougall recruited to assist him with construction and standardisation of tests – gaining access to schoolchildren for testing, in Oxford and later in Liverpool and elsewhere. In this great labour of quantification of attributes, a new kind of knowledge of the population was being constituted, not simply of its gross characteristics and crises – births, deaths, marriages, illnesses – but also of its more quotidian aspects. Eugenics was not responsible for the opening up of this new domain of knowledge, but it certainly did eventually come to establish the way in which a psychology of intelligence would be elaborated in England.

The importance for eugenics of producing a factor of general intelligence was its consonance with the postulate of a biological, variable, heritable basis for mental characteristics. Spearman recognised this, and explicitly allied his conception of general intelligence with Galton's earlier notion of a variable and heritable vital energy, which underlay and made possible labour and all the robust virtues.[20] Burt stressed a similar theme when he argued in relation to general intelligence:[21]

> we may eventually seek the psycho-physical basis, underlying this capacity, in a particular characteristic of general neural constitution; the accentuation of such a neural characteristic would then produce the type of mind known as intelligent, while its biological inheritance would form the condition of the transmissibility of the mental trait.

But although this psychophysiological basis was not yet specifiable, the demonstration of the innateness of general intelligence, once that had been given a precise definition, could serve the same function:[22]

> Once devised, once demonstrated to measure a general innate endowment, as distinguished from special knowledge and special dexterities, that is to say from post-natal acquisition, such tests will find yet a third direction for experimental investigation, namely the enquiry how far the capacity thus measured varies with Age, with Education, with Parentage and with Social Rank; and this further application of the methods of the 'tests' would provide at once an illustration of their practical importance and a corroboration of their theoretical validity.

I have already referred to the critical comments which have recently been levelled at Burt's later papers claiming to demonstrate the innateness of intelligence, and the publicity which has been given to the 'scandal' of his fabrication and judicious adjustment of his data.[23] But as we can see, what is at issue is not an isolated and regrettable aberration, but the formation of a systematic explanatory structure which made the claims of certain arguments so strong as to require little in the way of justificatory evidence. As Hearnshaw has pointed out, the argument which Burt puts forward in 1901 for the innateness of intelligence rests upon a series of dubious steps:

> (1) Bishops are brighter than butchers (obviously). (2) The sons of bishops are better at dotting and other similar tests than the sons of butchers. (3) These tests correlate highly with intelligence as judged by teachers. (4) These tests do not depend on prior experience and performance does not improve with practice, or on retesting after 18 months: therefore they must measure innate capacity. (5) The class differences cannot be accounted for by environmental deprivation, since the butchers could afford to pay 9d per week in school fees. (6) Therefore, we may conclude that the superior proficiency and intelligence of the bishops' boys is inborn. (Population: N = 43; 30 lower middle class; 13 upper class).[24]

This argument may indeed be guilty of the sin of *petitio principii* but the premises which contain its conclusions are fundamental elements of eugenic discourse. The postulation of a unitary function of intelligence, biologically based and innate, eminently inheritable, a common basis to all the attributes and qualities of the individual, manifested in social rank, was merely a reworking of themes which had been familiar since the publication of *Hereditary Genius*. It was not surprising therefore that Burt explicitly returned at the end of his article to the very terms of Galton's eugenic reutilisation of Booth:[25]

> we seem to have proved marked inheritability in the case of a mental character of the highest 'civic worth'.
> Parental intelligence, therefore, may be inherited, individual intelligence measured, and general intelligence analysed; and they can be analysed, measured and inherited to a degree which few psychologists have legitimately ventured to maintain.

So a method of assessment appeared to have been devised which would allow the discrimination and ascertainment required by the demands of administration. Underpinning this technique was the link which Galton had forged at the moment of conception of the psychology of the individual between statistical norms of population variation and social norms of conformity to required standards of conduct. Individual psychology would seek to diagnose social pathology in terms of deviation from statistical norms. Its conception of normal and abnormal mental functioning would be constructed from the point of view of a theory of populations, averages and correlations, not from a conception of the psyche itself. And similarly, methods of assessment would select their contents on the grounds of their ability to reproduce statistically a predetermined social categorisation and distribution – items being included only if they permitted a distinction between individuals which accorded with that already made on educational, moral or judicial grounds. The psychology of the individual was destined from the outset to construct its theoretical object in terms of norms of statistics and social adaptation rather than in terms of the normativity of psychic functioning. No wonder it was to become not so much a clinical as an administrative practice.

Yet despite the link it forged between social requirements and psychological assessments, despite its certainty of the possibility of assessing intelligence through the measurement of sensory functions, and despite the corollary that psychologists possessed the rights and capacities to adjudicate in cases of suspected pathology of the intellect, these claims fell on deaf ears as far as administrative procedures for diagnosing the feeble-minded were concerned. Not that diagnoses were not being carried out. But the procedures were not being operated by those versed in psychology but by doctors, and the technical device utilised was not based upon the assessment of elementary sensory and motor functions and their statistical treatment but was a test of a very different type.

We can trace this clearly if we examine successive Reports of the Chief Medical Officer of the Board of Education. By 1909 the question of the diagnosis of feeble-minded schoolchildren was already causing problems to School Medical Officers. The Chief Medical Officer included in his report a schedule for the examination of children in respect to this difficulty. This included not only tests of motor ability, sensory responses, emotional balance and will-power, but also 'tests of intelligence' involving the description of pictures, counting ability, handwriting tests and so forth. The Chief Medical Officer urged School Medical Officers on not with a eugenic argument, but because the task of ascertainment was vital in order to allow the feeble-minded to contribute to their own support, to save them from harsh treatment on the streets, to prevent them becoming drunkards, criminals and prostitutes and from giving birth to children who would certainly grow up to be a burden on the community.[26]

In the Report of 1910, a further familiar theme was deployed. The Chief Medical Officer advocated an organisation for the ascertainment and allocation of feeble-minded children in terms familiar from the Minority Report of the Royal Commission on the Poor Laws, when he remarked that 'the Day Special School is an indispensable agency both as an "observational centre" and a "sorting house" ', a place where children could be tested, classified and distributed to the appropriate place amongst a range of specialised agencies.[27]

It was within this familiar strategy of classification, distribution, socialisation or segregation that, in the Report for 1911, the 'psychological and educational tests associated with the name of Binet' were introduced for the first time into the schema of tests and recommended for the differentiation of the normal child from the feeble-minded.[28] It was now not so much the physical examination, though this still occurred, nor any of the other assessments, but *intelligence* which had become the fulcrum of adjudication, and intelligence had become what the Binet and Simon test measured. When the passage of the Mental Deficiency Act stabilised the administrative structure in the form it would maintain for many years, the Binet tests retained their central place in a versatile apparatus for the production and utilisation of scientific knowledge of intelligence and its pathologies.[29] Why should the Binet-Simon tests have succeeded in the hands of the doctors, while the psychologists and their measures failed to occupy the space they considered theirs by right? To resolve this question, let us consider briefly the formulation of these tests in France.

Like Galton, Binet from the outset considered the study of individual differences to be central to the construction of a scientific psychology. But unlike Galton, he eschewed any attempt to forge direct links between elementary sensations and individual abilities. Whilst the postulation of such links was, as we have seen, fundamental to any eugenic argument, Binet was not so constrained and moved directly towards the measurement of complex cognitive functions.[30] This object of measurement allowed a different *form* of measurement from that appropriate to the elementary sensory functions. The indices of mental functions that Binet used were partly physical and anthropometric: cephalometric studies, graphology, indeed any measure of this type which could provide a measurable range of differences between individuals. However, whilst such measures were compatible with those utilised by the British eugenicists, other measures of mental functions were not. They bore directly upon psychological faculties, and included assessments of mental images, of imagination, of attention, of aesthetic sentiment and so forth.[31]

But after ten years of work on this project, little had been achieved in the way of any straightforward means of assessing individual differences in intellectual ability. Claparede, reporting on this work as presented by Henri at the First German Congress for Experimental Psychology in Giesbach, stated:[32]

> The experiments made since [the 1895 programme] in the schools have shown that it is premature to look for tests permitting a diagnosis during a very limited time (one or two hours), and that, much to the contrary, it is necessary to study individual psychology without limiting the time – especially by studying outstanding personalities.

Sustained research had led to the failure of attempts to arrive at a brief measure for assessing individual differences in intellectual ability. Binet and his co-workers recommended instead lengthy and systematic investigations of particular individuals. There seemed, therefore, to be a division between the exigencies which administration imposed and the methods dictated by a serious scientific attempt to establish a theory of intelligence, produce the means of assessing it, and allow discrimination between individuals on the basis of such an assessment. Yet just thirteen months later the first metric scale of intelligence, consisting of only thirty items, was published in *L'Année psychologique*.[33] How can this sudden transformation from failure to success be understood? Was it perhaps a sudden upsurge of creative genius which was responsible for this remarkable leap forward in scientific techniques for the psychological assessment of intelligence?[34] On the contrary, what happened first of all was a consequence of a shift in the way in which the question of intelligence was posed. Beaunais commented upon this when he first announced the invention of the test, reading a paper by Binet and Henri at the First International Congress of Psychology in Rome:[35]

> The two authors of the present note have especially preoccupied themselves with methods that could be used to make the distinction between normal and abnormal children . . . methods that will permit a clinician to separate the subjects of inferior intelligence into categories verifiable by all; and second, that will permit commissions who decide on the admission of children into special schools to make an exact distribution.

In France, just as much as in England, the imposition of universal and compulsory education filled schools with numbers of recalcitrant children who were ill suited to the rigours and disciplines of the school, and unable to fill the role of subject in the pedagogic technology of the normal classroom. As a key member of the Society for the Psychological Study of the Child, Binet was involved in the philanthropic campaign demanding that government must fulfil its legal responsibilities by extending the benefits of education to *all* children including the mentally defective.[36] In 1904 the Ministry of Public Instruction appointed a Ministerial Commission for the Abnormal, the French equivalent of the Committee on Defective and Epileptic Children. Binet and three other members of the Society for the Psychological Study of the Child were among its members. The Commission was not successful in its principal task, which was to discover the number of abnormal children in France. The problems of definition and diagnosis produced such variation between the verdicts of the teachers who were doing the classifying that the information which was obtained provided no basis for useful conclusions. Nonetheless the Commission, which confined its activities to administrative and pedagogic questions, did recommend the use of a 'medico-pedagogic examination' in the diagnosis of abnormality, but 'could offer no criteria for methods to be used, observations to be taken, questions to be posed, or tests to be originated.'[37]

Binet and Simon turned their attention from the theoretical problem of devising a means of measuring intelligence in terms of the distinct faculties of the mind, to the practical task of devising a means of classifying individuals into one or other of a very limited number of categories: not the theoretical distinction of intellect into its different aspects and parts, but the ranking of individuals as a whole in relation to their fellows according to the actual abilities and behaviours which were pertinent to their educational progress. They were not isolated in this attempt. It was not a case of a unique concatenation of events which, when synthesised by an investigator of brilliance and creativity, allowed a definitive break with an old paradigm. It was the intersection of a particular conception of the psyche and a specific administrative demand which made possible the shift to the unilinear assessment of behaviours in terms of a single and simple numerical measure. The work of Blin and Damaye, for example, presented in *L'Année psychologique* in 1908, utilised a simple questionnaire to assess children on a range of tasks – reading, writing, arithmetic, general knowledge questions and so forth – and provided their results in terms of a single number on a scale from zero to one hundred, with suggestions as to which scores indicated particular levels of retardation.[38]

Binet's scale replaced the apparent arbitrariness of the Blin-Damaye procedure in many respects; perhaps the most significant being the role which age was allowed to play in the ranking of individuals. The comparison of idiots with young children in their abilities and behaviours was, of course, not new, but Binet reworked this in a way which was made possible by the existence of the institutions for which his procedures were designed. The observation of large numbers of children of similar ages in schools, and of large numbers of defectives in institutions, allowed the formulation of a double relation – firstly, despite individual variations, norms of performance could be established for children at particular ages, and second, defective children of particular ages could be seen to bear a striking resemblance to normal children some years younger. Whilst Binet refused to commit himself to an explanation of mental defect as an arrest of normal development, in pragmatic terms he recognised that the combination of these two arguments could lead to a classification of children in terms of a single measure – mental level – which, when compared with their chronological age, would give a simple indication of the degree of their defect. The virtue of such a criterion was all the greater in that it related directly to the field of problems into which it was inserted: the norms and expectations of the schools as to the performance of children of different ages in the classroom.

This was the crucial shift marked by the invention of the Binet-Simon scale – from measurement of faculties operating within a space internal to the subject, to the examination of behaviours in which measurement was concerned with the subject as a whole, and from the point of view of his or her ability to perform in relation to social norms. Behaviour was the link between the measurement of subjects and the administration of individuals; it was the common point upon which they were articulated.

Binet recognised at the outset that the problem to which his test of intelligence was an answer was not that with which he had struggled for so long. He did not believe that what he was measuring as intelligence in this new device was what he had been attempting to measure in his detailed studies of his two daughters and in his extensive observations and experiments upon children. Thus in *Les Enfants anormeaux* Binet and Simon stressed the utility of the test as an administrative device; they subtitled the text 'a guide for the admission of retarded children into special classes'.[39] They constantly emphasised the limitations of the test: its criteria were not theoretical but educational; it was to serve only as a first means for the teacher to use in singling out children who might be mentally backward for further detailed investigation by a number of experts; the test itself was only a guide and was never definitive. Yet at the same time as recognising these limitations – the test was merely a tool of administration – the authors were constantly beguiled into wishing to establish its claims to be something more. The test held a potent promise in its ability to transform previously unmanageable attributes into assessable, calculable quantities.

The first extension was from the pathological to the normal. What was originally a device for diagnosing the defective became a device for hierarchising the normal. The reference which the condensation of behaviours into a single number appeared to make to a hidden quality of the individual, together with the norms of development which provided the standard of assessment of deficiency, made it easy for the test to be extended beyond its initial point of emergence. By 1908 the test had changed its title – from 'new methods for the diagnosis of the intellectual level of the abnormal' to 'the development of intelligence among children'.[40] Mental deficiency, hidden within the psychological domain, beyond recognition by visible signs, physical stigmata or anthropometric indices, had provided the route for the formation of a psychological conception of intelligence and a technique of assessing it appropriate to every child. It was in relation to the question of the abnormal that a psychology of individual differences was established, and that a psychological conception of the normal was itself fixed and defined.

Despite the apparent virtues of the Binet-Simon test, its brevity, the simplicity of the calculations it entailed, the convenience of the result it provided, its direct orientation to pertinent educational norms of behaviour and performance, it made a very limited impact in France on its first publication. But after the 1908 revision of the scales was published the test, now oriented to assessing the intelligence of all children, rapidly came to define conceptions of intelligence and the means of measuring it for many decades – revised, restandardised, extended and modified but in its mode of functioning unchanged. The production of a simple numerical result was one advantage; another was that:[41]

> it runs its course according to an unvarying plan, it takes
> express account of age, and it assesses the responses by
> comparing them to a norm that is a real and living average.

By 1909 Binet was explicit about the central feature of his test, the fundamental reason why it could occupy the place it did in the structure of educational administration – that what it measured was *adaptation*:[42]

> We predict a new method for measuring the phenomena of
> consciousness; instead of measuring their *intensity*, which has
> been the vain and foolish ambition of the psychophysicists, we
> shall measure the useful effects of acts of adaptation, and the
> value of the difficulties overcome by them; there is here a
> measure that is not arithmetical, but one that permits a lineal
> seriation, a hierarchy of acts and of different individuals judged
> according to their effectiveness.

A measure of adaptation which allowed the serial ranking of individuals according to the effectiveness of the adaptations to norms which they demonstrated – could there be a clearer characterisation of the psychological conception and measure of intelligence which had now formed? Only one last hesitation remained – Binet's unwillingness or inability to combine together the elements of chronological age and mental level into a single figure. It was for William Stern to advocate this combination, and the calculation of a mental quotient. He recognised that the single figure disguised the most varied sorts of combinations of passed and failed items. But:[43]

> this very thing appears to constitute an advantage, rather than
> a disadvantage of the concept of mental age, for it gives
> expression to a fundamental psychological fact . . . there never
> is a real phenomenological equivalence between the intelligence
> of two persons: what we do have is rather a teleological
> equivalence – when measured in terms of the single function of
> all intelligence, namely, adaptation to new requirements. . . .

And the mental quotient allowed for comparisons between as well
as within age bands, for the summing up of the mental powers of
an individual in a single figure which would tell those who wanted
to know all they needed to know about them.

Perhaps it is true, as the familiar criticism goes, that with the
invention of the Intelligence Quotient, intelligence has become no
more than 'what intelligence tests measure'. But one must also
recognise that with the concept of IQ what has happened is that
social norms and expectations are internalised both within the
theory of intelligence and the technique of its assessment. The test
is not merely suited to the administrative demands placed upon it
because of the cultural bias of the test items, or the dependence of
performance upon experience, but because of its ability to produce
a single numerical measure of an individual's adaptation to social
requirements. The virtue of the Binet-Simon test was its tacit
recognition that for individual psychology to enter the space
where it could become an effective and functioning social
knowledge, it would have to concern itself less with the laws of an
internally organised mental domain than with the laws of the
adaptation of the subject to social and pedagogic exigencies, and
with the techniques of administration of individuals in respect to
the alignment or non-alignment of the registers of the mental and
the pedagogic.

It was for these reasons that it was the Binet-Simon test which
first provided the technical means of discrimination and ascertainment of feeble-minded children in England. And no doubt the
opposition of the English eugenic psychologists to this technique
was in part responsible for their failure to obtain the position of
adjudicating agency in respect to these questions. For, as we have
seen, despite the non-medical nature of the criteria which were
being used for ascertainment, and despite the self-proclaimed
'psychological' basis of the Binet-Simon test, it was doctors who

controlled the administration of children unfit for normal school from 1890 to 1975.[44]

Psychologists against doctors

Even as late as 1920 the psychiatric examinations carried out by the school medical officer were generally limited to measuring the size of the skull and inspecting the child for 'stigmata of degeneracy', 'cranial abnormalities', 'nerve signs', 'symptoms of malnutrition or other chronic deficiencies'. . . . Treatment was mainly physical; and, when that failed, the only remedy was held to be segregation. Mental symptoms, mental causes, and psychological or social methods of treatment were dismissed as the speculative fancies of the layman.

Gertrude Keir, 1952[45]

The doctors certainly came out on top in the first struggles over the pathologies thrown up by the school. This was not simply a question of their intransigence, their influence in high places or their superior status.[46] The school was not an accidental gain for medicine; from the start of compulsory and universal schooling doctors conceived of the school as a site which was as much medical as pedagogic. With the introduction of a universal system of education, a transformation could occur in the preventative and hygienist medical strategy which had been operative during the nineteenth century. By the end of the nineteenth century the language of contagious atmospheres of vice and disease, and the concomitant programmes of sanitisation of social space, had ceased to provide the terms for political arguments over 'the social question'. The new preventative medicine was a medicine of the clinic rather than the epidemic, a medicine of cases rather than spaces.

The first Annual Report of the Chief Medical Officer of the Board of Education put it thus:[47]

Preventative medicine . . . has become an appropriate medium for the solution of the problems of hygiene in relation to the education of the child . . . the centre of gravity of our public health system is passing, in some degree, from the environment to the individual and from problems of outward sanitation to problems of personal hygiene.

The school allowed a generalisation of the clinical experience to a whole class of individuals. It was a site which allowed the same sort of individualisation, comparison, statisticalisation and so forth as the hospital, but now not in respect of those few who had come to medicine for treatment, but to all those who, simply by virtue of being a certain age, became subject to medical investigation.

The earliest interest of medicine in education had, however, been of a rather different order. It concerned the potentially deleterious effects of education in schools upon the health of the child. Reading in poor light or with bad print could damage eyesight, sitting at cramped desks for long hours at crucial periods of growth could produce physical deformities, damage could be done by the 'mental over-pressure' which existed in the elementary schools of London.[48] When Dr W.R. Smith was appointed as Medical Officer to the London School Board in 1890, it was along these lines that his duties lay. He was to advise on those aspects of the school which might affect the health of the child – ventilation, lighting, sanitation and so forth.[49]

But three years later, when James Kerr was appointed in Bradford, a neo-hygienist strategy had begun to form.[50] It began to be recognised that the school could act as a mechanism to provide data on the health of all children in the population, and that this data could be of great value when processed, tabulated, and analysed in various ways. And, at the same time, the school was a site where individual diagnostic techniques could be applied to every child, and around which an integrated system of treatment could be organised. Doctors began to campaign for the social recognition of this medical function of the school. In 1896, the Society for the Promotion of Hygiene in School Life was formed; already, the nascent individual psychologists recognised the danger that this medical strategy was to pose to them. Sully, when requested to co-operate, declined and strove to maintain the separate existence of the Child Study Society.[51] But the movement of doctors was growing and international, and achieved further publicity in two International Conferences on School Hygiene, the first at Nuremberg in 1904, the second in London some four years later.

Neo-hygienism was the dominant strategy within the debate over national deterioration, as it took shape in the first decade of the twentieth century. It posed its explanations principally in terms of the deleterious effects upon health and physique of poor environment, bad food, poor personal hygiene and wasteful and ignorant habits of household management. It called for a programme of reform of habits of cleanliness, feeding, personal and household regimens; this would, if successful, improve health and reverse the deterioration of the national health and physique. The school was the ideal site for the coordination of such a strategy. Within it the question of mental defect and feeble-mindedness occupied a relatively minor position – it was simply one element in a complex of symptoms recognisable by a trained medical gaze. Problems of intellect always needed to be understood within the context of the general physical condition, health and cleanliness of the child and did not occupy any autonomous or exemplary place in relation to them.

From the Committee of Defective and Epileptic Children to the Inter-Departmental Committee on Physical Deterioration, the success of neo-hygienism accounted for the proposals which were put forward and the authoritative role which was accorded to doctors. The Inter-Departmental Committee's recommendations on schoolchildren were all in this vein: schools should be established for children whose ill-health made them temporarily unsuited to normal schools; every school authority should have the duty to make medical inspections of schoolchildren; authorities should be compelled to provide school meals for underfed children.[52] While the government balked at introducing the radical interventionist legislation which such recommendations enjoined, the Committee on Medical Inspection and Feeding of Children which reported in 1905 did nothing to provide any alternative, and indeed made the case more radical by implying that even medical inspection left untouched the question of the treatment of the conditions it revealed.[53] The Education (Provision of Meals) Act 1906 contained a clause which compelled local authorities to provide for the medical inspection of children. Thus, in 1907, the School Medical Service came into existence, with George Newman as head of a new Medical Branch of the Board of Education.

Within this neo-hygienist strategy, another shift occurred in the political concern with the population. It was now not a simple issue of numbers, of rates of birth and death, of major diseases, of differential rates of reproduction in the different classes. It was a matter of fine, and almost indelicate, detail. Height, weight, eyesight, hearing, vermin and lice, ringworm, washing habits and cleanliness of clothing – all were painstakingly investigated, recorded and analysed. The school was the surface upon which all the petty details of the lives of individuals could emerge as a domain of problems and objects for social reformation.[54]

The tactics of reform were two-pronged. Firstly, there were those directed at the child itself. The provision of school meals to the underfed was clearly aimed at direct and immediate improvement in health, and at long-term improvement in physique and fitness. But doctors were more involved in direct clinical intervention – diagnosis of a range of conditions from notifiable diseases, through sensory deficiencies of one type of another, to lice or general lack of cleanliness, each to be accompanied by recommendations for treatment. Newman was at the forefront of those who wished the clinical method of diagnosis in the school to be linked to an indigenous clinical machinery for treatment. This would avoid the vagaries of parental action or lethargy, or the problems of family doctor or hospital, intervening between these two indissociable aspects of clinical medicine. Whilst these clinics were slow to get established, the movement soon gathered momentum. The first school clinic was opened in Bradford in 1908, and by 1935, when Newman retired, over 2,000 had been established throughout England and Wales.[55]

But if this all sounds very much like individualised medicine, differing only in its universal application to all subjects within a given age range, the aspirations of the neo-hygienist strategy went far beyond this. For the second tactical prong was one which sought to utilise the clinical scrutiny of the child in a campaign for upgrading the hygiene and morals of the home and the space of personal existence outside the doctor-child encounter. Newman was quite clear on this, in his rebuttal of those who might think that to set up such a medical system was to relieve parents of important duties and hence to encourage irresponsibility:[56]

> One of the objects of the new legislation is to stimulate a sense of duty in matters affecting health in the homes of the people, to enlist the best services and interests of the parents and to educate a sense of responsibility for the personal hygiene of their children. . . . It is in the home, in fact, that both the seed and the fruit of public health are found.

This is what gave this neo-hygienist strategy a potency and

flexibility far beyond anything which psycho-eugenics could provide, with its impoverished tactic of ascertainment of intellectual pathology and segregation of those falling a certain way below the norm. For neo-hygienism, the school was the fulcrum of a mechanism which could be both universal and individualised, which enlisted the child and family themselves in the reformation of all the previously marginal matters of personal life – neck scrubbing, teeth cleaning, head washing and so forth. The mechanism allowed for the generalised insertion into the home, not only of moral principles and maxims concerning the virtues of cleanliness and so forth, but of the detailed behavioural techniques and modes of personal and household management in which they consisted.[57] It allowed for the monitoring of those transformations which did occur in the home through the continued scrutiny of the child who became, as it were, the symptom of the state of play in the personal domain. The school thus occupied a crucial position within a more general strategy of public health, indeed in two thirds of local authorities the School Medical Officer was also the Medical Officer of Health.[58] By the end of the first decade of the twentieth century this was no longer merely an ideal programme; it was a formidable apparatus, legally enforced, with School Medical Officers in every authority, with every schoolchild compulsorily inspected, with the whole enterprise supported by public funds, exploiting the existing conceptual and technical resources of clinical medicine, and linked in to the statutorily established system of public health.

It was not merely professional jealousy, then, which accounts for the opposition of doctors to the involvement of teachers or others in this apparatus, nor was it merely professional status which accounts for their success. It was a function of the way in which the strategy was set up, and the way in which it was to operate. From the Defective and Epileptic Children Committee in the 1890s to the debates over who should supervise Special Schools in the 1930s, doctors and teachers were at loggerheads, and doctors always won. Shuttleworth, Beach, Harris and others, in their evidence to the Committee, all stressed that only a doctor was capable of diagnosing defects, because this involved understanding the particular difficulties which a child was showing in the school within a spectrum of illnesses and physical defects which may have been causing them. This required an adjudication between one diagnosis and another, which could only be made on the basis of a clinical training from which teachers had not benefited.[59] The dominant role of medicine was enshrined in legislation. From the Elementary Education (Defective and Epileptic) Children Act 1899, through the 1907 provision for inspection of schoolchildren, to the Mental Deficiency Act 1913 and the Elementary Education (Defective and Epileptic Children) Act 1914 to the Education Acts of 1921 and 1944, it was always a medical officer of the local authority who was vested with the duty and power of ascertainment.

The English psychologists of the individual had failed in their attempt to isolate a non-medical space of diagnosis and ascertainment, and to adjudicate on the pathologies of the intellect which the school revealed. From 1905 onwards, the psychologists were vociferous in their criticisms of the use of the Binet test for the measurement of intelligence and the diagnosis of feeble-mindedness. The test, they claimed, was not based on any rigorous definition or theory of intelligence; it failed to link its measures to identifiable sensory or other variations in function; the measures it gave were unreliable and pragmatic; it was dangerous for those unversed in psychological knowledge and procedures to use this test as a mechanical device for identifying defect.[60]

Psychologists' historical accounts of this period make interesting reading. They tend to represent it as a struggle between psychological enlightenment and the outmoded and barbarous methods and beliefs of the doctors. Doctors, it is claimed, relied almost entirely upon stigmata and physical signs in the ascertainment of feeble-mindedness, and even utilised such absurd diagnostic procedures as the measurement of skulls. This is because they were under the sway of an organicist illusion – that all mental disorders were brain disorders – and they therefore explained educational backwardness in terms of cerebral inadequacy or specific brain lesions, of latent epilepsy or chorea, of inadequacies in the quality, quantity or distribution of the blood. They were, it would appear, implacable opponents of 'the new-fangled scheme of intelligence tests'.[61]

In fact the evidence suggests something rather different. The schedules utilised for the inspection of children referred to School Medical Officers on suspicion of mental defect certainly do refer to stigmata, but these occupy a relatively minor part of the examination. At least one third of the schedule which Newman included in his Report of 1909 concerns general history and family background, and one third is specifically devoted to 'psychological' questions: reactions of motor mechanisms, reactions to sensory stimulation, emotional conditions, 'tests of intelligence' and will-power.[62] And very soon the Binet-Simon tests were included within this schedule.[63] So it was not the lack of attention to familial or psychological intellectual matters which differentiated the neo-hygienist modes of ascertainment from those advocated by the psycho-eugenicists. The distinction was rather in the privilege which was accorded to the question of intellectual defect and the modes of conceptualising it in relation to pathology more generally.

For the psycho-eugenicists, the fundamental purpose of testing was to identify those who were intellectually defective and so should be subject to some measure of segregation, permanent if possible and certainly involving curtailment of reproduction; those not within this defective group were to be allowed to proceed unfettered. But for neo-hygienism, intellectual defect did not have this privilege as both the key index of defective stock and the sign of a potential threat of degeneration. Not, of course, that once a diagnosis of feeble-mindedness had been made, doctors were hesitant about advocating permanent institutionalisation and limitation of reproduction – though they disputed amongst themselves about the relative virtues of segregation and sterilisation.[64] But they refused to regard the diagnosis of feeble-mindedness as the central rationale for inspection, or the test of intelligence as the key diagnostic instrument. Mental defect was only one condition of concern amongst many, and institutionalisation was only one option within a range of possible tactics and a rather unproductive one at that, in that it failed to reach the home environment which was a major target of reform. To the extent that the Binet-Simon test took its place among the various investigations which doctors used, it was just one amongst many; the assessed mental level in and of itself never dictated a decision. This needed to be integrated with other symptoms of ill-health and processed through the expertise of a clinician before any course of action could be chosen.

Hence the doctors' opposition to the introduction of psychologists into this apparatus of ascertainment was posed in the same terms as their opposition to ascertainment by teachers. Psychologists were not trained in clinical methods and were not able to situate the intellectual defects which they might observe within the

complex of other signs and symptoms of illness which might be
present. Sutherland and Sharp quote the following comment from
a Medical Officer in 1912:[65]

> It is proposed that . . . the diagnosis required by the Act is
> really, if not nominally, to be entrusted to an officer who is
> without medical qualifications. A psychologist who is not an
> expert in medical diagnosis would be sure to over-look diseased
> conditions which a qualified medical man would discover and
> hence, in my opinion, the proposed course introduces a grave
> element of danger . . .

This comment was made during the discussions which did
indeed lead to the appointment of a psychologist, none other than
Cyril Burt, to the London County Council, to be involved in the
diagnosis of children with mental defect. But it would be
misleading to see Burt's appointment as evidence of the success of
the psycho-eugenic arguments over the neo-hygienists' prioritisation of the clinical gaze of medicine. The appointment of a
psychologist was, rather, a tactical compromise between a number
of competing positions. There certainly were psychologically
trained educationalists – mainly school inspectors trained on
Sully's textbooks and often veterans of the Psychological Laboratory of University College – who sought to break the hold of
medicine over the diagnosis of intellectual pathology. But there
were also teachers and administrators concerned with the
consequences of medical diagnosis. School Medical Officers were
thought to be too liberal in their ascertainments, considering that
every backward child would benefit from the small classes and
individual teaching methods of the special schools. Teachers
objected to what they saw as an over-extension of medicine into
properly pedagogic matters. Finance committees objected to the
expense involved. Parents objected to the stigma which allocation
to a special school attached to their children. And Burt's role was
to mediate between these pressures, and to act as a check upon
excessive ascertainment.[66] But whilst his appointment was not a
sign of the acceptance of the arguments which he and others had
been producing, the field of oppositions between doctors, teachers
and administrators opened a space into which individual psychology could be inserted.

The limits of psycho eugenics

Although Burt's part-time appointment did lead to the opening of what he termed a 'Psychological Clinic', which would examine and report on individual children referred by teachers and doctors, there was no question of any general displacement of medicine as the authorised diagnostic instance in cases of intellectual pathology. The aspirations of the psychology of the individual to an autonomous clinical role for psychology were not to be realised within this configuration around mental defect and its ascertainment. In the question of ascertainment, psychologists were not to become the professional agency of diagnosis, but merely to provide the technical means of investigation of intelligence. And this was not to involve a displacement of the Binet-Simon test, but a reformulation of the test to bring it into line with the theoretical demands of psycho-eugenics.

In 1914, Burt devoted a two-part article to a criticism of the Binet test, probably written at just the same time as his appointment to the London County Council.[67] Whilst he redeployed the familiar criticisms, he nonetheless could not fail to recognise the conflict between the force of these objections to the test and the practical role which the test had already obtained. Burt was trenchant in his enumeration of the limitations of the Binet test: its lack of theoretical clarity; the heterogeneity of the tests; the fact that test construction should come after the analysis of intelligence into its general and specific capacities; the dependence of the test upon acquired rather than innate characteristics, especially language; the need for correlational studies to eliminate the influence of the environment; the problem that to claim a relationship of intelligence to age implies a uniform and unilinear growth of intelligence and that the attempt to unify differences in intelligence along a single dimension cannot account for the heterogeneity of mental defect. On the basis of this catalogue of criticisms, which may come as a surprise to those today who recycle the same complaints against the work of Burt himself, he concluded:[68]

> Except for practical and popular purposes, then, Binet's intention of measuring native intelligence in terms of mental years seems impracticable. It is like measuring stature with an elastic rod, warped in two or three places along its length, and telescoped in upon itself at the upper end.

However, Burt was astute enough to recognise that, by now, replacement of the test was not possible. He adopted a more subtle and insidious plan of revision and standardisation, using the classical correlational techniques of psycho-eugenics, in order to shift the Binet test into line with the biological, psychological and statistical requirements of the eugenic strategy. Burt's work at the London County Council was largely an attempt to realise this plan. And, by 1920, the task had by and large been accomplished: the synonymity of intelligence with what the test measured, but now backed by a theory of intelligence as a normally distributed, innate, heritable, general cognitive capacity. The influential Report of the Consultative Committee on Psychological Tests of Educable Capacity and their Possible Use in the Public System of Education exemplifies this new synthesis.

The Committee, which was chaired by Haddow, had Ballard, Myers and Spearman amongst its members; its Report was mainly written by Burt. The Report was clear about the advantage of mental tests for 'comparing children in respect of their inborn capacity ... selecting the best candidates for higher instruction, and sifting out defectives and dull children for treatment by special educational methods'.[69] And, in addition, tests minimised environmental conditions, were a basis for the prediction of educational capacities, provided an objective standard of judgment, took account of age, and required less time for administration than other forms of examination. Not only did the test possess all the advantages which Burt had claimed it lacked ten years earlier, but they now reached to that very core which was the target of psycho-eugenics: 'What tests of intelligence measure, therefore, is inborn, all round, intellectual ability.'[70]

It is not surprising that Burt was now able to accord the test the very ability and function which he had denied and criticised for so long. At the beginning of his now classic *Mental and Scholastic Tests*, in which his revised and standardised Binet-Simon tests were first published, he wrote:[71]

> No appeal is more often addressed to the psychologist than the demand for a mental footrule. Teachers, inspectors, school medical officers, care committee visitors, the officers of the juvenile criminal courts, all have long felt the need for some such instrument. . .

And in the revamped, standardised intelligence test, individual psychology had established the congruity between social norms and statistical norms which was fundamental to its theoretical existence, its classificatory tactics, and its strategic aspirations.

The 1920s saw a flood of literature on tests and testing, new standardisations, surveys and experiments, guides for the use of the tests in diagnosis.[72] Though the tests were modified, restandardised, new content introduced and old items dropped, the technique of the test, and the conception of what it was that it measured, was to remain virtually unchallenged for some forty years. Phillip Ballard was, perhaps, not far from the truth when he wrote in 1920:[73]

> Binet's crowning glory is, not that he got together a medley of heterogeneous tests for the detection of the feeble-minded, but that he invented a scale. In this he resembles Saul, the Son of Kish, who set out to look for asses and found a kingdom.

The tests were, indeed, the gateway to the psychological kingdom. The technology of quantification of qualities, of scaling of attributes, has undoubtedly been the basis of psychology's social vocation. But the technology of testing was not sufficient to found individual psychology's claim to provide an alternative theory, method and practice to medicine. Individual psychology was to become not a clinical science, but an administrative technique.

Of course, testing had functions beyond the field of mental defect, for the field of application of the instrument in the eyes of the English psycho-eugenicists was always across the whole span of human ability. The two other principal fields of application of testing were in vocational guidance and in selection for secondary education. In respect of the former, undertaken by C.S. Myers at the National Institute of Industrial Psychology, Burt again was active, as part-time head of the Vocational Section.[74] The main work on group tests of intelligence was carried out by Godfrey Thomson.[75] It has been estimated that 70 out of 146 local authorities used group tests of intelligence for the purposes of selection at some point between 1919 and 1940, most commonly the Moray House tests which Thomson devised.[76] Much has been written on the future of tests of intelligence in selection and streaming after the installation of the tripartite system of education in the Education Act of 1944.[77] But however successful individual psychology was in providing the technology of measurement and allocation, this was not equivalent to the establishment of an autonomous field of judgment and operation in respect of mental pathologies. Here the psycho-eugenic strategy had reached its limits.

By the mid-1920s, the centrality accorded to the problem of mental deficiency in social and political argument was on the wane. Not that legislative activity ceased.[78] The Wood Committee was set up jointly by the Board of Education and the Board of Control in 1924, particularly to examine the confusion which had been created in the earlier Acts over the division of powers between different authorities in provision for defectives, especially for children; before it reported, the Mental Deficiency Act 1927 had tinkered slightly with the Act of 1913. When it finally reported, in 1929, it attempted to reconcile the conflict between the demand for segregation of defectives and the advantages of non-institutional supervision, and the conflict between the growing emphasis on environmental and social factors in the production of mental deficiency and the commitment of the expert members of the Committee, who included Tredgold, Burt and Pinsent, to the notion of inherited and irremediable defect calling for compulsory curtailment of reproduction.[79] Following Tredgold's classification, the Wood Committee distinguished between primary and secondary amentia. The latter was non-heritable, individually caused, through illness or injury, and ameliorable through some form of intervention. The former, however, was the real problem. Primary amentia was the last stage of inheritance of the degeneracy of the subnormal group. Far from being a tiny minority, this subnormal group constituted the lowest tenth of the population – the insane, the paupers, the criminals, the alcoholics, the prostitutes and the unemployables. Here the Committee rehearsed the familiar eugenic argument – the group must be prevented from propagating its own kind and dragging down the rest of the community; segregation or sterilisation were the only methods possible. It was vital that the work of ascertainment of mental defect, so often carried out in a hurried and partial way by school doctors looking only for the physical signs of deficiency, should be made more rigorous, and that the criteria used in ascertainment should not be physical or educational but be those of social inefficiency. Only then would the 'social problem group' be identified for compulsory and certain treatment.

The Wood Committee equivocated, largely on practical grounds, on the question of legalising sterilisation for defectives; the Brock Committee, set up by the Board of Control to consider this question, reported in 1934.[80] Whilst hedging their bets on the question of causation in any individual case, the Committee was clear that mental disorder and defect was transmissible in the majority of cases, and that, when it was hereditary, it was linked to the familiar forms of degeneracy from insanity to epilepsy. They also concluded that mental defect was more frequent in the lower stratum of society, where inherited conditions played a large part in the conditions of the social problem group: that 'relatively small section of the community the families of which show a high incidence of chronic pauperism, physical disease, infantile mortality, neglect of children, habitual crime, mental disease and mental defect.'[81] The Committee recommended that sterilisation should be legalised, though on a voluntary basis and subject to legal safeguards. But while they concluded with what was perhaps the last official plea for a eugenic strategy, their recommendations were never turned into legislation, and their plea already sounded outmoded.

It is true that the events in Nazi Germany sounded the death knell for the claim of such a eugenic strategy to respectability. But it is worth asking why it was that the psycho-eugenic programme had such a limited impact over the whole of its active life in the first thirty years of the twentieth century, despite the influence of its promoters, the vigour of its publicity, the apparently propitious time of its launching and its substantial theoretical back-up. No doubt one could put this down to natural revulsion, and the temptation of hindsight is to feel that such a scheme was never compatible with our native notions of justice and humanity. Yet such an anachronistic judgment fails to account for the fact that the proponents of the eugenic schema saw themselves as humane and enlightened, and the opposition to them was seldom posed in these moralistic terms. Certainly the opposition from the medical neo-hygienists who were installed in key positions by legislation was crucial. But what was it about this neo-hygienist strategy which allowed it to function and extend itself whilst the eugenic strategy ran into a cul-de-sac? An explanation in terms of the superior status of the medical profession seems to assume what it sets out to demonstrate, and ignores the fact that whilst neo-hygienism was certainly a medical strategy, many doctors supported psycho-eugenics from positions of power and influence

– Tredgold was a key example. And the eugenicists played such a central role in the official enquiries we have just discussed, yet still to no avail.

One answer can be constructed in terms of bourgeois liberties and individual rights – the argument that the economic and political systems of bourgeois democracies depend upon the existence of individuals equipped with personal rights. The degree of curtailment of such rights necessary for the effective implementation of a full-scale programme of negative eugenics, involving everything from compulsory segregation and sterilisation at one extreme to the licensing of marriage and procreation at the other would be incompatible with such a fundamental doctrine. But even so, fairly radical measures of compulsion and intervention *were* proposed and implemented at the turn of the century, and such an argument would find it hard to explain why even the limited eugenic proposals in respect to mental deficiency obtained so tenuous a hold on reality.

Eugenics entails a direct coercive intervention into the sphere of personal existence, an intervention which operates by, first of all, ascertaining who is pathological, and how many such individuals there are, and secondly by removing and isolating these dangerous elements to prevent their number increasing still further. This strategy works by an attempt to subtract, as it were, the pathological from the normal: it is negative and deductive. It leaves the 'normal' untouched, and where it does intervene into families to remove individuals its objective is to prevent such families from functioning, or rather malfunctioning, spawning more defective progeny and acting as a focus of illness, vice and defect. The identification of pathology is thus the occasion for disabling the family. But we have already seen that the neo-hygienist strategy is both wider in scope and more flexible in application than this. It certainly has disablement and segregation as one of the weapons in its armoury. But it does not limit itself to the neutralisation of this pathological minority; it aims rather to utilise its clinical expertise in a preventative way, through moralising, training, reforming those who fall within the range of the normal. To inject new norms of health and household management into the home through the instrument of the child. To make the family take on to itself the responsibility for its own hygiene – not merely to urge this as a moral or religious duty, or for the sake of propriety, but to produce it at the level of the detailed techniques of washing, body maintenance, habits of eating and defecating and so forth. And it is also a strategy more compatible with the doctrine of personal autonomy and individual liberty, for what are urged as duties and responsibilities will also have to be accepted by family members as their own desires.

It is along these lines of development that social policy proceeded during the 1920s. A strategy of this type was adopted and generalised. It entailed not ascertainment and segregation of the socially inefficient but the promotion of family welfare, the production of beneficial behaviour, habits and wishes within the 'private' space of the family, aided by a growing number of professionals with expertise in these areas which could be called upon. It was here that a new space opened for the operation of psychological agents, techniques and theories in the period after the First World War. This space formed in the network of relations between the school, the family and the juvenile court. The new objects which were produced here were not the mental defectives but children with disorders of temperament, emotion and behaviour: maladjusted or delinquent children. Around them was created a new institutional form – the Child Guidance Clinic – and a new psycho-social strategy.

6
Hygiene and welfare

Recent advances ... have shown the growing importance of the individual – of his heredity, upbringing, habits, and physical training, his rest and work, his hours of labour, and his innate and acquired powers of resistance to disease. In order to secure a healthy nation we must first obtain healthy individuals. This is the reason why – almost imperceptibly – we are moving from external conditions to personal characteristics, from the study of the environment to the study of the mother, the child, and the adult; or, in other words, to the problems of maternity, of child welfare, and of insurance against ill health of the individual.

George Newman, 1914[1]

Neo-hygienism transformed the field of public health through the individualisation of preventive medicine. Public health was no longer a matter of the relationship between passive and receptive bodies and an environment which might or might not be pathogenic – entailing action at the level of clean air, pure water, sufficient and suitable food, satisfactory housing and improved domestic sanitation, though these remained important. It was now also a matter of health as a positive value, as something to be achieved through detailed scrutiny of individuals and the relations between them, both at the social level – as in the attack on tuberculosis and venereal diseases – and at the level of family regime and individual habits.[2]

The principal terms of this strategy were hygiene and welfare: the hygienic management of one's bodily functions, of one's habits, of one's personal environment, of one's encounters with others; the welfare of those whose health depended upon the hygienic conduct of others. A whole range of social problems appeared in terms of hygiene and welfare, the lack of them, the need to promote them. Of particular significance were the decline in the birth-rate in the early decades of the twentieth century, the loss of life in the First World War, and the further decline in births in the 1920s and 1930s. Around these issues the old concern with infant mortality and the conservation and promotion of the health of the population in general, and children in particular, was re-awakened, but it was now construed in neo-hygienist terms.

'The family' was a central focus for neo-hygienism. The family was an apparatus for the physical care and hygienic management of the child and for its moral and social education – in short, for its *welfare*. The object was not merely the conservation of children, but the production of physically efficient bodies and socially productive habits. The means was the training of mothers in diet – with the provision of both guidance as to nutrition and dietary supplements if necessary – the inculcation of the habits of cleanliness and the techniques for achieving it, the promotion of maternal efficiency in so far as the requirements of a healthy child were concerned, and the constitution of the mother as the individual responsible for the proper management of the home. Children were to be regularly scrutinised, not simply for the purposes of diagnosis of illness and remedial action, but also to pick up signs of family malfunctioning. Steps could then be set in hand for the remedy of such malfunction; where it proved intractable the child was to be removed and relocated in a substitute family. School medical inspection and school meals, discussed in the last chapter, formed one prong of this family strategy. The infant and child welfare movement formed another.

The hygienic mother and child

The many conferences, reports and publications concerning infant mortality in the early decades of the twentieth century saw the high numbers of infant deaths as both indicative of the low physical efficiency of the population and as a particular squandering of a resource which the nation required both for its defence and for its industry. Whilst deaths in the first month of life were largely a consequence of the unfitness of the infant itself, and thus both difficult to prevent and eugenic in their consequences, deaths subsequently were the result of infectious disease, poor diet and lack of hygiene. These were themselves the result of failures of motherhood and were to be prevented through the construction of an elaborate apparatus of scrutiny and rectification. Hence the occasion and objective of intervention was the child, but the instrument was the mother.

The strategy sought to bring all new-born infants into the field of inspection, enabling the mothers to be reached through their babies. It entailed a number of elements: promotion of the use of trained and salaried midwives; compulsory notification of births; employment of health visitors to visit the homes of all new-born babies whose birth had been notified; setting up infant welfare centres, 'Baby Welcomes' and schools for mothers to which new mothers could be directed for the inspection of children and for the instruction of mothers; provision of milk and food for necessitous mothers and infants; establishing day nurseries where appropriate levels of hygiene could be maintained and the progress of children could be monitored. Voluntary organisations proliferated: by 1916 there were over 160 branches of voluntary organisations and 35 local authorities running infant welfare centres, backed by the urgings of the Local Government Board and the Chief Medical Officer of the Board of Education. And in 1918, the Maternity and Child Welfare Act required each local authority to set up a maternal and child welfare committee, and empowered them to provide the other functions for which some central funding was to be made available.[3]

The target of this strategy of scrutiny and instruction was the working-class mother. Whilst some reckoned the middle-class mother was equally ignorant, but that her superior standard of living ameliorated the malign consequences, no similar counter-vailing influences existed for the mother of the working class. As Newman put it: *'the principal operating influence is the ignorance of the mother and the remedy is the education of the mother'*.[4] The main cause of infant mortality was diarrhoea, which resulted from contamination in the home, dirty feeding bottles and dummies and other removable evils which were to be counteracted by raising maternal efficiency, persuading mothers of their maternal duties and educating them in the ways of carrying them out. There were three main channels through which influence could be brought by the State to secure the physical efficiency of children: through the promotion of healthy motherhood by attention to the physical condition of the mother; through the promotion of healthy infancy, by instructing and training the mother in how to bring up her child after its birth, and providing assistance when she was not able to care for it efficiently; through the promotion of healthy childhood, by means of systematic medical supervision and education in hygiene during school life.

Mothers-to-be could be educated in the schools – the Board of Education first issued its Memorandum on the Teaching of Infant Care and Management in the Public Elementary School in 1910. This advocated instruction of schoolgirls in the domestic arts of proper feeding, temperance, housekeeping, infant care and the dangers of domestic dirt. But more immediately, the Schools for Mothers, Baby Welcomes and Infant Welfare Centres combined individual scrutiny of babies and advice on management – in Infant Consultations – with classes and instructions designed to convey information, instil responsibility and encourage pride in the home and family. Since attendance at such centres was voluntary, and unlikely therefore to reach those most in need of intervention, the centre was also utilised as the base from which a more comprehensive scrutiny could be undertaken. To each centre were attached health visitors, who would visit all homes where births were notified, classify them according to the efficiency of the mother, repeat visits as often as necessary (ranging from once a month or more for the bad homes to not at all for the better-class homes). If inefficient mothers could not be persuaded to attend the centres, instruction would nevertheless reach into the heart of the home itself.

McCleary gives some idea of the scale of this exercise. At the end of 1933, 2,938 health visitors were employed by local authorities, 2,546 by voluntary associations. Together they undertook 505,674 visits to expectant mothers that year, of which 179,682 were first visits; 3,316,903 visits to children under one year of age, of which 570,830 were first visits; and 4,437,300 visits to children between the ages of one and five.[5] Middle-class mothers were moralised through child care manuals, the blandishments of experts on motherhood and of the manufacturers of baby products.[6] Feminist organisations espoused the new doctrines of motherhood, emphasising the need to protect the 'mothers of the race', and therefore also to eliminate, through ante-natal care, the dangers associated with childbirth. But the central focus of governmental neo-hygienism was the working-class family.

Generalised yet individualised inspection was the first element in the strategy. As we saw in the last chapter, the clinic was not only a site for the organisation of treatment; in it conditions could be documented and recorded, norms could be established and individuals classified in relation to them, specific diseases or departures from norms of functioning could be identified, and signs of lack of hygiene could be picked up which were important not so much in themselves but because they were symptoms of a lack of welfare in the home.

The home was the crucial site of prophylaxis, where ill health could be prevented, and where good health could be promoted through the insertion of hygienic norms of conduct. Whilst in the schools and treatment institutions individuals could be instructed in appropriate modes of behaviour, the home was the object *par excellence* of the neo-hygienist strategy. For it was here that pathological conditions could operate or be prevented as a consequence of hygienic management by mothers. And it was here that welfare could be promoted through the adoption of a correct dietary regime, and correct techniques of washing, cleaning, clothing, as well as the avoidance or suppression of such harmful habits as coughing, spitting and sneezing.

The child was, of course, the stake in the whole business. What was the child for neo-hygienism? The answer must be in terms of the body. A body which conformed to normal standards of development in terms of height, weight, muscular co-ordination and so forth. A body unmarked by caries, rickets or incipient tuberculosis. A body uninfested by lice, and free from the conditions in which such infestations might flourish. A body, therefore, which conducted its personal habits in a hygienic fashion. But a hygienic regime of the body did not limit its aspirations to the production of fodder fit enough for the demands of the battlefield or the factory. For the moralisation of the everyday which was entailed in the promotion of hygiene and welfare had effects more directly moral as well. The habits and conducts of the body which were to promote its physical welfare were also moral, in the traditional religious sense of rules of right conduct and in the nineteenth century sense of pertaining to the space of character. To promote physical welfare, the child was to be trained up in cleanliness, regular habits, avoidance of excess and intemperance and so forth. Ignorance and fecklessness were to be turned into conscientiousness and responsibility. Hygiene and welfare entailed the active co-operation of individuals in the promotion of their own bodily efficiency.

Inspected in the school clinic or moralised through the school curriculum, the older child could carry back to the home appropriate norms of conduct in matters such as personal cleanliness and the management of various bodily functions. However, it was the mother who was the key to the technical possibility of neo-hygienism. The neo-hygienist mother was not so much an individual as the embodiment of the home itself. As Newman put it in his report for 1914, 'The environment of the infant is its mother.'[7] Her role was to actualise the instructions of the pedagogues of home and child management in the regime of the home itself. The mother was construed as a mere assemblage of habits – bad budgeting to be turned into good, an indifference to household dirt to be transformed into a campaign against it, the use of feeding bottles and dirty dummies to be replaced preferably by the breast, but if not at least by instruments and contents duly boiled, diluted, delivered according to instructions. The efficient mother was one who conducted the tasks of welfare in an hygienic manner – and that was virtually all there was to it. Thus if women were the particular targets of the neo-hygienist doctrines of motherhood, this was largely because neo-hygienism believed that the nurturers of children were nearly always women. The relationship between women and motherhood was almost contingent – a consequence of the fact that it happened to be the case that women looked after infants and children during the period crucial for their hygienic development.[8] The domain of the maternal was exhausted by the hygienic duties assigned to the mother.

The welfare of families

In neo-hygienism, the space between family, school and clinic was traced out by the operations of welfare work. Welfare workers established paths of interchange between the domestic, conjugal and child-rearing arrangements of working-class families and the different sites of inspection or treatment. During the inter-war period there was an impressive proliferation of social devices concerned to promote and regulate health, hygiene and welfare.

The social devices were dispersed and based upon specific problems – in the field of public health, education, the welfare of children, the penal system and so forth. Around these issues aggregated a heterogeneous series of agents, some employed by statutory agencies, some voluntary but attached to committees established by statute, some working for private charities or in other voluntary organisations. Professional organisations of these different branches of welfare work began to be set up, journals and books were published in great numbers.

Eileen Younghusband's investigation of employment of social workers, conducted at the end of the Second World War, allows us to make some sort of inventory of the social field.[9] If one disregards those schemes which had been established in wartime, one finds the following at the end of the inter-war period. There were health visitors, of course, who have already been referred to. There were almoners attached to hospitals, Public Health Departments and clinics. There were child-care workers attached to residential institutions of one sort or another – approved schools and hostels, remand homes, orphanages run by voluntary societies (Doctor Barnardo's, National Children's Home and Orphanage, Church of England Waifs and Strays Society and other orphanages and homes run by religious orders). There were child care workers involved in visiting homes 'in which a child is living because something has gone wrong, whether the "something" be a need for dental treatment or criminal neglect of the child by his parents.'[10] There were adoption officers working with courts with regard to the adoption of children for whom a local authority or voluntary society is acting as guardian *ad litem*. There were welfare and after-care officers visiting homes of those discharged from approved schools. There were care committees, concerned with follow-up work in connection with the school medical service and with children in need of clothes or school meals, with a paid organiser directing the activities of voluntary workers engaged in home visiting and liaising between home, school and clinic.

We also find moral welfare workers, often employed by the church, part paid by local authorities, who dealt with children living in conditions of moral danger or who had been the subject of sexual assaults. Juvenile Employment Officers were involved in vocational guidance of young unemployed juveniles, and in finding them employment. School Attendance Officers were responsible for visiting the homes of children absent from school for any length of time, for undertaking enquiries for juvenile courts, supervising boarded out children committed to local education authorities as Fit Persons and undertaking duties under the Adoption of Children Act, 1926. Special Enquiry Officers performed similar tasks but were attached to the juvenile courts. And there were workers involved in settlements and wardens of community centres.

There were family case workers – most notably from the Charity Organisation Society, but also from a range of other organisations including those formed for specific purposes such as the care of the handicapped, the single 'fallen' or ex-service personnel. Characteristic of all such case work organisations was that relief was provided to certain classes of persons based upon individual investigation and assessment of need, and with a view to promoting the self-reliance of those individuals rather than merely providing indiscriminate charity or small doles. There were voluntary associations for domiciliary assistance and welfare to the blind, to whom local authorities had devolved their responsibilities under the Blind Persons Act 1920, and others, with no statutory links, for the deaf and cripples.

There were probation officers, responsible to the local probation committees of the courts of summary jurisdiction in England and Wales, or, in the Metropolitan area, to the Home Office via the London Probation Service. Probation officers dealt with cases such as children brought before the courts as beyond the care and control of their parents and subject to supervision, children given a probation order for a minor offence, adults in similar circumstances, matrimonial problems and elderly persons charged, for example, with indecent exposure. There were Discharged Prisoners Aid Societies. Finally there were a few 'mental welfare' workers and psychiatric social workers employed by mental hospitals, by local authorities, by voluntary associations and by child guidance clinics and responsible for obtaining family histories, home visiting, after-care, domiciliary supervision of mental defectives in their homes or boarded out.

This social field was clearly heterogeneous in a number of respects. Firstly in respect of the formal status of the agents and agencies concerned – statutory, voluntary and so forth. Secondly in terms of the mode of designation of their objects – a specific problem, a category of individuals defined by age or status, an institution or whatever. Thirdly in terms of the specification of their field of action – an individual prisoner living alone, a child in a residential institution, a family. But despite this heterogeneity, there was a coherent and consistent rationale to welfare work. We can see this clearly if we consider what some of these welfare workers actually did.

The task of the almoner is typical:[11]

> The almoner supplies knowledge of the patient's circumstances, social as well as economic, both as a guide to what he can be expected to pay and for purposes necessary to treatment for the use of the hospital staff; she serves as a link with all outside agencies – State, municipal or voluntary – which may be utilised for the benefit of the patient.

That is to say, the almoner was to act as a link between the patient, the medical site, professional and social agencies and public authorities. Additionally, the almoner was to give friendly and sympathetic information especially as to available benefits, facilitating attendance and continuance at hospital or clinic, diffusing instruction as to home management, cleanliness and hygiene, budgeting, debt and problems with obtaining suitable employment.

And as for the health visitor, her role was pretty much the same: to advise on the proper care, nurture and management of children under five including the promotion of cleanliness. Her tasks were clear from the regulations for training issued by the Board of Education in 1919. Courses were to cover: theoretical and practical instruction in elementary physiology; artisan cooking and household management; hygiene, infectious and communicable diseases; maternity; infant and child welfare; elementary economics and social problems. Additionally, the task of the health visitor, like that of Care Committee workers, was to act as a liaison officer rather than a practitioner: the complexity of modern society had, according to Macadam, called into being a new type of service, 'social work' or 'social administration', in order to establish rational linkages between its various social provisions.[12]

The welfare worker was a pedagogue and go-between, one who carried information, acted as a relay between different agencies, and served to inject norms of care and management into the home. 'Welfare' construed the family as a mechanism for the construction of physical health and sober habits, for the provision of clothing, food and shelter for family members. Hence welfare workers provided advice and evaluation in respect of finance, employment, housing, hygiene, diet, education, clothing, budgeting, the requirements of different family members – mothercraft, household management. And welfare agencies were the means of linking the family with the other specialised agencies involved in these issues – medical, housing, relief, school, court and so forth. At issue was the physical conservation and maintainance of the population at high levels of efficiency, able to do its duty in industry or in war.

Over the next two decades, this neo-hygienist strategy was to be displaced, and a new conception of the family, the child and the means and objects of intervention would take shape. Histories of social work usually argue that this shift 'from welfare to social work' occurred principally after the Second World War, as a consequence of the belated input of psychoanalysis, the evidence from the wartime separation of children from their families, and from institutionalisation, and the effects of the 1948 Children Act.[13] Such accounts pass over the welfare activities of the inter-war period as merely a hiatus, a bleak period between the individualised case-work of the nineteenth century and the psychoanalytically inspired family social work which burgeoned after the Second World War.[14] But nineteenth-century case work was not the origin or precursor of the social work of the 1950s, and welfare was no mere absence. It was based on a definite strategy, conceptual apparatus and set of objectives. The new psychosocial strategy took shape in the tension between what neo-hygienism made possible, and what led to its decline.

A number of factors in the inter-war period conspired to reduce the salience of neo-hygienism. The deepening economic depression made it increasingly difficult to maintain the linkage between character and unemployment, and between personal habits and social problems. Even the Charity Organisation Society had to accept the necessity for 'out relief' and the fact that many cases of distress had as their sole cause the absence of employment consequent upon conditions of trade.[15] The particular *bêtes-noires* of the proponents of individualised case work were the 'socialist' insurance based schemes which were being established for sickness, unemployment and old-age pensions. These effected a separation between the register of financial provision and that of personalised case work with needy individuals and families, thus sidestepping the principle that relief should be conditional upon scrutiny and having the objective of establishing self-reliance.[16]

Of course, the development of the schemes of unemployment benefit throughout the 1920s was accompanied by debates over means-testing and scroungers, and the necessity and significance of a 'genuinely seeking work' test. But the scrutiny that was carried out pertained, initially at least, only to willingness to enter paid employment and the nature and arrangements of the family unit were pertinent only in so far as they affected the financial status of the claimant. Relief was either given unconditionally or refused – there was no intermediary state of attempted individual reformation, although, towards the end of the inter-war period, officers administering unemployment benefit were increasingly urged to assess willingness to enter employment in terms of 'the state of the applicant's mind'.[17]

The strategic emphasis upon individual responsibility and individual reformation found itself very much on the defensive. For the middle class with a conscience, social service rather than scientific philanthropy was the order of the day. Social service located social evils not in the individual but in the structure of society itself, particularly in the unequal distribution of wealth. To work with the poor, in the Settlements or elsewhere, was an expression of citizenship, in which all parties enjoyed social rights and equality of status. It gave first-hand experience of working-class life to those who would make policy. It helped to break down class barriers and to spread education and cultural values. And it involved the educated and the working class together in the project of constructing a better society.[18]

In the 1930s the notion of social service gave way to another which stressed the need for collective planning and management of all aspects of social and political life and the expansion of the social services – a middle way between capitalism and socialism. Political and Economic Planning (PEP), founded in 1931, stressed the need for efficiency and modernisation and centralised planning in its report on the social and health services and other issues.[19] The Next Five Years Group in the book it published in 1935, proposed an Economic General Staff, a National Development Board, public investment in housing and electrification, town and country planning, the location of industry in distressed areas, and the co-ordination of the social services to achieve a National

Minimum.[20] Doctors and nutritionists began to stress the relationship between income, poverty, diet and health, as opposed to concentrating upon the part played by individual, family and maternal hygienic management.[21] And Eleanor Rathbone, a leading light of the Next Five Years Group, gained further support for the campaign for the endowment of motherhood.

This campaign had its origins following the end of the First World War and crystallised in Rathbone's *The Disinherited Family* of 1924.[22] It stressed the deleterious effects of the existing wage system on family and home life, especially on working-class mothers and their children who were suffering severe under-nourishment and poor health as wages were unrelated to the needs of families. In the 1930s this campaign was linked in to a growing concern with the decline in the birth-rate. The neo-hygienist strategy slipped from prominence as it began to be argued that, accompanying the fall in infant mortality which had been achieved in the 1920s, there had been a reduction in the birth-rate from 28.3 per 1,000 in 1901-5 to 15.3 per 1,000 in 1931-5. Population projections predicted the 'twilight of parenthood'.[23] Economists and others adopted 'under populationist' positions and discussed the damaging effects of low population on empire and industry, and the consequence for the age structure of the population – with a growing number of old people supported by a declining number of producers.

But more worrying were the consequences of differential decline, with the greatest reduction in births and family size amongst the well-to-do and professional classes. Whilst the earlier negative eugenicist response to this was certainly present – with calls for compulsory sterilisation of defectives and so forth – as we saw in a previous chapter, this achieved little success. The campaigns for birth control promoted especially by Marie Stopes and the Society for Constructive Birth Control and Racial Progress, and later by the National Birth Control Association, were no more successful.[24] Their arguments tended to be positive rather than negative, stressing birth control as a means of securing the health of mothers and babies through the spacing of births, as well as its use to prevent the diseased and defective from procreating. Whilst Stopes advocated birth control as a means of promoting racial improvement and limiting the working-class birth-rate, these arguments had little effect on government policies in this period. The old eugenic opposition between the virtues of action at the level of procreation and the limitations of action at the level of environment had begun to break down. A new 'positive eugenics' became active which combined the call for family allowances with the arguments that the provision of a basic minimum of food, clothing, shelter, medical care and maternity services would increase the welfare of families and children generally, encourage the thrifty artisans and professional classes to have more children, and provide an antidote to those forms of disorderly living which promoted excessive and dysgenic breeding. Universalism of provision no longer produced the fear of promotion of reckless breeding amongst poor and degenerate stock and its consequences.

The new strategies of planning, insurance, allowances and so forth were thus not linked to a system of individual scrutiny and reformation. They turned problems of health and welfare into technical questions of types and levels of allowances and benefits, generalised provisions of services, and their consequences at the level of the population. But in effecting a separation between the register of financial provision and that of personal case work, they freed the level of personal and familial malfunctioning for its elaboration within a discourse and practice in which material difficulties were symptoms of a problem rather than the problem itself. It was here that the new social work would form, initially through the application of the language of hygiene and welfare to problems posed by disorders not of bodily function but of conduct.

The hygiene and welfare of the mind

> insanity is, after all, only a disease like other diseases . . . a mind deranged can be ministered to no less effectively than a body deranged. . . . The keynote of the past has been detection; the keynote of the future should be prevention and treatment. . . . The problem of insanity is essentially a public health problem to be dealt with on modern public health lines.
>
> Royal Commission on Lunacy and Mental Disorder, 1926[25]

Neo-hygienism sought to promote health as a social value to be maximised and as a personal responsibility to be fulfilled. When such a strategy was applied to mental pathology in the period following the First World War, it had consequences for conceptions of madness and the social responses appropriate to it. New tactics for the social regulation of disorders of conduct were constructed within a strategy of mental hygiene and mental welfare. And the new problems of childhood, which individual psychology would attempt to address, were shaped within this strategy.

From the first Report issued by the Board of Control after the First World War, through the Report of the Royal Commission on Lunacy and Mental Disorder of 1926, to the Report of the Feversham Committee on the Voluntary Mental Health Services published in 1939, mental hygiene and mental welfare set the terms of analysis and proposals.[26] The link between mental disturbance and 'socially inefficient conduct' – criminality, immorality, unproductiveness and so forth – was reconstructed in terms of the new preventive and hygienic medicine of public health. Mental hygiene and mental welfare were construed as attributes of the population to be maximised, and mental illness as a source of inefficiency to be minimised, in order that society could function at its highest efficiency.

Most significantly, it was argued that major mental disturbances were preventible by early recognition and treatment of all the minor troubles from which they grew, and by promotion of correct habits of mental hygiene in the family. One certainly needed medical investigation of persons who were clearly socially inefficient, such as those who had broken the law, to see if their conduct was a consequence of mental pathology and therefore required treatment. But one needed to extend the field of surveillance in order to pick up minor troubles before they developed into major ones. This could be done by linking up, co-ordinating and educating the various statutory and voluntary agencies who might come into contact with such individuals. It also required the development of new sites of treatment; of measures to encourage individuals to scrutinise their own mental state, and that of family and friends, for signs of minor trouble; and the development of the obligations and opportunities for those with mental disturbances to have voluntary treatment. Mental welfare was to be a new objective of social regulation. It was also to be a family responsibility and a personal value.

A number of interlinking arguments were put forward, all of

which had the object of removing constraints and hindrances upon the early recognition of disturbances of the mind, with a view to promoting early intervention and remedial action. Two related problems were seen to be standing in the way of the promotion of mental welfare. The first was the stigma surrounding lunacy. The second was the disjuncture between the nature of provision for disorders of physical function and those of mental function. Not only did the elaborate legal measures surrounding admission to a lunatic asylum, the association with the Poor Law and so on, serve to prevent ill individuals obtaining early help, they also made it difficult for doctors to provide it. The 1890 Lunacy Act had allowed asylums to take only certified patients, and certification could only be accomplished with the direct involvement of the legal authorities – Justices of the Peace. This, it was argued, prevented early treatment of mild cases, discouraged doctors from utilising asylums, and turned asylums into places of incarceration for those considered beyond hope.

The key move in the new strategy of mental hygiene was to establish the continuity of disorders of mind and body, and hence to seek to extend to the former the new preventive and therapeutic techniques which had worked so well for the latter. 'Lunacy' was a particular form of illness and not a condition which should be separated off, stigmatised, feared. It should be treated in institutions which had as their model not the prison but the general hospital, for they were places for the treatment of a type of disease. In any event, it was argued, the separation between the mental and the physical was misleading – all mental disturbances no doubt had physical concomitants, physical disorders had mental concomitants, and in many cases it was a matter of judgment which predominated. So lunacy should be termed mental illness – a disease whose symptoms were mainly derangements of mind rather than of physical function. And asylums should be mental hospitals – hospitals specialising in the treatment of certain kinds of disease.

This would not only be a correct recognition of the nature of the disorder, but it would also facilitate mental welfare by removing the stigma associated with the old terminology, which had discouraged individuals from seeking assistance. The fears concerning the liberty of the subject which had underlain the legalism of the 1890 provisions were clearly no longer appropriate; what was involved raised no more problems of liberty and its infringement than did the measures which were routinely taken in the treatment of disorders of physical function. The whole legalistic paraphernalia which required certification before treatment was an anachronism which acted as a drag on the promotion of mental health. Treatment should be available on an in-patient basis without certification in public hospitals.

But further, clinic-based facilities for out-patient treatment of those with mild disorders should be set up as a means of preventing the development of mental illness by the treatment of those with incipient insanity; general hospitals should themselves participate in this activity which did, after all, simply represent one of their specialisms. To these clinics, people would come voluntarily, once educated in the recognition of the early signs of mental illness, free of fear as to stigma or incurability; taking responsibility for their own mental health. These clinics would also act as the bases for a more extensive system; they would be centres *into* which individuals would be directed, and *from* which other mental welfare activities would radiate. Welfare workers, statutory and voluntary, and other agencies, once properly aware of the links between mental illness and social inefficiency, would direct individuals to the clinics for assessment and treatment. The new mental medicine would radiate out of its institutional sites and begin to act also upon the circumstances and conditions of the lives of patients, ex-patients and potential patients. There was to be mental after-care, there was to be work with out-patients, there was to be enquiry into the home circumstances and lives of patients, and there was to be general public education as to the habits likely to promote hygiene of the mind. To this end there should be co-ordination of the various statutory and voluntary bodies concerned with different aspects of the problem in order to promote a coherent and exhaustive programme of mental welfare.

The new strategy did not remain merely at the level of recommendations. It was instantiated in the construction and objectives of the Maudsley Hospital. The building of this hospital was completed in 1915 by the London County Council, with an initial gift from Henry Maudsley which included the conditions that the hospital should deal exclusively with early and acute cases, have an out-patients department, and teach and research on psychiatry in the context of medicine. The strategy underpinned the use made by the London County Council, from 1919, of the Mental After-Care Association, to carry out early-care and after-care work. It was what led to the change of name and tactics of the Central Association for the Care of the Mental Defective, which became the Central Association for Mental Welfare in 1923, and changed the title of its journal from *Studies in Mental Inefficiency* to *Mental Welfare* in 1925. When the Royal Commission on Lunacy and Mental Disorder was set up in 1924, it appears that it was principally intended to allay public anxiety over safeguards, administration and conditions of detention in lunatic asylums. But the recommendations which it made were in line with the strategy of mental hygiene; they were put into legislation in the Local Government Act 1929, which gave local authorities a wider responsibility for providing lunacy and mental deficiency services, and in the Mental Treatment Act 1930. This Act renamed asylums 'mental hospitals' and lunatics became, in most cases, simply 'persons of unsound mind'. It allowed the reception of patients into in-patient treatment on their voluntary application. And it authorised local authorities to make provision for the establishment of psychiatric out-patient clinics at general or mental hospitals, and to make arrangements for after-care. Soon after the outbreak of war, effect was given to the recommendation of the Feversham Committee, to set up a National Council for Mental Health to co-ordinate the voluntary societies, and to work in partnership with the statutory authorities, in the fields of after-care, work with mental defectives, early treatment, and children's troubles with the law and at school.

The strategy of mental hygiene also underpinned the establishment of the provisions which we will discuss in more detail in the next chapter – private psychiatric out-patient clinics such as the Tavistock Square Clinic founded in 1920, the Child Guidance Council, set up in 1927, and the Mental Health Course, for training psychiatric social workers to be based in the new clinical sites, which started at the London School of Economics in 1929. And it was this strategy which the National Council for Mental Hygiene sought to co-ordinate and promote in the inter-war years.

The National Council was founded in 1922 and included an array of prestigious names amongst the membership of its various committees.[27] The strategy of mental hygiene provided a new framework for debates concerning mental disturbance from a range of different perspectives, thus active members of the National Council ranged from psychoanalysts, through individual and industrial psychologists, to organicist psychiatrists, doctors, magistrates and welfare workers. The prestige of such an enterprise is indicated by the proportion of these who were, or would be, knighted or otherwise honoured by the Crown. The Council sought to promote the study and effective treatment of mental disorder with a view to its prevention, to introduce the routine medico-psychological examination of persons charged with crime and to investigate the role of mental disease or defect in other forms of socially undesirable behaviour. But it also sought to promote positive measures for the development of mental health, to educate in the factors producing good mental health and to remove all barriers which made early treatment of mental disease more difficult – including the stigma around 'lunacy' and the legal constraints which inhibited those in need from seeking help. It particularly worked for the establishment of out-patient facilities.

Its rationale for all this was straightforward – major disorders had precursors in minor disturbances, early treatment of the latter would reduce the incidence of the former. Thus an Appendix to the Annual Report for 1927-8 sought to draw attention to the inadequacy of provision for those suffering from 'Minor Mental Maladies' or 'nerves', that is:[28]

> emotional and mental instability characterised by such
> insidious and apparently trivial symptoms as depression,
> anxiety, impaired powers of initiative and concentration, loss
> of interest, irritability, self-distrust, sleeplessness,
> hypersensitiveness, shyness and seclusive tendencies, hysterical
> manifestations – the latter especially in the young – and other
> symptoms of a like nature.

These apparently trivial symptoms were insidious not on their own account but in what they pointed to and would lead to – they were often the early stages of much more severe disorders. But fortunately new methods had demonstrated that treatment, if carried out early enough, had a good chance of success; hence it was vital to encourage all measures to increase the availability and likelihood of early treatment.

Nowhere was it more important to recognise these issues than in relation to the disturbances of childhood. Here were the earliest signs of future trouble manifested; here were the chances of averting such problems greatest. And here, in childhood, in the school, was the opportunity for a universalised scrutiny of conduct with a view to identifying problem cases. It is in this light that we can understand the emergence of the new objects around which a new psycho-social strategy would form – the maladjusted schoolchild and the delinquent juvenile.

The maladjusted schoolchild and the delinquent juvenile

What made the maladjusted schoolchild and the delinquent juvenile possible objects for a psycho-social strategy was the way in which they were linked. Starting soon after the end of the First World War a regular connection in argument began to be made between children who showed disorders of behaviour at school and children who would later end up before the courts. The disturbed schoolchild would become the juvenile delinquent, the juvenile delinquent was, or had been, also a disturbed schoolchild. If this was the case then the detection and treatment of disturbances of behaviour in the school had a significance beyond itself, in its preventive and prophylactic function. The school could now be seen as a generalised site of scrutiny and intervention with regard to problems not of physical health and deterioration, not of intellectual defect and degeneration, but of all sorts of social inefficiency resulting from mental illness. If it was the case that what ended as major problems in the judicial sphere – disregard of the law and criminal behaviour – began as minor disturbances in the moral sphere – anything from excessive emotionality to minor transgressions such as lying – then the school had as important a function in crime prevention as it did in the promotion of physical health and the recognition of mental defect.

This new class of problem child emerged hesitantly at first but then with growing regularity alongside problems associated with physical or sensory handicap, ill health or weakened physical constitution. Initially designated nervous, neuropathic or unstable, this class of children came to be referred to as 'maladjusted'. One can trace this emergence from the successive reports of the Chief Medical Officer of the Board of Education. In 1920, the Chief Medical Officer drew attention to the neuropathic child, who could be found throughout the educational system but without any special form of treatment being available. Neuropathic children might be normal or even super-normal in school progress, but their behaviour was:[29]

> marked by certain psychological characteristics, a tendency to quarrel, to make violent friendships, to engender bitter dislikes, to attend unduly to [their] bodily functions, to night terrors, to unreasonable fears, grief, abnormal introspection and self-examination, and to separation from family and friends.

Whilst these behaviours were often accompanied by minor physical symptoms, the condition was a psychical one and school life itself, as well as sympathy and relief from strain, might bring about recovery.

By 1927, it was the specific link with delinquency which was prioritised. Apparently Healy's work with delinquents in the USA had 'revealed how long and complicated, in many cases, was the history behind the delinquent act, and attention was drawn to abnormal traits in behaviour generally as they showed themselves in childhood'.[30] The conception of a child guidance clinic, as promoted by the Child Guidance Council, and as established in a number of places in the mid 1920s, rapidly set the terms in which the *educational* issues posed by 'unstable' and 'difficult' children were to be posed and organised. The difficult child was gradually re-conceived in terms of maladjustment: a child 'whose conduct in school and home reveals a lack of harmony and stability leading to delinquency or nervousness'. The child guidance clinic was to play the role with regard to mental hygiene that the School Medical Service filled with regard to physical hygiene. If the latter sought to ascertain and treat early and slight departures from the normal in order to prevent them becoming major defects, the primary duty of the child guidance clinic was 'the ascertainment, study and correction of minor abnormalities, which if left to themselves, may eventually lead up to gross aberrations of conduct, delinquency and crime'.[31]

Thus all these minor deviations of behaviour gained their pertinence less on account of the disruption which they constituted to the normal activities of the school, than because of the sign which they fortunately gave of the imminence of future disorder. Abnormal behaviour, antisocial conduct, neuroses, eccentricities, making friendships too easily or not at all, quarrelling or being withdrawn, grieving or fearing too much or too little – all these departures from the norm could be linked together as maladjustments, and as predictors of troubles to come.

This prospective analysis in terms of mental hygiene linked up with a retrospective analysis which was based upon the Juvenile Court.

It is, no doubt, true that there was a long-established connection between criminal forms of juvenile conduct and other aberrant conduct which was not in itself criminal but might lead to criminality if left unchecked. It is commonly accepted that the conception of juvenile delinquency began to emerge in the mid-nineteenth century. In the eighteenth century and early nineteenth century, the criminal child was treated in the same way as an adult, subject to the same processes of trial and the same punishment on conviction, graded by offence and precedent.[32] Capital sentences were often commuted to imprisonment or transportation but this was so for adults as well as children. When a child was proceeded against at law it was considered to be merely a juridical subject, that is, the subject of an act deemed to have transgressed a given law. To be the juridical subject of such an act, however, it was necessary to be competent to bear the rights and responsibilities of such a subject. A juridical subject must be able to distinguish right from wrong and hence form a guilty intention. There was thus a strict analogy at law between children below the 'age of discretion', madmen and natural fools, to the extent that they were all incapable of forming such an intention, and hence could not be found guilty of a criminal offence. From Blackstone onwards the arguments of jurists with respect to the principle of *doli capax* stabilised.[33] Children below the age of seven were automatically deemed *incapax*; over fourteen they were deemed *capax* unless proved insane. Between seven and fourteen, the prosecution had to demonstrate the existence of discretion. Whilst under the Code Napoléon in France it would appear that it was customary to seek expert opinion on the state of development of the discriminative faculties of infants, in England, the matter was left to the judge and jury to decide on the basis of such factors as malice, revenge, craft, cunning, other evidence of a mischievous discretion and the extent to which punishment was a necessary deterrent for a particularly heinous crime which children were both capable of and tempted to commit.

As execution and transportation gave way to imprisonment in the early nineteenth century, children were intermingled with adults in the prisons. Reform took as its theme mass corruption; children and other juveniles did not appear as a separate class, and the prison reforms of 1823 introduced a classification not by age but by nature and seriousness of offence. The opening of Pentonville in 1842 marked a shift in the aims, objects and techniques of punishment.[34] Punishment now sought to transform the convicted individual through the detailed regulation of time, space, and activity. The behaviour of the prisoner was subject to a constant judgment and evaluation in relation to norms of conduct and techniques of rectification. Hence the reformatory regime of the prison, like that of moral treatment in the asylum, was individualising – it focused not upon the act or even upon the offender, but upon the character of the delinquent and it directed its action and evaluation to that moral space which organised action and was liable to reformation. Hence this type of prison entailed the assessment and distribution of offenders to the types of regime most appropriate for their reformation. Prisons now began to be indicted for the specific effects which they had upon the young: they were not reformed but 'hardened to prison life'; imprisonment scarred them with a stigma which made respectable employment more difficult to obtain and forced them back into crime; detention was too short for reformation but long enough to remove the fear of prison; in addition, state maintenance of children in jail acted as a premium upon parental irresponsibility.

The moralising philanthropy of the mid-nineteenth century singled out young actual and potential criminals as a special class. With the rise of the statistical societies, the setting up of a regular police force, the division of large towns into police districts, and the gathering and publication of figures on the quantity and distribution of crime, it began to be argued that juvenile crime in particular was on the increase.[35] Moral topographers sought to link this to the moral and physical milieu, conceptualising criminality on the model of the causes and spread of epidemic diseases. Thus William Beaver Neale, writing in 1840 of Manchester, argued that there existed a class of juvenile delinquents concentrated in a particular area where moral and physical contagion, encouraged by parental irresponsibility and neglect, led children to delinquency, petty theft, and ultimately a life of organised crime.[36] And Mary Carpenter argued that crime diffused 'a subtle, unseen but sure poison in the moral atmosphere of the neighbourhood, dangerous as is deadly miasma to the physical health.'[37] The child was seen as a complex of learned habits which were contracted from the examples given in the home, from bad company, and from experience of vice and corruption in the streets.

Reformers in the last half of the nineteenth century established a separation and relation between two classes of children. On the one hand there were those who were already 'dangerous' – who had committed an offence of some sort and who, if left in the immoral atmosphere of the rookeries and dens of vice would spend their adult lives as paupers, prostitutes or felons. On the other hand, there were the children in danger, 'perishing' as Mary Carpenter terms them – without homes, in bad company, neglected by their parents or lacking discipline in the home. Despite the fact that they had not yet committed a crime, they were incipient criminals; further exposure to moral contagion would demoralise them still further, and make criminals of them for life. A series of Acts over this period, beginning with the Reformatory Schools Act, 1854 and the Industrial Schools Act, 1857, empowered magistrates to commit such children to Reformatory and Industrial Schools respectively. Reformatories were modelled on the agricultural colony established at Mettray, France in 1839; industrial schools on the so-called 'ragged schools'. By 1894, 17,000 children were in industrial schools – not simply vagrants, those who frequented the company of thieves, without settled abode or having no visible means of subsistence, but also those deemed 'in need of care and protection' and 'beyond parental control'; a further 4,800 were in reformatories. In each of these types of school the principles were the same. The children were to be resocialised in substitute family and cottage based systems, away from their old haunts where their old habits could be broken down and new habits of honesty, discipline and industriousness could be inculcated through the application of a sort of moral treatment.

At one level, the famous Children Act of 1908 represented merely a continuation and extension of this strategy.[38] It further attenuated the relations between the prison and the juvenile. It maintained the distinction between Industrial and Reformatory schools and the separate circumstances under which magistrates could commit children to each. It applied to children the provisions of the Probation of Offenders Act 1907, allowing the court to discharge an offender who voluntarily entered into recognisance to be of good behaviour, and allowing this to be subject to certain conditions, including that the offender be under the supervision of a probation officer for a specified period. The Children Act also consolidated the various pieces of legislation concerned with infant life protection – inspection of people other than parents looking after infants, laws on neglect, cruelty and sexual or economically prohibited use of children, and their access to alcohol and tobacco. And the establishment of Juvenile Courts was a further move to separate delinquent or neglected children from the taint of the adult criminal justice system. But in consolidating the legislative provision around children, in establishing a discrete site of adjudication and disposal in the Juvenile Courts, the 1908 Act provided the conditions for a shift in the way in which regulation of children and families would occur.

Throughout the nineteenth century, social regulation of the family had entailed a discontinuity between the promotion of morality in the household itself and the coercive action of the penal-legal apparatus. The former was undertaken by private philanthropic activity, having as its concern a perceived breakdown in the moral order of the cities, and seeing the family as a potential means of action upon those deficiencies of character manifested in prostitution, intemperance, vice, indigence, adult and juvenile crime, and pauperism. Leading activists in this field were those bourgeois women who had themselves been so recently inculcated with all the virtues of domesticity. Women from the various voluntary charitable organisations, 'missioners' attached to the courts and sanitary organisations, housing reformers associated with the name of Octavia Hill and others sought to construct the family as a moralising apparatus. The poor were to be encouraged to marry, not because of an affront to Christian morality, but as a means of producing responsibility. Marriage was to control and restrain the moral and financial profligacy of men and women, and household economy was to be enjoined as a moral duty. The mother was to become the agent of moralisation – attracted from the streets and the gin palaces into a domestic unit, her role supported and valorised. The adult male was to be attributed responsibility for financial provision, thus promoting prudence and discouraging him from indulging in gambling, drinking, brawling and all sorts of vice and crime. The child was to be inculcated with the habits of industry, self-reliance, discipline and temperance, its behaviour was to be watched, checked and monitored through the agency of its mother. The object was to promote a private, domesticated unit which would be self-reliant and so organised as to 'automatically' produce in its members the responsibility to care for themselves rather than placing burdens upon the state.[39]

But there was a disjuncture between this philanthropic moralisation of the family and the element of compulsion provided by the machinery of government. Initially, in the Reformatory and Industrial Schools Acts, it was only when the child had been found by a court to be in moral danger itself, or a danger to others, that the voluntary activities of moral familialism were provided with a coercive back-up. The child could be removed from its family and placed in an institution for its moral reformation. As concern began to focus on the consequences of the decline of the birthrate, it became possible for a new problem to emerge for legal regulation. This concerned the deaths of children in foundling homes or being reared for gain – on account of the squandering of national resources which was involved. Measures of compulsory regulation of children *outside* their families were initiated in the Infant Life Protection Act of 1872. Much of the argument concerning these measures focussed upon the issue of the rights of the State to intervene into matters of parental duty, the consequences both for the freedom of the individual and for the sense of responsibility which parents felt towards their children. And the same arguments were used in the debates which finally led to the passage of the first Act allowing compulsory intervention into the details of the upbringing of children in the 'natural' home itself – the Prevention of Cruelty to Children Act of 1889.[40] However, these compulsory measures were discreet and dispersed, families only coming to light as the result of investigation by the voluntary organisations, or through contact with relief agencies or the police. And the role of the state was limited to negative intervention in cases of intractable failure. This involved the removal of the child and the disabling of the family unit, which was the 'natural', but not unique, locus for the preservation of life and the inculcation of morality. Its essential functions could be reproduced elsewhere – in a substitute family or reformatory institution.[41]

With the new configuration around the Juvenile Court, there was no longer a disjuncture between coercion and moralisation, or between different measures concerning different aspects of the troubles of children. The magistrates in the Juvenile Courts now received before them children who, by virtue of their separation from others appearing in the courts, and the common procedures and provisions applying to them, could be seen as a single group which extended all the way from those neglected or in need of care and protection on the one hand to those who had committed serious crimes on the other – a continuous dimension of unfortunate children. And the magistrates had before them an analogous dimension of disposals, ranging from unconditional release, through release on condition of accepting supervision from a probation officer whilst living at home, through to removal into an institution. The Juvenile Courts thus established the linkage between familial scrutiny and moralisation on the one hand and the penal system on the other which remains until today, providing 'voluntary' interventions into the lives of families and children with the coercive back-up necessary for them to operate.

In the 1920s, the arguments put forward by magistrates, probation officers, the Home Office Children's Branch and the Reports of various committees of enquiry were remarkable for their consistency. The terms of their analysis were enshrined in the Children and Young Persons Act, 1933. Probation with supervision was the first choice with respect to children coming before the Juvenile Courts and institutionalisation was only a last resort, appropriate only when probation had failed or had no chance of success and to be maintained as a warning of the consequences of disobeying probation conditions. A check on juvenile delinquency was best effected by supervision in one's own family rather than reformation in isolation from the home environment.[42]

Further, it was argued that the distinction made by legislation between the neglected child and the delinquent child was an artificial one. It was merely a matter of chance whether a child came before the court as a wanderer or a thief, and hence the distinction in the ways in which they could be dealt with, between Reformatory and Industrial Schools, made no sense: 'The tendency to commit offences is only an outcome of the conditions of neglect and there is little room for discrimination either in the character of the young person concerned or in the appropriate method of treatment.'[43] In each case the particular behaviour involved was not the issue – the act, whether it be crime, vagrancy or truancy, was not so much a problem as a symptom of a psychological condition which had its roots in the home:[44]

> It matters little whether a boy or girl of twelve is charged with
> 'found wandering', petty larceny or persistent truancy. . . . In
> nearly every case the root cause of the trouble is the fact that
> the child is living under such home conditions as have not led
> to a right upbringing. . . . Under right influences most children
> respond and do well. . . . The treatment of the young offender
> is entirely a psychological problem.

But this psychological problem was not conceived in terms of
psycho-eugenics. The first Report of the Home Office Children's
Branch was typical in arguing that too much importance should
not be attached to heredity. The majority of offences were
committed by normal children who had not been brought up
correctly. In particular, these children had not been trained to
control their impulses; as we shall see, this question of impulses
will come to underpin a new psychological strategy. The 1927
Report considers that the 'mental equipment' of some delinquent
children manifests an inherent overdevelopment of the instincts.
Other 'inherent' causes, such as chorea, epilepsy, encephalitis,
syphilis, defects of vision, hearing or speech, tuberculosis, enlarged
glands or mental defect were sometimes, though rarely, involved.
But more important were the 'external' causes – that is to say
'environment': parental neglect, bad housing conditions, bad
companions, want of rational amusement, defective education,
want of employment, special temptations and poverty.[45] It was
these external causes which acted on the congenital characteristics
of the child to construct a character of a certain type. Within such
an analysis, the home was just one part of the 'environment'
which contributed to the training of character; family relations
were pertinent only in the lessons which they taught the child in
duty, respect for property, habits of obedience and so forth. If
crime was a mental symptom of a psychological problem, this
problem was, therefore, the lack of correct training, and the
psychological domain was thus still construed as the domain of
habits and of learning, albeit learning to control inherent
impulses. Treatment was to compensate for the early absence of
such control by providing compensating corrective 'influences'.

These questions of causation and treatment were important
because the Juvenile Court sought to become an instance which
made its decisions upon the basis of 'the welfare of the child', and

which decided in relation to that objective on an appropriate
mode of 'treatment' of the children that appeared before it.[46] The
principles of reformation and treatment which the Gladstone
Report of 1895 had proposed as the general rationale of the
system of administration of justice must, it was argued, be applied
with even greater force to the young offender whose character was
still plastic and thus the more readily moulded by wise and
sympathetic treatment.[47] Thus children were not to be 'tried',
'convicted', 'sentenced' as criminals – 'what is needed is not the
dramatic staging of a trial for a crime, but the provision of the
best means for ascertaining and remedying evil tendencies' and the
question should be 'not "what has the child's past conduct
deserved in the way of punishment?" but "what past conditions
have led up to this conduct?" '[48] As Cyril Burt put it:

> The question that has to be asked is not – who committed this
> crime? but – why did he do it? Investigation is still essential;
> but the point to be investigated changes. A psychological rather
> than a judicial enquiry is the primary need.[49]

Magistrates had before them a variety of children who were to
be dealt with not on the basis of the details of their illegal acts but
with respect to the origins of their pathological conduct. Not an
act to be punished but a disorder to be treated. Treatment
depended upon the allocation of the child to the appropriate
option selected from the range of possible disposals – different
types of school, probation 'in the open' and so forth. And to make
this treatment decision, it was necessary to *understand*.[50] It is thus
that the Juvenile Court begins to establish relationships between a
number of previously dispersed elements. Officers of the local
education authority were required to provide the courts with
information as to the home conditions, school career and medical
record of the child.[51] Probation officers were, where necessary, to
make special enquiries into the home and family background.
Children were to be remanded in special remand homes, where the
probation officers could visit them in order to get to know the
character and tendencies of children who might eventually be
placed under their care. And in these homes the children could be
systematically observed and thoroughly examined as a matter of
routine before being brought to the court for a decision. The
routine psychological examination of children had been urged not
only by Hall and Burt, but by Sir Robert Armstrong Jones, Dr

Hamilton-Pearson, Dr MacNamara, Margery Fry, the People's League of Health, the National Council for Mental Hygiene, the Juvenile Organisations Committee and the Home Office Departmental Committee.[52] William Clarke-Hall had introduced it into his court very early on, Burt and Shrubsall had examined children in the London County Council area when requested by the courts, and the Tavistock Clinic had established a tradition of giving free advice to the Shoreditch Court.[53] A new psychological jurisdiction had begun to form.

Around the children in danger and the dangerous children, around the Juvenile Court, a new strategy had thus taken shape. It was one in which the court would act to bring into relationship previously dispersed practices of investigation and regulation of childhood behaviour, family life and transgressions of the law. The criminality of children had become the symptom of a psychological problem, minor disturbances of behaviour had become precursors of later criminality, each sort of problem had its origin in defects within the home. The role of the agencies of social regulation in respect of these problems was not one of punishment but of treatment, and treatment required knowledge not of what the child had done, but of who the child was. What was it in his life, in his personality, in his constitution, in his experiences, which had caused this particular bit of aberrant conduct? The allocation of the child amongst a range of possible disposal options required the court to be provided with information of two types. Information as to the child itself, to be provided by a psychology of the clinic. Information as to the home circumstances, to be provided by welfare work. Psychologists and welfare workers together were to provide the court with the information it required in order to understand the child sufficiently to make its diagnosis and decide upon its treatment. And later a new psychology and a revamped welfare work together would act in relation to this treatment as well.

Through its alliance with the juvenile court, the psychology of the individual had begun to establish its rights to adjudicate on behavioural disorders, at least insofar as it could provide the specialised knowledge upon which such decisions relied. It had extended its sphere of influence through its relations with probation officers. And it had simultaneously established a number of localised and specialised sites for its activities – in remand homes, in the approved schools themselves, but also, and increasingly over the 1930s, in a place separate from either but servicing both – the child guidance clinic.[54]

7
The psychological family

The practices of investigation, diagnosis and reformation of maladjusted and delinquent children which developed in the 1920s and 1930s, entailed a new conception of the family, the type of problems which it engendered, and the nature and objectives of intervention into it. The family was a field of dynamic interchanges between husbands and wives, mothers and fathers, parents and children, brothers and sisters. And the relations between family members did not so much concern health and habits as feelings and emotions: love and guilt, dependency and jealousy, beliefs and fantasies. A child's own family, its 'natural' family, was, in most circumstances, a uniquely appropriate emotional economy for its normal healthy development. But families did go wrong, and when they went wrong this engendered problems in the child. The way in which families went wrong was not through having bad habits or inculcating bad habits or failing to inculcate good ones. They went wrong at the level of their emotional economy. And when children showed problems of behaviour – nerves, maladjustment, delinquency – these were symptoms of this disturbance of family relationships. They were symptoms that disturbed family relations had produced a disturbed child by producing a disturbed psyche. Rectification hence required something different from the instruction of family members or disturbed children in correct habits and moral ways of conduct. It was similarly no longer appropriate, except as a last resort, to remove the child from his natural family and to place him in a 'home', which lacked the very elements with which the problem was bound up – mothers, fathers, love and so forth. The objective of intervention was to preserve the family, to get its emotional economy running along the right lines through acting on the inner feelings of family members.

The disturbances of childhood

As far as the medical psychologies of the nineteenth and early twentieth centuries were concerned, mental disturbances of childhood were not a distinct object of concern.[1] Early nineteenth century texts did recognise disorders of the mind in infancy and childhood, but throughout the nineteenth century they were accorded a somewhat ambiguous status. On the one hand, the child had a kind of immunity from insanity, on account of its under-development, simplicity and freedom from stress.[2] Where children did suffer insanity it was of simple form: infancy was not exposed to many of the predisposing and exciting causes which operated at other periods of life; fewer faculties had developed and therefore fewer faculties were likely to be assaulted by disease; the delicacy of the infant brain made it likely that morbid changes would lead to death.[3] However the *in utero* period and that of infancy and childhood did have a significance in relation to mental pathology. The child would inherit a particular constitution from its parents which might be sound or already enfeebled, but influences at conception or during pregnancy could affect this constitution. Thus Browne argued that illness in the mother, or injury while the child is *in utero*, can produce insanity, as can the longings, desires or habits of the pregnant mother. A tendency to epilepsy could be produced in a child whose pregnant mother was shocked by the sight of a person in an epileptic fit. A child could inherit a drunkard-like walk from the acquired habit of the mother. And in general, those who had led an immoral life, 'who have perpetrated self-abuse, who have given themselves up to licentiousness, lust and passion, to the vice of intemperance, to the pleasures of the table, or to any nervous excitement in excess,' would not only suffer themselves, but would 'entail upon their progeny numerous and grievous ills – none more numerous and grievous than psychological disorders'.[4] Management during infancy and childhood could also have an effect which might be permanent not only as far as the character of the adult was concerned but also on the constitution handed down to future generations, which might be improved or injured by techniques of infant management by parents or wet-nurses, especially poor feeding or excessive indulgences.[5]

As the opposition between heredity and environment began to establish itself, children's disturbances of mind *per se* became marginal, rarely warranting a specific mention. Insanity inhered in a damaged or underdeveloped nervous system. Influences on the aetiology of mental disturbance spanned generations through heredity. This inherited tendency of the nervous system was laid down at conception and resulted in a brain insufficiently equipped with nerve cells or association fibres. After conception the nervous system might be subject to damage from direct or indirect stress. Direct stress entailed injury, toxins or lack of nutrition to the brain. In the category of indirect stress were reworked all the moral causes of insanity familiar from the earlier texts – anxiety, worry, misdirected education, financial concerns, intemperance, sexual excess, religious fanaticism and so forth – now operating on the brain through the medium of bodily processes such as impurities in the blood or exhaustion of nervous energy.[6]

Whilst mental disorder could occur at any period of life, it rarely manifested itself in childhood due to the absence of such indirect stresses. However, if indirect stress could provoke the onset of actual insanity in those with a hereditary predisposition, careful management in infancy and childhood might produce a character and habits which would minimise the risk of such stress. The nostrums elaborated within moral medicine were reworked within the new conception of the nature and aetiology of insanity – the necessity for careful control of diet, avoidance of stimulation, training in obedience, proper habits of thought, feeling and behaviour, self-denial, avoidance of food fads, tobacco, alcohol and religious fanaticism.[7]

It was such a conception of the innate organic foundations of childhood disturbances that led Henderson and Gillespie, in 1927, to assimilate these problems not to insanity but to mental defect.[8] They described the existence of a kind of mental defect designated 'emotional defect', most commonly shown as emotional instability. This condition manifested itself in temper tantrums as a child, being bullied and unhappy at school, rapidly changing emotions and inability to sustain efforts. Emotionally defective children indulged in kleptomania, pyromania and pathological lying, grew up with poor judgment, were improvident financially and liable to alcoholism. Such children made up a considerable proportion of delinquents and moral imbeciles and, claimed Henderson and Gillespie, since the condition was inborn, treatment held out few hopes. They did not lay much emphasis upon the utility of inculcation of correct moral habits to avoid the precipitation of disorder. Training was important, but such emotionally defective persons would often have to be placed under institutional care.

But by the time of their third edition in 1932, something appeared to have changed which had thrown into question this hereditarian and organicist pessimism and placed the mental disturbances of childhood in a new light. The separate chapter which they introduced on the psychiatry of childhood was announced in the preface as a consequence of 'the welcome growth of Child Guidance work [which] has shown that the topic must now be considered an important part of the psychiatric domain'.[9] It now appeared that many adult disorders were a cumulative result of mental habits which had been acquired and ingrained during the years of childhood and adolescence, when the plasticity of the child's mind made it so likely that the innumerable traumata of childhood would leave an indelible mark – indeed the wonder was that so many children grew to be reasonably normal adults at all. Disturbances of childhood, they now warned, should only be attributed to innate factors when all environmental and personal events had been ruled out, and all therapy had failed. Childhood now had its own specific repertoire of disorders: disorders of personality (timidity, obstinacy, irritability, lack of sociability, etc.); behaviour disorders (truancy, temper tantrums, lying, stealing, cruelty or food fads); habit disorders (nail biting, thumb sucking, incontinence, stammering); 'glycopenic' disorders (migraine, insomnia, night terrors and so forth). So troubled children called for a detailed study by a skilled psychiatrist who could make a diagnosis and effect a cure principally by investigation and reformation of the environment of school and home but particularly of family relationships and the habits and manner of training the children.

But in addition to seeking to establish the rights and competence of psychiatry in this new domain, the principal theme of the chapter was, paradoxically, to argue against the necessity of a detailed examination of, or therapy with, the psyche of the child itself. Childhood problems were not, they repeatedly insisted, located in the depths of the psyche, but 'arise at the surface of contact, so to speak, of the child's environment with his aims and desires'.[10] Why the sudden concern to pose the problems of childhood in this way in relation to this domain previously marginal to psychiatry?

Adjustment and maladjustment

In the early years of the twentieth century, a new focus emerged
for medical psychiatric and neurological debate – the neuroses:
types of mental disturbance which did not themselves amount to
insanity, but were nonetheless severe enough to disrupt normal
functioning.[11] Nervous fatigue, neurasthenia, 'nerves', were not
discovered in the asylum, and asylum psychiatrists rarely encoun-
tered them. They owed their discovery to all those places where
problems could come to notice which seemed to prevent the
individual concerned from complying with prescribed tasks or
social expectations, but without completely disabling them. The
army, the factory, the school and the courtroom – these were the
places where the subjects of this new theoretical attention
emerged: the shell-shocked soldier, the fatigued or inefficient
worker, the maladjusted schoolchild and the delinquent juvenile.

Whilst the traumas of war allowed these problems to be
conceived in a specific way and the problems of industry were the
focus of a continuous debate, the school clinic, the Juvenile Court
and the mental hygiene movement gave the disturbances of
childhood a particular significance and urgency. It was now clear
that children with even mild neuroses or nervous disorders might
develop into insane or criminal adults, and, as a corollary, that the
likelihood of insanity or delinquency might be recognised in the
mild disorders of childhood. And these disturbances were not
merely the earliest manifestations of the presence of an untreatable
organic condition. Whilst they would almost certainly lead to such
severe troubles if left untreated, they *were* treatable. The minor
troubles of childhood had became a specific object of theoretical
concern and therapeutic intervention.

How was the problem thus formed to be conceptualised?
Psychiatry sought to retain an analysis in terms of the effects of
stress upon an inherited neuropathic tendency throughout most of
the 1920s. Some paediatricians, notably Hector Cameron, did
however seek to differentiate the problems of the 'nervous child'
from these organic conditions, and to locate them in a psychological sphere. The conduct of the nervous child, he argued, was a
product of suggestion from the mother. The child loved attention
and hence delighted in the distress caused, for example, by refusal
to sleep, to eat, or to go to school. It was thus the *parent's* pride,
nervousness or opposition which produced the *child's* disturbance:

'Stripped of all that is not essential we see the problem of the management of children reduced to the interplay between the adult mind and the mind of the receptive suggestible child.'[12] Hence Cameron sought an alliance between doctors and well-to-do mothers in promoting mental hygiene by avoiding that restlessness, instability and hypersensitivity in children which passed insensibly into neuropathy in adult life. But whilst the notion of suggestion was to play a part in the new way of conceptualising childhood disturbances, this was not within Cameron's conception of the psyche as simply a kind of register of emotional impressions. There was, rather, a much more fundamental shift in the conception of the psyche, one in which emotions, wishes and actions were linked up in a three-dimensional space organised by flows of instinctual energy, channelled into adaptive or maladaptive forms by childhood experiences of family emotional relationships.

Psychoanalysis came to England quite early, and proceeded under the steadfast and loyal helmsmanship of Ernest Jones. Jones founded the London Society of Psychoanalysis in 1913, and this was re-born as the British Society for Psychoanalysis in 1919. The London Psycho-Analytic Clinic, later the Institute of Psychoanalysis, was founded in 1924. The principal works of Freud became available in translation from 1909 onwards. A small but steady stream of people trained and practised as orthodox Freudian analysts, and a number of faithful secondary texts were produced.[13] Thomas Mitchell, whose own orthodox Freudian *Problems in Psychopathology* was published in 1927, was editor of the *British Journal of Medical Psychology* from its foundation in 1921 through to 1934.

Yet the debates in its pages indicate how far Freudian psychoanalytic theory was from exclusive occupation of the new terrain of psychology. Indeed, over the 1920s and 1930s, classical psychoanalysis as a doctrine of the psyche and a clinical method was very much on the defensive.[14] It was vilified by small heretical factions – those promoting the doctrines of Jung and the Zurich school from the Analytic Psychology Club and by Adlerians who founded the Medical Society of Individual Psychology in 1931. Its theoretical bases and therapeutic methods were attacked by organicist psychiatrists like Alfred Tredgold and Edward Mapother of the Maudsley Hospital, and investigated by the British Medical Association after a particular scandal in 1925.[15] A further line of theoretical and practical opposition came from a group of English doctors and psychologists, many engaged in therapeutic work, who, whilst recognising the revolutionary discoveries of Freud, sought to dispense with certain of the central concepts of his system and combine the remainder with theories drawn from other domains. This school termed itself 'the new psychology'. In the face of this opposition, Freudian psychoanalysis retained its presence in the literature and the private consulting room, but largely withdrew from the public domain of social and political disputation.

The 'new psychology', however, was not so modest. Its formation was contemporary with the incursion of psychoanalytic orthodoxy into Britain in the immediate pre-war period. The writings and lectures of Bernard Hart and William Brown sought to promote what were considered to be the fundamental principles discovered by Freud, whilst expressing reservations about certain of his doctrines, and effecting a judicious replacement of these elements by others more acceptable or at least less scandalous.[16] What was accepted was the energy model of the psyche, notions of unconscious mental processes and unconscious motives, repression, regression, mental conflict and complexes. What was discarded, explicitly or tacitly, was the conception that libidinal energy, or the 'sex instinct', was the organising principle of mental life and conation, together with the associated doctrines of infantile sexuality and the sexual origins of the neuroses.

The effects of the First World War enabled this non-organicist theory of neurotic disorders to be organised into a distinct and active body of argument and therapeutic techniques. An alarmingly high proportion of the casualties in the first months of war were suffering not from obvious physical injury, but from 'shell shock' – 7-10 per cent of officer casualties and 3-4 per cent of other rank casualties by December 1914. The number of such cases over the whole war was estimated at 80,000 and in 1921 some 65,000 ex-servicemen were still receiving disability pensions for 'shell shock'.[17] Treatment was mostly given near the fighting, and the majority of cases were returned to active duty within three weeks, but the more serious cases were sent to special hospitals in England – Maghull, Nettley, Craiglockhart, and Denmark Hill were the best known. Whilst many senior military officers considered 'shell shock' to be only a disguise for cowardice, to be minimised by improved morale, good officership, and, where necessary, the firing squad, organicist physicians such as Mott initially considered the condition to be a consequence of minute cerebral haemorrhages caused by the blast.

But the doctors and psychologists who were employed in these hospitals contested the therapeutic pessimism which this would imply. They began to deploy various versions of the therapeutic techniques developed in Paris by Janet and in Vienna by Freud, and used their apparent success to dispute organicist theories of the aetiology of neuroses. The war neuroses provided the opportunity of extending to these 'minor disorders' of the mind the type of practice which had made clinical medicine possible, and hence of disputing the medical theories themselves. As Hadfield put it:[18]

> The cases presented by war are so simple in their aetiology and the factors which contribute to their production so well-defined and uncomplicated in character, compared with those in civilian cases, that we have the opportunity of studying them almost under laboratory conditions. Moreover, so many of these are practically identical in origin and symptoms, that they constitute excellent material for testing and comparing the various methods of treatment.

But they also appeared to confirm the early doubts and scepticism concerning the emphasis on sexuality in Freudian psychoanalysis and the exclusivity claimed for the analytic method itself.[19] In order to understand these neuroses it was necessary to infer the reality of processes which resembled conscious mental processes in every way except that the patient could give no account of them. These processes were the results of repression: a forgetting by the conscious mind (consciously or unconsciously effected) of some intolerable or irresolvable mental conflict. But it was not necessary to 'pervert wholly the meaning of sex or sexual' or to see the origins of neuroses in some 'very hypothetical sexuality of infancy' to understand these repressions.[20] These elements were replaced with a theory of multiple instincts drawn variously from William McDougall's 'hormic' psychology, William Trotter's conception of a 'herd instinct' and the concept of 'sentiments' put forward by Alexander Shand, often together with a conception of neuroses in terms of dissociation drawn from Janet.[21] Thus, for example, W.H.R. Rivers attributed the war neuroses to a repressed conflict between the instinct of self-preservation and the call of duty, and

McDougall saw the symptoms of paralysis, muscle tremors, headaches, giddiness, lassitude, lack of confidence, insomnia and so forth as the consequence of the conflict between the repressed energies of the complex and the repressing energies of the rest of the personality which could not let this complex into consciousness.[22] And a range of therapeutic techniques were deployed – the choice depending upon the nature of the case – ranging from occupational training, through persuasion, suggestion and rational re-education to a form of psychotherapy which used hypnosis or free association to discover the nuclear incident which had been the precipitating cause of the disorder, to bring to consciousness the conflicting feelings and emotions which had accompanied it, to reveal the links between this repressed complex and the symptoms, and hence to provide relief and cure by liberating the affect and energy which had been blocked and by allowing it to be directed into other channels.[23]

In the decade following the end of the First World War, the new psychology was elaborated in numerous texts with varying degrees of sophistication.[24] What is significant for our purposes is not the degree of subtlety with which the different authors expounded the new psychology, nor the fine details of the disputes which traversed it. Rather the question we must ask is this: what was it that the new psychology made thinkable? The answer is in terms of the alignment which it forged between the register of personal happiness, that of family relations, and that of social adjustment.

Within McDougall's purposive psychology, in which mind governed action in the light of experience in order to direct it to certain ends, an instinct was defined as:[25]

> An innate disposition which determines the organism to perceive (pay attention to) an object of a certain class and to experience in its presence a certain emotional excitement and an impulse to action which finds expression in a specific mode of behaviour in relation to that object.

McDougall identified twelve such primary instinctual dispositions, each of which involved *cognition* – the mind taking cognisance of the object – *affect* – the specific emotion aroused – and *conation* – the mental tendency or set towards appropriate action. These primary dispositions were flight, repulsion, curiosity, pugnacity (associated with fear, disgust, wonder and anger), self-assertion and self-abasement (associated with positive and negative self-feelings), the sex, parental and gregarious instincts (passion, tenderness and a general heightening of pleasant feeling), feeding, construction and acquisitiveness.

Not everyone accepted McDougall's views completely. Some preferred Shand's terminology, and his argument that over the course of development, action became governed by 'sentiments' which were complex organisations of different emotional dispositions that directed action in particular situations.[26] Others sought to displace McDougall's instinct of gregariousness with Trotter's more powerful 'herd instinct'. This referred to the innate disposition of the normal mind automatically to obey suggestions and influences arising from the herd or social group, and the unhappiness consequent upon being different or separate from the group.[27]

The significance of this proliferation of instincts and the form in which they were specified is that the impulse to social adjustment was inscribed in the individual at the psychical level. Thus the parenting instinct and the emotional disposition of tenderness was, for Tansley:[28]

> the great psychical bond which binds the mates to one another and their children. . . . Its biological function is to hold the family together for mutual protection – in the first instance probably the mother to her children, then the husband to his wife, the father to his children, and the wife to her husband.

The natural family was now a biological necessity, a social value and a realisation of individual will. And, from its evolutionary origins in the physical safety of the group, the herd instinct bound the individual into obligations to morality and authority at the level of dispositions and in the register of pleasure versus unhappiness – though it also explained allegiances to such 'partial herds' as crowds, class, political and religious groupings.[29] Unlike the psychoanalytic postulate of a single libidinal energy with no given form of satisfaction, instinct theory construed individuals as pre-organised towards social adjustment, for psychic energy was such that it sought discharge in directions which were advantageous both to the species in terms of social adjustment, and to the individual, in terms of the satisfaction of a wish and the experience of pleasure. And where Freud was to write, in 1930, of the unease inherent in civilisation, the new psychology was to be a science of social contentment. Personal happiness and social adjustment were now two sides of the same coin.

For the new psychology, character was no longer merely an aggregate of acquired habits. Under the pressure of experience, inherited nervous temperament and innate primary dispositions were organised into sentiments, which were themselves organised into an harmonious and integrated system: character. The most important experiences were those which the child gained in its family. It was here that primary instincts and emotions were channelled and connected up into constellations containing cognitive, affective and conative processes and attached to appropriate objects or ideas. The normal family provided the environment in which these impulses were smoothly and harmoniously organised and directed towards the right objects, ideas and persons, producing a harmonious and adjusted character. Parents did this through encouraging correct habits, certainly, but also through their own psychological relations with their children, through the processes of suggestion whereby the feelings and emotions of the parents towards actions and objects would be incorporated into the suggestible mind of the child. Also crucial was the operation of the child's experience upon the sentiment of self-regard: the master sentiment of the will, made up of the paired instincts of self-assertion and self-abasement, which organised action and directed volition. By respecting and directing this sentiment of self-regard, socially adjusted and happy individuals would be produced, and the individual's impulse to self-realisation would be fulfilled through the formation of abiding sentiments of right habit and good conduct.[30]

A psychological rationale had been superadded to the moral rationale for the existence and promotion of the family, but simultaneously the family that was to be promoted had been limited to the *natural* family, for it had something which was not present in any substitutes. The natural wish of men and women was to be husbands and wives, parents and home-makers. And the natural place to raise a child was its own family, since here the wish of parents to have a child and the need of a child for its parents coincided. A new type of family history had been made possible, one where the relations between the biological, the psychological, the moral and the social were not direct – as in degeneracy and eugenics – but indirect. Nonetheless, the biological and evolutionary grounding of the instincts acted as a reality-justification for the promotion of particular familial relations. The social adjustment of the individual was at one and the same time a self-realisation – since it was towards this that the biological urges were directed – and the consequence of a good psychological family.

The conception of the normal psychological family was formed from the perspective of pathology. The discoveries of the new psychology induced normality from an analysis of abnormality, the mechanisms of adjustment to social life from the study of the maladjusted. As Brierley wrote, 'When a hitch occurs in the process of adjustment of the individual to his psychical environment, its workings are revealed, – discoveries that might never be made if all went smoothly.'[31] And if the normal family was characterised in terms of a harmonious and adjusted channelling and expression of psychic energy, this was because pathology was a consequence of repression.

Repression was a consequence of an environment where dispositions were not channelled, and energy not expressed, but where it was blocked and forced into the unconscious. A family could provoke or produce conflicts in wishes and emotions, or deny them expression, or associate them with shame, guilt or other unpleasant feelings. Repression could also be produced by the parents expressing their own fears, hopes, anxieties, guilts and disappointments in relation to the child's feelings, wishes or actions. The child, who was so suggestible, would incorporate these into its psyche, and the displeasure so caused would conflict with the pressure of conation and its associated emotions and ideas. This conflict would be resolved by forcing the ideas, feelings and wishes which had provoked it into the unconscious. A similar process would occur if the parents feared the child's independence and positive self-regard, playing on its fears and anxieties in order to keep it dependent. The repressed complex would not, however, lie silent outside consciousness. The energy attached to it would find distorted expression in dreams, nervous disorders or abnormalities of conduct, in compensatory phantasies, projection of the repressed conflict on to others, anxiety and so forth. If the normal family was construed in terms of adjustment and happiness, disturbances in the psychological relations of the family produced social maladjustment and personal unhappiness. As the new psychology began to construe the family at the level of emotions and wishes, the possibility opened up for emotions and wishes to be inscribed within the field of social regulation.[32]

For the new psychology, the organisation of dispositions into sentiments and character was one that was produced in the real, as a result of the actual experience by the child of its interactions with its parents, and the actual – even if unconscious – feelings, emotions and wishes that the parents had in relation to it.[33] Similarly, real events were the causes of its troubles, neuroses and maladjustments. They arose from a conflict generated by the real experiences and events in family life which had been coped with by repression. The function of the neurosis was to provide a defence against the conflict and to conceal that which had been repressed. The function of therapy was to reveal to the individual his own unconscious motive and to enable him to cope in consciousness with the conflict that had generated it. Thus on the one hand therapy could proceed by a kind of abreaction in which energy was freed as these real repressed events were reinserted into consciousness and simultaneously removed from their troubling unconscious existence, and on the other hand norms of family relations could be constructed, and types of family relations evaluated, in terms of their likelihood to promote or hinder the production of a normal, adjusted psyche. The insistence of the real provided the possibility of constructing psychological norms of healthy child-rearing and a normalising practice of intervention and therapy.

It was around this question of the real that one focus of dispute between psychoanalysis and the new psychology was organised in the late 1920s and early 1930s. For the new psychology, phantasy was often harmless childhood daydreaming, sometimes the outcome of conflict, a way of escaping from an unpleasant reality which should be dispelled by bringing the real problems into the open. But as orthodox psychoanalysis extended its techniques to the actual analysis of children, rather than inducing the psychical relations of childhood from the results of adult analysis, the priority of reality over phantasy in the mental life of the child was reversed. Hermione Hug-Hellmuth's techniques of analysis with children, dating from 1913, were reported in English in the *International Journal of Psychoanalysis* in 1921. Melanie Klein's extension and development of these techniques for very young children were increasingly the focus of a developing and disputatious tendency in British analytical circles. These arguments were popularised beyond the field of professional psychoanalysis by the writings of Susan Isaacs based upon her work at the Malting House School and, from 1933, as Head of the Department of Child Development at the Institute of Education in London.[34]

The work of Isaacs was widely disseminated through the training of infant school teachers to which her department contributed, through pamphlets and through her answers to parents' questions in the journal *Home and School*.[35] The conclusions which she drew from theory and observation of young children entailed a denegation of the real which appeared to rule out the possibility of psychoanalysis providing general norms of conduct for parents in order to rear healthy and well adjusted children. As she wrote in 1930: 'Our real behaviour [to children] and the actual conditions we create, are always *for them* set in the matrix of their own phantasies.'[36] In blurring the line between experience and its psychical consequences, as a result of the significance accorded to primitive wishes and phantasies within the child itself, these English developments of psychoanalysis in the inter-war years provided no easy schema for the mapping of the disorders of childhood on to real maladaptive types of family relations. Thus they problematised the project of normalising the latter in the service of the former.

If the emphasis of the new psychology was to resolve a problem in the child by action upon the family, in these developments from psychoanalysis this balance was reversed. Thus Isaacs did not provide parents and teachers with a set of instructions or advice as to conduct, because the meaning of any particular situation, action or event to the child could never be specified in general, and varied according to individual circumstances and the child's mental life. Mothers could, however, be alerted to the inevitability of fears, phantasies, jealousies, angers and conflicts in the mental life of the young child. They were to recognise these as the products of the child's own beliefs and imaginings, not a product of real events or persons, but nonetheless more real to the child than any external facts. So norms of parental behaviour could not be prescribed in specific terms; only the general presumption that leaving the child free to express itself in its own way was usually preferable to constraint or direction. An understanding, liberal, tolerant attitude was to be encouraged to the vicissitudes of the mental and emotional growth of the child.[37] As psychoanalysis provided the motive and the vocabulary for the study of the smallest fancies of the child's mind, elaborating on the significance of play, dreams and phantasy, stressing the developmental functions of these aspects of the child's imagination, and privileging the 'point of view of the child', the links which welded together the constituents of the new psychology began to dissolve.[38]

At the same time McDougall's hormic psychology was increasingly called into question, with each author generating his own inventory of instincts, and others beginning to question what it was that held together the various aspects of behaviour aggregated as a single instinct, apart from the fact that they were all labelled with the same name. As the 1930s progressed, the conceptual alliances which had constituted the new psychology began to look increasingly shaky, and the modes of explanation which it had provided were increasingly annexed to medicine and psychiatry. And it was to be doctors rather than psychologists who controlled the practice which formed around the mental troubles of children.

In the post-war period, the new psychology would be replaced by a revamped and normalising psychoanalysis. This took as its central concern not so much the emotional relations between all family members as the specific relationship between the mother and the child, or rather between the child's need to be mothered and the woman's desire to be a mother. It is often suggested that this emphasis upon the importance of the early mother-child relationship for healthy psychological development was an ideological legitimation for the closure of wartime nursery provision, the removal of women from the labour market and their re-domestication. But the arguments concerning the damaging effects of separation of babies and young children from their mothers ante-date the famous post-war studies of children reared in institutions, and the requirements of post-war economics, indeed these arguments played only a small part in the decisions to close the nurseries.[39] We must look elsewhere for the social conditions which led to such a concentration on the bond between the mother and the child. The work of Bowlby, Winnicott and the other celebrants of maternality had its foundation in the new psychology and the Child Guidance Clinics. Before the war, Bowlby and Winnicott both cut their teeth in the child guidance movement, and they maintained many of its normalising aspirations, founded now upon an emphasis upon the specific importance of the child's first object relations in the formation of the ego. Bowlby's famous study of 'Forty-Four Juvenile Thieves' which claimed to establish the link between early separation from the mother, an Affectionless Character, and juvenile theft, though not published until 1944, was carried out at the London Child Guidance Clinic during the years 1936-1939.[40] The Child Guidance Clinic was the site which made this new theory and practice of the genesis of childhood disturbances possible.

The young delinquent

If the new psychology was to lead to a clinical role for psychological knowledge from the direction of the minor mental disturbances of childhood and the perspective of mental hygiene, it was to intersect with another path which also prioritised the establishment of the psychological clinic. The issue for this second line of development was not so much the maladjusted child who would present worse problems in the future but the delinquent child and the past origins of his conduct. This problem was formed in the debates around the juvenile court and in the texts of Charles Goring and Maurice Hamblin Smith. But the leading advocate of this tendency, and promoter of the role of individual psychology, was, once again, Cyril Burt.

In the decade following the passage of the Mental Deficiency Act 1913, there was a consistent attempt to extend the hereditarian explanations concerning idiocy and feeble-mindedness to the problems of delinquency and crime, through the notion of 'moral imbecility'.[41] Many psychiatrists, notably Mercier, Tredgold and East, sought to uphold the argument that there was indeed a class of defectives who suffered from an inherited or congenital defect in their moral faculty – without necessarily an accompanying defect of intelligence – which was manifested by aberrant conduct in childhood leading to delinquency and criminality, and that these children should be dealt with in the same way as other defectives, for the condition made them unreformable.[42]

It is paradoxical at first sight that Burt, architect of psycho-eugenics, should have been at the forefront of the opposition to this application of the familiar strategy to a new domain. Especially since he had himself, in 1917, described a class of unstable persons who were a definite type of mental defective –

defective in character rather than in intellect.[43] But this opposition is intelligible on at least two counts: firstly, as an attempt to claim the disturbances of childhood and their relation to delinquency as a field of psychological rather than medical expertise; and secondly, because these conditions were to be attributed to factors other than heredity, to allow psychology a space of action beyond that of mere ascertainment of an inborn state of affairs – to allow it, that is to say, a role in therapy and reformation.

Burt took as his targets two notions which he reckoned to underpin the 'medical' view – the notion of an inbuilt 'moral faculty' and the argument that crime ran in families.[44] There was no inborn condition of 'moral blindness', he argued, but rather an inherited temperament which was shaped and channelled through family life. And family histories, he claimed, showed that the proportion of delinquents with a family history of transgression of moral rules was low, and in any event delinquency was more likely to be transmitted by family life than by inheritance.[45]

Burt proposed a conception of delinquency and its origins which would lead to a new claim for a clinical status for psychology. It combined a theory of conduct drawn from the new psychology with a Galton-like energy theory of the psyche. The problems that the unstable might produce were a consequence of their high level of 'general emotionality' – analogous to 'general intelligence'. But whether this led to delinquency or to brilliance and/or originality depended not upon the excessive level of emotionality itself, but the way it was channelled by the discipline of the home and family. Properly directed, it could lead to the following of a highly useful and productive life, ill-directed, to perversion, morbidity, impulsivity and criminality. The problem, that is to say, was neither physical nor inborn – it was a psychological problem, with psychological causes, that admitted of psychological solutions.

Burt at first argued that, if the family was not channelling energy correctly, the child was better off being removed from it and located in a colony, conceived of along the lines of a new form of moral treatment. The unstable child was to be placed in a free-running, self-disciplining community, along the lines of Homer Lane's Little Commonwealth or the Riverside Villages. But this was not a reactivation of the old psycho-eugenic demand for segregation. For in the colony, free from interaction with an unstable mother, without arbitrary discipline and repression which blocked energy rather than channelling it along useful lines, immersed in country life with its uniformity and orderly progression of sensuous, natural and impersonal interests, aided by adults playing the role of 'sympathetic psychoanalysts', the child could truly be reformed.[46]

Burt sought to claim this new field of problems for the psychology of the individual.[47] On the one hand, in that these problems arose in a psychological domain, psychologists rather than doctors were the appropriate diagnostic agents; and whilst doctors conceived of the problems as intractable to reform, psychology could both explain their genesis in the life of the individual and prescribe a therapeutic regime. On the other hand, traditional psychology had little to offer here. The majority of psychological textbooks were engrossed with the processes of sensation; the remainder dealt with the general principles of perception, memory and association. These had about as much value to those handling concrete cases as a knowledge of plant cells had to the gardener bedding out begonias. But the psychology of individual differences was another matter. It was concerned, like practitioners themselves, with the nature of mental differences in different individuals, the signs by which they might be recognised, the causes which produce and remove them. So it was *individual psychology* which was to be 'the master science' for all those who dealt with troubled or troublesome individuals and had to take decisions in the light of their character and personality.[48]

The Young Delinquent, first published in 1925 and going through four editions in the following twenty years, at one level merely systematised these arguments and sought to substantiate them by reporting the results of a study of some 200 young delinquents and a matched group of 400 non-delinquents.[49] It appeared to align individual psychology with the new psychology and with the types of analysis and practice which it suggested. But at another level, in wishing to incorporate these within the theory, methods and expertise of individual psychology, it attempted to recast the new psychology in terms of the variation of emotional characteristics across a population, and hence make it amenable to the statistical techniques, scalings and assessment methods which had come to define, at the most fundamental level, what could count as a scientific psychology of the individual. Here the seeds were sown of the failure of individual psychology to become the dominant instance in the Child Guidance Clinic.

The delinquent act was a symptom: its causes were fundamentally mental. Hence the object of investigation – if these causes were to be discovered – and treatment – if they were to be removed – was the inner mental life of the delinquent. Physical conditions or defects might be involved, as might environmental factors, but since criminal activity sprang ultimately from the mind, these could operate only through the moral or emotional reactions which they produced and which might persist, even after the relevant condition no longer existed. But the psychological field pertinent to delinquency was not that of the intellect. Only a small proportion of delinquents were defective in intelligence; others were of dull, normal or even above-normal intelligence; intellectual factors were usually accessory rather than the main causes of delinquency. They did not furnish the motive for the act; they simply removed some of the checks, based on prudent or rational insight, which prevented the normal mind from giving way to desires whose fundamental source was an inner instinct or impulse. Unstable and delinquent children had prioritised a new domain for psychological conceptualisation – that of temperament and character: 'the sum total of all those personal qualities of mind which do not constitute, or are not pervaded by, intelligence'.[50] Within this framework the demands of social existence could be linked up with the biological and psychological laws of development of the psyche.

Burt allowed that there were cases in which children were 'emotionally defective' in the sense in which Henderson and Gillespie used the term. But such cases were rare; in most cases delinquents were either temperamentally normal or else temperamentally unstable. Instability, however, was neither the cause of delinquency nor irremediable, nor a justification for permanent segregation. What was inborn was a set of biological instincts, and a level of energy which 'fuelled' them. In some cases specific instincts might be overdeveloped, producing particular types of misconduct: an overdeveloped sex instinct was linked to promiscuity; anger to violent offences; acquisitiveness to theft and so forth. But more often what was involved was a generally high level of energy which sought discharge through all the instinctual channels. Problems arose when this energy was misdirected within the family, producing anti-social habits. In such cases, treatment was most effectively carried out by removal from the home environment, into one where the old habits by which the impulses were directed could be broken down, and new and constructive ones formed.[51]

But also, events might cause energy to be blocked or repressed, leading to the formation of unconscious 'complexes'. This was related not so much to actual home conditions as to the peculiar mental life of the child: foolish phantasies stemming from doubts about the love felt by parents or rivalries with siblings; conflicts between pairs of opposing instincts such as gluttony and fear around the purloining of food; conflicts between sexual temptations and social taboos. Here something unpleasant is blotted from consciousness, and that which has been repressed may return through other channels of discharge – stealing, violence, running away – in which the substitute act is linked to the original temptation through a connection unknown to the delinquent. Burt claimed that he had found traces of such repressed complexes in 57 per cent of his cases – most often where intelligent persons with no obvious reasons or motives of gain had taken to a life of crime. Here, none of the usual methods of treatment was appropriate; what was needed was 'psychoanalysis':[52]

> The object of psychoanalysis is to loosen the twisted knots in which the soul is entangled. The analyst must strive to disengage all the implicated motives of the child, unconscious as well as conscious, so that both the child and himself may become fully aware what hidden bonds encumber him.

Psychoanalysis, for Burt, was thus a kind of practical re-education of the psyche to free repressed energy and to rechannel it along socially acceptable and constructive paths.

At the very beginnings of *The Young Delinquent*, Burt had staked the claims of psychology, rather than medicine, for jurisdiction over the behavioural disorders of childhood, on account of their mental origin. He wrote:[53]

> And there is now a definite body of ascertained knowledge, tracing mental symptoms to their causes, just as medical knowledge tracks down the sources of bodily disorders, and so can prescribe for each its proper treatment or appropriate cure. The study of the criminal thus becomes a distinct department of this new science – a branch of individual psychology; and the

handling of the juvenile offender is, or should be, a practical application of psychological principles.

And a vital sub-plot of *The Young Delinquent* was to demonstrate the variety of the factors that could produce delinquency, and the need for, and efficacy of, psychological analysis, investigation and conceptualisation if one was to understand the complex workings of these factors in the mental life of the child. It thus led naturally to a reactivation of the demand for a site of operation for this psychological expertise, not now in relation to the defective, but to the disturbed and the delinquent. The psychological clinic, for which Burt provided a detailed model in an appendix, was intended to install individual psychology as the integrating instance in a complex of investigation, adjudication and treatment which spanned home, school and court, social work, medicine and probation, with options ranging from permanent segregation, temporary committal to a reformatory colony, probationary supervision in the home, and psychoanalysis.[54] If these aspirations of individual psychology were not to be realised, it was nonetheless the case that such sites were established, and provided the means by which a form of psychological knowledge would underpin a new strategy of regulation of children and families.

8
Psychology and the clinic

The Child Guidance Clinic formed at the intersection of a number of different axes. The mental hygiene movement, the Juvenile Court, the new psychology, and the psychology of delinquency all proposed the establishment of such sites for early assessment and/or treatment. The Child Guidance Clinics which were founded in the 1920s and 1930s were formed in the image of the new psychology. This psychology entered into an alliance with welfare workers, providing the rationale for a new theory and practice of social work. The psychosocial strategy which took shape entailed a way of conceptualising the family, pathology, and the objectives and techniques of reformation which was very different from that involved in welfare work within neo-hygienism. But individual psychology was neither the master science of this strategy nor the dominant instance in the clinical site which it had promoted for so long. With a few exceptions, the role of psychologists, professionally and practically, was subsidiary and limited. It was confined to the mundane activities of mental testing, supplying its results to others for action in both diagnosis and treatment. Psychometrics, not psychotherapy, was the destiny of the psychology of the individual.

The psychology of the clinic

The aspirations of psycho-eugenics to a clinical role were largely thwarted, although at least one local authority had set up a 'psychiatric clinic' by 1913, equipped with the paraphernalia of anthropometrics, and with the role of identifying feeble-minded schoolchildren.[1] The move to a psychology of the clinic really began not in relation to problems of the intellect, but problems of nerves. Hospital children's departments began to concern themselves with 'nervous' children soon after the First World War.[2] By the early 1920s, a number of separate and specialised clinics had been established for the treatment of children and adults with what were now being termed 'functional nerve disorders'.

It appears that the first of these was the Medico-Psychological Clinic of London, which opened in 1913.[3] It was run by Jessie Murray, a doctor who had attended Janet's lectures in Paris. The publicity material for the clinic used neo-hygienist language, describing it as 'a fresh adventure in the field of *Preventive Medicine*, viz., in *Mental Hygiene*'. It argued that attempts to discover and treat the earlier manifestations of disorders of the brain and nervous system were of far-reaching significance, as these disorders were present in a large proportion of those in prisons, reformatories and workhouses as well as those who were recognised as insane. And it claimed that modern research had demonstrated the efficacy of new therapeutic measures if they were applied at an early stage. Principal amongst these measures was psychoanalysis, and apparently it was disputes over the exclusivity of its adherence to orthodox Freudian analysis, and its affiliation to the British Society of Psychoanalysis, that led to the demise of the Clinic in 1922. James Glover, its director at the time, went on to become an orthodox Freudian analyst; a number of those who had worked and trained at the Clinic, however, transferred their allegiance to the Tavistock Clinic.

The Tavistock Square Clinic for the Treatment of Functional Nerve Cases was established in 1920 by Hugh Crichton Miller, 'pioneer of the new psychology'.[4] It was the new psychology which provided its practical, theoretical and therapeutic orientation, and the link which it established between the psychical, the familial and the social was instantiated in the way in which the Tavistock combined diagnosis and therapy in the clinic itself with the investigation of family relations in the home. Nowhere was this clearer than in its work with children. Children were treated from very early on, and in 1926 the Children's Department was opened under Dr W.A. Potts. This was an affair involving many disciplines. Initially, a doctor would examine and interview the children, and a voluntary social worker would investigate home and family conditions. For this latter task the Tavistock had the full-time services of Doris Robinson, who was amongst the first batch of British social workers to be sent out to America for training as a Psychiatric Social Worker. The Clinic utilised psychologists, but they were not involved in diagnosis or therapy, which was strictly a medical matter. Their role was the carrying out of psychological tests, and the ascertainment of intelligence quotients, the result of which would be fed into the diagnostic process. In 1928 a psychologist, Constance Simmins, was appointed to the staff, to be joined by other psychological assistants in the 1930s, but the role and function of psychology in the Tavistock team changed little.

Children came to the Clinic from a number of sources – 'nervous' children from middle-class families unable to afford high private fees; maladjusted children having trouble at school; children referred from the Juvenile Courts. The Tavistock struck up an intimate relationship with the probation service. It worked closely with the Shoreditch Court, and held frequent meetings and training courses in which the doctrines of the new psychology were disseminated to the attending probation officers. In the late 1920s and early 1930s *Probation*, the journal of the National Association of Probation Officers, became virtually a Tavistock house-journal, with contributions on topics such as 'The Unconscious Motive of the Juvenile Delinquent.' Whilst, to the disappointment of its founder, the Tavistock Clinic itself failed to provide the model for similar institutions throughout the country, the same was not true of its Children's Department. Its work increased and it established links with the psychologically minded inspectorate of the London County Council – people like C.W. Kimmins, whose psychological education was through Sully's textbooks and the psychological laboratory of University College.[5] It gave evidence to the Home Office Committee on Persistent Offenders and, as a consequence, was asked to supply regular advisory attendants at children's courts.[6] And the pattern which it established was generalised through the emergence of Child Guidance Clinics.

Like the Medico-Psychological Clinic of London, the Tavistock promoted itself in the language of mental hygiene.[7] It collaborated in joint ventures with the National Council for Mental Hygiene.[8] For the mental hygiene movement, the Child Guidance Clinic was both the foremost of the measures for early and preventative treatment, and one which could be the centre of a system of child welfare embracing 'the nursery, the home, the school, the playground and the courts'.[9] The history of the child guidance movement in England is well documented. What concerns us here is the way in which the child guidance movement acted to integrate a range of diverse concerns and orientations into a coherent framework of argument and practice.[10]

The Child Guidance Council was set up in 1927, through the collaboration of a number of organisations and individuals. Amongst those involved was Burt, who had long been an advocate of psychological clinics. Dame Evelyn Fox was the Honorary Secretary, representing the involvement of the old National Association for the Care of the Feeble-Minded, now retitled the Central Association for Mental Welfare. The National Council for Mental Hygiene represented the more general social aspirations of the child guidance movement. The links with social work were formalised with the involvement of the Institute of Hospital Almoners and the Charity Organisation Society. And the concern with delinquency was manifest in the participation of the Howard League, which had published articles in 1924 urging the setting up of psychological 'laboratories' for the assessment of young offenders.[11]

The chronological histories pay much attention to the visit that a magistrate, Mrs St Loe Strachey, paid to the United States of America in 1925 and the impression that was made upon her by the child guidance work with young offenders which she saw.[12] The American pattern, in which a team of psychiatrists, psychologists and social workers carried out medical, psychiatric, psychological and social investigations of individual children, had been established by William Healy in 1909 when he set up the Chicago Juvenile Psychopathic Institute.[13] It received widespread publicity with the publication of *The Individual Delinquent* in 1915.[14] The model was copied by the Boston Psychopathic Hospital, which actually appointed social workers to its staff – Healy had made use of other social agencies – and which invented the designation 'psychiatric social worker' in 1915. A private benefaction – the Commonwealth Fund – collaborated with the American National Council for Mental Hygiene to set up the first American Demonstration Clinic in 1922 – its aim was 'to develop the psychiatric study of difficult pre-delinquent and delinquent children in schools and juvenile courts, and to develop sound methods of treatment based on such study'.[15]

The first English Child Guidance Clinic to open was explicitly modelled on the American pattern. This was the East London Child Guidance Clinic opened by the Jewish Health Organisation in 1927, under Dr Noel Burke and Dr Emanuel Miller.[16] A year later Margaret Lowenfeld founded the Children's Clinic in West London, which renamed itself the Institute of Child Psychology in 1931. But the Institute set itself apart from other organisations, and felt that its orientation was unique. It argued that it was because of some unsuccessful direction of emotion *in the child itself* that environmental influences produced neuroses, social and emotional maladaptation, delinquency and criminal tendencies, as well as chronic physical ill health; the treatment should be of the child itself, was inevitably a lengthy business, and should consist of a 'scientific adaptation of free play'. In the playroom of the Institute, the child would use specially constructed or adapted materials to give expression to his conscious and unconscious phantasies and his primitive impulses would be re-directed under the supervision of the Psychological Director.[17] The Institute was also a centre for training and research, and the observations carried out in it formed the basis for Lowenfeld's book *Play in Childhood*, published in 1935.[18]

Yet another form of clinic was represented by the Institute for the Scientific Treatment of Delinquency, which was established in 1932 and opened its clinic a few years later. This was inspired by the radical programme for the psychologisation of penality put forward by Grace Pailthorpe, whose controversial report was published by the Home Office in 1932.[19] Pailthorpe had investigated the psychology of criminals, and compared them with inmates of non-penal institutions. Although she was hampered by the lack of adequate means of assessment of character, she claimed to find the presence of mental imbalance – mostly stemming, it appeared, from something wrong in their families – in a large proportion of cases in both types of institution. And she condemned the prison for its lack of reformation, because it did not try to investigate, diagnose or treat the psychological problems which had led to crime. The Institute, which was directed by Edward Glover, sought to apply scientific methods of diagnosis and treatment to delinquents.[20] Associated with it, in one capacity or another, was virtually everyone who had been active in the new psychology, and it applied the whole range of psychotherapies to delinquent individuals referred, in the main, from the Juvenile Courts and the probation officers. Such a psychologisation of crime would have a bright future after the Second World War.[21]

But the type of clinic which began to spread during the inter-war period was not an exclusive site for the treatment of delinquents, nor based on Lowenfeld's quasi-Kleinian model, nor (despite the fact that financial support came from the Common-wealth Fund) on that developed in the United States. It was rather the Tavistock model, grounded in the new psychology. The Child Guidance Council opened its first Demonstration Clinic in Islington in 1928 with Dr William Moodie as its director, and Dr Lucy Fildes as its psychologist. The range of children referred exemplifies the systematisation of the field of childhood pathology which the child guidance movement had established; backward children referred from the schools, delinquents coming from the courts, children referred for nervousness, being unmanageable, lying, stammering and so forth. Although the London County Council declined to finance the Islington Clinic when Common-wealth Fund money ran out in 1933, by that time the principle of local education authority clinics had been established, by the foundation of a clinic at Birmingham.[22] In 1935, when the private funding which had made this possible ran out, the Board of Education approved local education authority funding, thus establishing the principle of State-maintained clinics. It also empowered local education authorities to contribute to voluntary Child Guidance Clinics in respect of services provided for children referred by school medical officers. By 1939 there were 17 clinics wholly maintained and 5 partly maintained by local education authorities, in addition to a number of clinics established by voluntary bodies or hospitals.[23]

The various publications of the Child Guidance Council in the period from 1931 to 1939 enable us to make a kind of synopsis of the way in which the clinic was supposed to function.[24] The clinic would receive children across the whole range of pathologies and from all the institutional sites where such children came to notice. In addition to performing treatment itself, it might distribute the child to one or other of available forms of specialised agency, or provide reports and advice to other agencies of allocation. Agents attached to the clinic or working closely with it – social workers, psychiatric social workers, probation officers, school attendance officers and so forth – could use it as a focus, radiating out from it into the environment and the home, moving between the sites of assessment, treatment and prophylaxis, beginning to sketch out the contours of a psychosocial strategy of regulation. At the level of their organisation, therefore, Child Guidance Clinics made it possible to apply something like a neo-hygienic strategy to questions of mental health, with an extension of inspection to larger categories of individuals at an earlier point in their lives, thus allowing the intervention to represent itself as preventive. This was made possible by the increasing scope provided by links with schools, courts, social work and other specialised agencies, which made it plausible to regard the clinic as the fulcrum of a comprehensive programme of mental welfare.

The clinic was not simply to be a site of diagnosis and treatment, or of the organisation of services – it was to be a place for research and investigation. It would allow the coordination of the knowledge gleaned from work with specific individuals and families in order to produce statistical information on the psychological development, psychiatric disorders and relationships of individuals, knowledge of the links between circumstances, symptoms, treatment and consequences. This would therefore provide the conditions for the construction of *clinical* knowledge of the mental disturbances of childhood. It would allow the construction of classifications and of norms, and hence of diagnosis in terms of deviation from normal behaviours, characteristics, abilities or developments. It would allow the move from the abnormal to the normal, as experience showed the absence of any firm boundaries between normality and pathology. It would make clear the links between minor aberrations and major disturbances both statistically and developmentally, hence allowing one to address within the same framework 'the problem of the normal child'. And the clinic itself, with its programme of training by a kind of apprenticeship, allowed the consolidation of this new knowledge and technique in the act of its transmission.

The clinics, and the knowledge produced in them, provided the basis for a concerted attempt to disseminate the norms for happy families and contented children which the new psychology had made possible. In radio talks and popular texts, as well as advice to teachers and others dealing with children, the same guidance was given – how to promote adjustment and prevent maladjustment, nervousness, night terrors and all the other troubles of childhood by a judicious adjustment of family regime. Thus Emanuel Miller edited a book on *The Growing Child and its Problems*, with contributions from child guidance experts from the Tavistock and elsewhere, designed to bring to the attention of readers 'the sorts of mild disorders which tell us that the child is troubled or maladjusted', to help them understand the nature of the early impulses and fantasies which inform the child's acts, the ways in which unconscious parental attitudes, feelings and the actions they lead to can provoke conflicts and repressions, and the means of bringing these out into the open. The book attempted therefore to 'show how best to meet these difficulties, so that children may enter adult life on a path which has been cleared for them by the benevolent insight of those who guide them.'[25]

The Home and Schools Council was a further important element in promoting the new psychology of child management. The Council, a federation of parent-teacher associations, published a monthly magazine, *Parents and Teachers*, and a series of books under the title *The Home and School Library*. These were guidelines for parents, teachers, nurses and others to use in studying young children and bringing them up. The techniques advised were to promote Confidence, Helpfulness, Dependability and Thoroughness, avoid Fear, Cruelty, Stubbornness and Jealousy. And, as elsewhere, the main contributors were those working in the field of child guidance.[26]

Parents and teachers were now being urged to accept the responsibility of regulating not their habits or morals, but their feelings, wishes and anxieties, if they were not to produce troubled and troublesome children. Two sorts of continuity were now established. The first was from generation to generation. If parents had problems with their own emotional life, if they had repressed conflicts, anxieties and so forth, they would build these unconsciously into their attitudes and relations to their children, and hence provoke and produce those same difficulties in their offspring. And there was also a continuity of the normal and abnormal, for if families did produce normal children this was because they regulated their emotional economy correctly. For the new psychology, normality was conceived as the absence of symptoms and the lack of unconscious conflict.[27] But the line which divided correct and incorrect emotions was a narrow one, and the slight exaggeration of normal feelings and wishes which might come from one's own difficulties was sufficient to disturb the harmony of the child. It was thus all too easy for major problems to develop from minor and normally inconsequential upsets if they were not handled correctly. A constant awareness of one's feelings, a constant willingness to discuss, to recognise, to evaluate the emotional interchanges of family life was what was required in the name of mental hygiene of the individual and society.

And the new psychology of the clinic had yet wider social aspirations. A series of talks on the BBC instructed the nation on *How the Mind Works*, including discussions not only of the problems of child development, by Emanuel Miller and William Moodie, but also of the way in which a knowledge of the mind could help one understand the problems of politics, religion and nationalism.[28]

But if such activities were principally directed towards politicians, intellectuals and well-to-do families, the Child Guidance Clinic offered also a more specific and directed opportunity for psychology. This had as its target the working-class family, whose children so often showed problems at school, and were so likely to become delinquent. In the clinic there was the possibility of the development and promulgation of a new type of practice in which psychology would provide a clinical expertise independent of medicine though linked to it – one in which medicine would occupy a subsidiary and delimited role. A site had emerged where psychology could become an effective social instance, not on its own but in alliance with non-medical agents – social workers – in a new psychosocial strategy.

The psychosocial strategy

It was in the new ensemble of relations established by the Child Guidance Clinic that the old welfare rationale for social work began to be transformed. What was the new psychosocial strategy?

When William Moodie considered the role of the social worker in his discussion of child guidance by teamwork, it was clear that her role was still the familiar one of co-ordinator and relay. The social worker conveyed 'advice and instructions from the psychiatrist which he could not himself afford the time to discuss', discussed practical difficulties with the parents, obtained information on home conditions and 'had the duty of discovering and arranging all necessary social activities, Scouts, clubs and so on'.[29] Yet over the 1930s this role began to transform.[30] Leading ideologues of the Tavistock Clinic, the Mental Health Course, the Central Association for Mental Welfare and similar groupings actively sought to promote a way of conceiving of social work which would legitimate a claim to professional status and an independent role in therapy. The new psychology provided the theoretical code upon which this claim, and this role, would depend.[31] If the problems of the child lay in the wishes, feelings and beliefs of the parents, it was the social worker who was most directly in touch with these. And if this was so, then social workers could be more than conveyors of information, psychiatric aids: they could have a directly therapeutic role.

Social workers attached to Child Guidance Clinics would go into the homes, talk to the parents – or usually the mother – about home conditions, material circumstances and so on, and try to explain the work of the clinic. These workers found that a sort of emotional tie-up was developing with the mother, which initially seemed to be a problem as it was hampering the objectivity of the information gained. Instead of finding out what actually happened, one would find out what the mother wanted the social worker to think had happened, or what she wanted to happen, feared would happen, or thought would happen. But from the perspective of the new psychology, this apparent disadvantage was actually a valuable opportunity. For a link could now be drawn between the child's problems and these beliefs, wishes and fears of the mother. Suddenly describing material circumstances, arranging appointments and so forth seemed by the way. For it was not in circumstances that the problem lay, but in feelings about circumstances. What was going on in the social worker's interview was not the gathering of information but the manifestation of feelings – a sort of transference. These were feelings which the mother herself was not aware of – unconscious beliefs and wishes, feelings of guilt and disappointment and so on – which had their roots in her own emotional relationships with her parents. A new form of family history could now be constructed, where problems could be transmitted across the generations without invoking hereditary mechanisms. And simultaneously a therapeutic familial case-work had been invented, and one which centred upon the mother-child relation. For in the relationship with the social worker these unconscious aspects could be made conscious, the mother could be made aware of her phantasies, desires, conflicts which had been at the root of the disturbances of the child and hence remove herself and the child from their sway. In short, the relationship of the social worker to the mother could become therapeutic.[32]

Early attempts to incorporate these insights into a theory of social work maintained a separation between the register of the familial and the register of the psychical: the environment was made up of all those things outside individuals which impinged upon them in the form of experience, hence facilitating or obstructing the appropriate channelling of the instincts.[33] But for the psychosocial strategy to be able to operate, the environment would have to be re-construed in terms of *other people* – their attitudes, emotions, wishes and fears – and the psyche as an extension of this relational space of the family.

Reading through this literature, one rapidly becomes familiar with the range of family parables without which no article is complete. There is the story of the regressive juvenile to whom infantility and mothering have become too attractive and who therefore is afraid to grow up and of responsibility. There is the tale of the unwanted child, who steals because she feels she is not wanted, not loved or valued for her own sake – because she is illegitimate, or a girl whose parents desired a boy child. There is the case of the child who uses delinquency as a weapon against his parents because they have projected the disappointment and feelings of their own lives on to him or because he is jealous of the loss of his mother's love to a younger sister or brother. The troubles of childhood, that is to say, are the outcome of the many sad ways in which love can go wrong: to be loved too much, not to be loved enough, not to be loved for what you are. To be delinquent or withdrawn, to lie or to bite your nails, to not sleep or to wet your bed was to be the victim of the emotions of your parents. In their desires, their disappointments, their frustrations and fears were to be found the roots of maladjustment.[34]

It is true that British social work of the inter-war period did not produce any sustained theoretical and practical account of this new psychosocial analysis and technique – no English Mary Richmond or Virginia Robinson.[35] The numbers of those trained and practising the new 'psychiatric social work' were small. The Mental Health Course at the London School of Economics, which began in 1929, turned out only 165 people over the next decade, and it was unique.[36] Many of those who taught on the course – for example, Mapother of the Maudsley, and Tredgold –

were no proponents of the new dynamic psychology, and were actively hostile to psychoanalysis.[37] Psychiatric social workers were viewed with suspicion by mainstream welfare workers, operated only in the specialised institutions of mental hospital and clinic, and organised in a separate professional association. Sybil Clement Brown was clearly stating a wish more than a fact when she wrote in 1939 that the 'kind of social worker we have come to describe as "psychiatric" represents, to my mind, a stage of development of social case-work as a whole, rather than a distinct profession.'[38] But her investigations illustrated that such social work was on the increase before the outbreak of war. Of the 80 case records which she studied in her comparison of 1924 and 1934, those of the earlier date were apparently principally concerned with such kinds of behaviour as cleanness, honesty, sobriety and with material conditions. Those from 1934, she claimed, were concerned on the other hand with aspects of personality and with the specific nature of family relations. The change presumably resulted, she commented, 'from the growing conviction that social problems are more dependent upon the attitudes and intimate social relationships of the individual than upon his superficial habits and surroundings'.[39]

Social work was becoming concerned less with recording circumstances and events, and more with interpreting the unconscious wishes which gave those events a meaning for the participants. The terms of analysis were now far from those entailed in the psycho-eugenic conception of character, or the neo-hygienist conception of welfare. What were salient now were not sobriety, diligence and thrift, nor cleanliness, healthy diet and hygiene. They were fears, early experiences, anxieties, attitudes, relationships, conflicts, feelings of persecution, wishes, desires, phantasies and guilt. The way of resolving problems was not segregation or sterilisation, nor moralisation by instruction in virtue and technique. It involved 'becoming aware of the conflicts', 'learning to handle the problem', 'coming to understand oneself', 'sorting out one's real needs'. This was the psychosocial strategy, through which psychological knowledge would provide the rationale for a complex and expanding system of social regulation of personal life in the post-war period. But the psychologists themselves remained in a secondary and subordinate role in the clinic, testing but not diagnosing, supplying information but not directing treatment. Why should this have been?

The temperament of individual psychology

Cyril Burt had seen the Child Guidance Clinic as a site in which psychological expertise would be dominant, co-ordinating and integrating information from the other disciplines, diagnosing and directing treatment.[40] But in England between the wars this was not to be. By 1939, only two of the forty-three English clinics were directed by psychologists; the others were all under medical direction.[41] The opposition between the claims of medicine and those of psychology, which had been set up around feeble-mindedness, was extended to these other behavioural disorders of childhood.[42] From the early 1930s the medico-psychiatric position was in the ascendancy in the clinic. The division of labour was clearly laid out. Psychiatry was the directing science of the clinic. It was a branch of medicine which covered the normal and abnormal mechanisms of the mind, their diagnosis and treatment. Psychology was essentially the study of the operations of intelligence and its measurement by standardised techniques, but included also testing using other devices – psychology was the technique of mental testing.[43]

As Henderson and Gillespie had hoped in 1932, psychiatry had indeed become the expertise competent to manage the behavioural disorders and emotional troubles of childhood. In the medical arguments, explicit and implicit, for such a role one sees the reactivation of those points which had succeeded in relation to the inspection of school-children and the ascertainment of feeble-mindedness. One had before one a troubled child, and the cause of these troubles might be anything from a physical illness, through an organic mental illness, to a 'family neurosis' or troubles at school. One needed information on physical, mental, familial and social conditions supplied by all the various members of the child guidance team. But the diversity of sources and professions made it all the more important that one person was responsible for integrating all this information and taking a decision in relation to it, and only a medically trained agent was competent to assess the weight of all the different factors involved, to make a differential diagnosis, and to decide on treatment in that light.[44]

Indeed psychiatric medicine seemed to have assimilated the lessons of the new psychology. The first section of the 1939 *Survey of Child Psychiatry* discussed the influence of physical diseases upon maladjustments of behaviour, Winnicott contributing a paper suggesting that the potential depressive was often mistaken for a rheumatic and proposing a sort of psychoanalysis of pain.[45] The second section discussed problems relating to mental illness, ranging from psychoses (organic and untreatable, according to Gillespie) to 'the family neurosis'. Bowlby's paper on hysteria stressed the need to look for physical causes such as smouldering appendicitis, as well as the child's personality and the emotional atmosphere in the home – quarrelling parents, fussy mothers, mothers playing on their children's affections and trying to buy their children's love. And William Patterson Brown described, in familiar terms how 'Neurosis is a family problem . . . the seeds of neurosis are sown in childhood in a neurotic family setting.' The articles on family, school and social maladjustment, and juvenile delinquency were also contributed by doctors, and construed the problems in similar terms.

Physical factors and diseases had to be considered, diet taken into account, there were differences in the mental apparatus of the child itself, these differences were affected by the way in which the parents managed the rituals of waking, sleeping, feeding, bathing, urinating and defaecating, and by the play of their own fears, anxieties and hostilities across the psyche of the child. If all these failures of adjustment were caused through such a complex interaction between social, familial, mental and physical conditions, and if each case was the consequence of a unique concatenation of such factors, medicine was surely the only instance capable of differential diagnosis, for it was the only one which possessed a clinical expertise. Psychology had a role which was specific, delimited and subordinate: to supply information on the mental equipment of the child derived from the administration of mental tests.

The notion of psychology as the science and technique of mental measurement was certainly not anathema to the individual psychologists. Indeed, despite the occasional urging, by those who had abandoned the new psychology in favour of psychoanalysis proper, that psychologists in the clinic should free themselves from the limitations of testing, psychology accepted this role as if it was its destiny.[46] It had been formed as an effective discursive practice in the image of the test; measurement was the horizon of its thought and it could not think outside it. This is not to say that psychology wished to limit itself to the assessment of intelligence. The existence of the clinical site, and its rationale, provided the impetus and the possibility for the extension of assessment along two interconnecting lines: the notion of development as a principle of organisation for psychological thought; and the notion of temperament as a new object for psychological quantification.

The clinic and the nursery school made a psychology of development possible. Of course the mind and behaviour of the growing child had been an object of psychological discussion prior to the 1920s. The new psychologists of development ritually acknowledged the pioneering detailed studies of the development of individual infants and children undertaken by Darwin, Preyer, Shinn, Sully, Claparede and Stern, as well as the observations collated under the impetus of the child study movement.[47] But the problem with such investigations was their idiosyncrasy, their anecdotal quality, their lack of systematic observation, the absence of consideration of the effects of surroundings, their variable methods, their lack of comparability – in short, their lack of scientific rigour. However suggestive their reflections and observations on the ways in which the abilities of children changed over time, they did not themselves found a psychology of childhood.

But what the clinic and the nursery school made possible, it was argued, was precisely such a psychology. For they allowed the observation and collection of data covering numbers of children of the same ages, by skilled psychological experts, under controlled, experimental, almost laboratory conditions. They thus simultaneously allowed for standardisation and for normalisation – the collection of comparable information on a large number of subjects and its analysis in such a way as to construct norms. A developmental norm was a standard based upon the average abilities or performance of children of a certain age on a particular task or in a particular activity. It thus not only presented a picture of what was *normal* for children of such an age, but enabled the normality of any individual child to be assessed by comparison with this norm. In the movement that was characteristic of the psychology of the individual, the individual subject in its uniqueness and variability could become the object of scientific investigation when it was viewed from the perspective of the population of which it was deemed a part.

The psychological conception of childhood was essentially developmental. The gathering of data on children of particular ages over a certain span, and the organisation of this data into age norms, enabled the norms to be arranged along an axis of time, and seen as cross-sections through a continuous dimension of development. Growth and temporality could become principles of organisation of a psychology of childhood. And normalisation and development enabled individuals to be characterised in relation to such norms in terms of this axis of time – as 'normal', 'advanced' or 'retarded'.

Whilst the construction of the test of intelligence had made this possible in the restricted sphere of the intellect, it was now feasible to utilise a fundamentally similar approach in a much wider domain.[48] The first steps were taken in the USA. The work of Arnold Gesell and his collaborators is testament to the potency of this new mode of conceptualisation for the generation and organisation of vast quantities of psychological data on childhood into a coherent conceptual schema. This work was initiated at the Yale Psycho-Clinic which had opened in 1911 for the observation and treatment of children having problems at school. The Clinic was used as the basis for the selection of a sample of children of certain ages, who were visited and assessed at home, as well as for the detailed observation of children, involving the invention of various technical devices to keep the observers hidden from those whom they studied. Behavioural items characteristic and distinctive of the various age levels were defined, and organised into four scales – motor, language, adaptive and personal-social – with a specification of the ages at which a given proportion of children could achieve various levels on each scale. Gesell's work thus brought non-intellectual behaviour within the sphere of psychological evaluation: norms of posture and locomotion, of vocabulary, comprehension and conversation, of personal habits, initiative, independence and play could now be deployed in evaluation and diagnosis.[49]

In the following years, others attempted to utilise the same tactics.[50] Katherine Banham Bridges adapted the method of Gesell for the nursery school, which, she asserted, served as a laboratory for the study of children's development. But whilst Gesell's scales merely sought to normalise different sorts of behaviour which children manifested, Bridges organised social and emotional behaviour in the familiar terms of adjustment: the development of socially accepted responses to social situations. The criterion of social approval and the conception of adjustment enabled the developmental normalisation of the scale to comply with the requirements of a socially normalising practice of evaluation and intervention.[51]

The Bridges scale did not meet an enthusiastic reception in England. Susan Isaacs commented on Bridges' work acerbically that 'the rate of change in children towards behaviour which is considered desirable is not more significant psychologically than the actual behaviour which they do show at any given stage.'[52] Even Isaacs, however, could not fail to recognise the value of the scale in introducing normativity into development:[53]

> It will not only provide norms for individual development, with far reaching effects on educational standards and techniques. It will also suggest significant inter-relations of psychological processes, by showing which aspects of development tend to hang together, and outlining the changing picture of their inter-relations at succeeding ages (in the way intelligence tests have done for certain aspects of intellectual development).

But, whilst Isaacs gradually introduced discussion of Gesell's norms of development into her advice to parents, she argued that the scales produced by Bridges oversimplified and homogenised psychologically distinct aspects of behaviour, implied a single and unbroken axis of development towards adjustment, and were founded on the belief that behaviour could be measured outside the specific concrete situations in which it occurred and which gave external events their inner meaning and significance in the psychic life of the child.

In fact Gesell himself had argued in a somewhat similar way about the use of his scales. Whilst stressing the value of the scales in encouraging the cultivation of the normative and comparative thinking necessary for clinical work, much of his text of 1925 was a polemic against psychometrics, for substituting the mechanical application of a partial measure for the complex process of interpretive diagnosis which a clinical psychology required. But nonetheless it was the psychometric objections which formed the other, and probably more influential, prong of English opposition to the scales. A scale is not, after all, a test. Bridges reckoned that one month of daily observation was required to complete the schedule for her scales. And the scale was linked only in a tenuous and *ex post facto* way to a theory of what it was supposed to be measuring in terms of the inherited or acquired mental capacities of the child. When English psychology approached the new problem with which it had been presented by the clinic, this was the issue that concerned it – the development of techniques for measuring the non-intellectual mental capacities which were manifested in the behavioural disturbances of childhood and the delinquencies of youth. The problem was one of devising a test of the manifestation of instincts and energy in dispositions, sentiment and character – of constructing a test of temperament.

In the late 1920s and early 1930s, the psychology of the individual sought to constitute a new object – the temperament. Though initially somewhat hesitantly designated (character, temperament and personality were given different significance in the different texts) this referred to that which the old faculty psychology had designated 'will' – the domain of strivings, of drives and instincts, of purposive behaviour. Of course there was a venerable philosophical and psychological literature on the issue of the will, its nature and development. But the problem for the psychology of the individual was a new one. It was one of measuring the nature and force of 'will', characterising its direction and its strengths and weaknesses, assessing that of one person in relation to another, or to the population at large. Individual psychology could conceptualise this domain only insofar as it was measurable, differentiable, insofar as one could submit it to the techniques which had been so successful in the annexation of intelligence to psychology. But temperament proved less tractable to psychologisation, and in this fact was grounded the interruption of the development of clinical psychology.

In fact the United States of America was the place where the psychology of the will really got off the ground. There was a proliferation of 'dynamic' theoretical systems, of synthetic texts of one sort or another, and of techniques of assessment. Authors vied with one another to promote catalogues of personality types, character dimensions and temperamental traits. When Raymond Cattell, who like McDougall went to work in America, published his attempt to establish the primary traits of personality in 1946, Lewis Terman estimated in his introduction that the past twenty-five years had seen over one thousand publications in the field of personality, including over one hundred on a single test.[54]

Compared to this massive American psychological colonisation of the domain of the personality, the developments in England might appear somewhat meagre. It is true that no major schools vied with one another, no lasting theoretical syntheses were published. What occurred was more modest, more practical and, in the end, more constraining. For it was organised around the search for a means of assessment which would solve the problems faced by all those who were interested in character and temperament because they had to take decisions in the light of it – in the work of vocational guidance, in decisions as to the treatment of juvenile delinquents and in the Child Guidance Clinics. From about 1925 onwards, regular papers began to appear in the pages of the *British Journal of Psychology* on the development and evaluation of tests of temperament. Authors agreed that the existing state of techniques for the assessment of temperament was something like that which had characterised the evaluation of intelligence at the beginning of the twentieth century – none of the available devices was reliable or exact enough to be of much practical service in the diagnostic activities of the clinic or elsewhere. But whilst Cattell minimised the problems in his practical compendium and handbook for psychologists, the domain of temperament, emotions and will proved strangely resistant to psychological normalisation.[55]

In *The Young Delinquent*, Burt proposed a version of the word association test based on some early work by Galton and a method developed by Jung.[56] Jung used word associations in a large-scale testing programme to investigate the existence of unconscious complexes. He observed the appearance of delay in response to certain words, coupled with various 'indicators' of the existence of a 'repressed complex' – blushing, coughing, sighing, stammering and so forth – and not only suggested that such techniques could be used as a starting point in analysis, but also that one could use them in personality typing. Burt put this test to a more prosaic use, interspersing items such as 'money', 'anger' and so on in the list of words, measuring reaction times, and comparing results from delinquents with those from a thousand 'normals'. But, whilst useful 'to lay bare the man's deeper emotional interests, but also to unveil a guilty consciousness of some specific crime', this hardly provided the standardised and normalised assessment technique which individual psychology desired.[57] Attempts to use variations in psycho-galvanic reactions in a similar context proved no more successful. The use of this and other devices – such as those for measuring reaction time – for this new purpose had a number of major drawbacks: one didn't

know what one was measuring and such investigative devices did
not admit of ranking, scaling and the comparison of individual
scores with population measures in order to effect a diagnosis.[58]

Other methods were tried for detecting and measuring
'complexes' – such as the Pressey Cross Out Test and the
Rorschach Test – but, despite valiant attempts, they proved
similarly unhelpful for standardisation and normalisation.[59]
Collins felt that the Will-Temperament Test – which analysed
handwriting produced in various test situations to produce a 'will-
profile' of the individual – 'differentiates the strong character from
the weak, the careful from the careless, the quick from the slow'
and was certainly tapping innate qualities. But others pointed to
the low reliability of the test and its lack of correlation with any
independent estimate of personality at all.[60]

Some were attracted by 'moral tests' like the Kohs Ethical
Discrimination Test which attempted to measure moral judgment
by noting how often the child singled out moral reasons for
actions in preference to others. For example in the sub-test on
Offence Evaluation, the subject had to evaluate different actions
by saying whether they deserved a response of praise, nothing,
scold, jail, prison or kill. The test, which, of course, provided the
right answers, allowed for the calculation of a moral age and a
'moral IQ', but was considered problematic because it involved
intelligence as well as character, and one couldn't really assume
that what a subject said in the clinic about questions like these
was a good indicator of what he or she would do on the street.[61]

The line of enquiry which would eventually claim success
utilised complex statistical techniques to resolve the problem to
which theoretical enquiry and practical investigation appeared to
have no solution. Webb, as early as 1915, had carried out a
factor-analytic study of ratings of students and schoolboys on
various qualities of character and concluded that there was a
general factor, which he called *w* (for will) involved in all the
moral qualities and deeper social values. In the 1920s and 1930s a
number of investigators tried to refine this and provide it with a
theoretical basis, usually by linking it to a McDougall-Shand
notion of instincts and emotions, and by analysing covariance
between ratings on character traits derived from their inventories.
Burt, Cattell, Oates and others sought to establish the existence of
a single general, and possibly innate, factor, harking back to
Burt's earlier notion of a 'general emotionality' (Cattell promoted

the term 'surgency') which underpinned all those oppositions like extravert/introvert, cyclothyme/schizothyme and so forth, coupled with a number of smaller and more specific group factors. There was a sort of common fund of energy powering all the instincts, together with more specific and non-interchangeable funds attached to specific instincts – the particular combinations accounting for the temperament. But all this complexity did not lend itself to simple measurement, and hence the technique appeared to fail to satisfy the demands which had sparked off the search. A further impetus would be required before the various multi-factorial personality assessment devices would be produced in a form amenable to diagnostic use.[62]

So, despite all this labour, all that the English psychology of the individual had to offer to the clinical requirement for the assessment of character and temperament was precisely what it had sought to replace – observation of behaviour and the personal interview. It did, of course, try to put a respectable gloss on this residual position. The most ingenious idea was to offer the intelligence test itself as the solution to the problem which it had at first appeared to ignore. It now, apparently, could allow for the assessment of temperament too, by providing a standard situation in which behaviour could be observed and compared as between subjects. One could look for disparity, for example, between scores on verbal and non-verbal items in order to identify the presence of a 'verbal neurosis'. Or one could simply observe behaviour while the subject was undertaking the test, looking for such things as perseverance in the face of difficulty.[63]

Burt himself preferred a psychologisation of the interview. He prepared a classified list of temperamental and moral qualities and, during the course of such an interview, rated the disturbed or delinquent child on each quality, using a five-point scale – holding in his mind, as he assured his readers, the standard deviation as the unit of classification. But other psychologists, of a critical inclination, cast doubt upon the validity of even these techniques.[64] In the end, it appeared, all the psychology of the individual had to offer in relation to the novel domain of character, temperament and personality which had been offered up to it by the new problems of maladjustment and delinquency was a version of procedures long utilised by medicine – and one not enriched but reduced and etiolated by the attempt to assimilate it to the impoverished conceptual structure of psychometrics.

At the very beginning of *The Young Delinquent*, Cyril Burt had confidently asserted that 'what the method of mental testing does for the study of intellectual capacity, that the method of psychoanalysis performs for the study of the growing character.'[65] But what he had in mind was the use of psychoanalysis as some sort of diagnostic tool which would enable the construction of population norms of character, personality and temperament and the assessment and diagnosis of individuals insofar as they could be located by the degree of their deviation from such norms. However, orthodox psychoanalysis was a 'science of the individual' in a very different sense. Not only did it problematise the links between conformity to social norms and the absence of physical disturbances, it also eschewed the possibility of specifying general norms for evaluating psychic 'health' at all. The new psychology *could* form the basis for a normalising social practice by establishing precisely this link between conformity to the requirements of social and moral standards, personal happiness, and psychological health defined in terms of the absence of troublesome symptoms. But its diagnostic judgments were made within a clinical practice in which 'normality' was a standard which did not need to be assessed or bolstered through comparison with the variations of particular qualities in the population as a whole. The whole project of individual psychology, however, depended upon such a congruity between norms of healthy mental functioning, norms of social demand and expectation, and statistical norms of the distribution of variations in a population. The psychology of the individual founded itself in the belief that the normalising intentions and evaluations of social regulation could find their objective grounding in the laws of large numbers and a congruence between statistical and social conceptions of populations and their variations. Its limits were marked out by the type of explanation in which 'to diagnose' was construed as 'to measure'.

In his famous paper on *The Problem of Lay Analysis*, published in English in 1928, Freud looked forward to the prospect of analytically trained 'social workers' combating the neuroses of civilisation, and of analytic educationalists treating the inconspicuous neuroses of children as a method of prophylaxis.[66] If something of this has come to pass, the conditions for it were established in England in the period between the two World Wars in the events which we have been discussing. The consequences of these developments for the rationale of government and for the regulation of social and personal existence have been revolutionary. But it was not simply the professional dominance of medicine, nor the success of its tactical manoeuvres, however important these might have been, that precluded the psychology of the individual from occupying the role of secular healer of souls which Freud had proposed. One major condition for the failure of the psychology of the individual to achieve a clinical status was the mode of conceptualisation of normality and abnormality upon which it was founded.

Conclusion

The events which we have been tracing are not the *origin* of the modern scientific enterprise of psychology. The intellectual projects and social vocation of the various branches of contemporary psychology cannot be *derived* from this analysis of the formation of the psychology of the individual. But this does not imply that the investigation which we have undertaken has nothing to offer *vis-à-vis* the present state of psychology.

The history of psychological modernity

> From colour theories to defence mechanisms, from the functions of a white rat's vibrissae to the mystic's sense of unutterable revelation, from imaginary playmates to partial correlations, wherein lies that unity . . . which leads us to speak . . . of 'contemporary psychology'?. . . In a sense it is true to say that through all this vast melange the very birth cry of the infant science is still resounding. In another sense psychology is as old as civilization, and this seething multitude of investigations and opinions springs from a rich and variegated history. . . . Whatever difficulties there may be in finding unity in the various psychological disciplines, there is at least one unity to which we can cling for orientation and perspective, for appreciation and synthesis; and this is the tranquil unity of history.
>
> Murphy and Kovach, 1972[1]

Many have been troubled by the lack of unity which is presented by contemporary psychology. It is fractured into specialisms which often exist in isolation from one another, addressing distinct problems and issues, and which have no common language or explanatory schema. There are psychologies of motivation, perception, cognition, learning, development, personality, social interaction and so forth, studying not only humans but also animals ranging from the higher apes to the lowly laboratory rat. And within each specialism, psychology appears to lack the coherence of the sciences it takes as its models. It is divided into rival and competing schools – functionalism, behaviourism, gestalt psychology, psychoanalysis, physiological psychology. One might almost regard each as having a distinct paradigm, each conceiving of its objects and problems differently, utilising different explanatory schemes and conducting different types of research.[2]

And overarching this division is another, between 'pure' and 'applied' psychology. For the qualified psychologist is more often a professional outside the university than an academic within it, and outside the university, the philosophical, biological and epistemological doubts which perplex the academy are answered peremptorily or swept aside. In the educational system, the factory, the prison, the army and the hospital, the psychologist is presented with two classes of subject. There are those who, for one reason or another, have failed to adapt themselves to institutional existence. And there are those who seek to know to which sector of institutional life they are best adapted – or for whom others desire this information: which school, which job, which role in the armed forces, which type of penal regime. In either case the response of the psychologist is more or less the same: the selection of one or more psychological tests from the growing armoury of such devices; the application of the procedures to the subject in question under specified – if inherently unprogrammable – conditions; the calculation of a score utilising the scoring systems and scales which the devisers or marketers of the test have standardised on target populations – of course, under the aegis of the ubiquitous and all powerful normal distribution curve.

But despite appearances, many have sought to establish that the discipline of psychology is, could or should be unified. Perhaps the most ingenuous are those histories of psychology which wish at one and the same time to establish the scientific credentials of psychology by reference to its ancient tradition and excuse its scientific incoherence on the grounds of its youth. The remark of Hermann Ebbinghaus is popular: 'Psychology has a long past but only a short history.'[3] Such histories tell a tale which might appear convincing, if only because of the frequency with which it is repeated.[4] Man and his mental life have always, it would appear, been objects of fascination for the enquiries of philosophers, intellectuals and savants, and yet for many hundreds of years their deliberations contained little that might count as scientific knowledge. In this 'long past' of psychology the proper object of a psychological science suffered a repeated reduction – either through a philosophical appropriation of the psyche into the closed circles of metaphysics, or through an organicist reduction of the psyche to the biological processes of the body. Either mind was divorced from the body – the latter, at least by the eighteenth century, a possible object for scientific study, the former too noble for such an enquiry, the privileged arena of religion and metaphysics. Or else mind was reduced to body, to no more than the mechanical interplay of sensations and associations. In either case the investigation of the mind could not be scientific; it proceeded only by deriving the necessary principles of human mental activity from a series of speculative premises.

Then, in the middle of the nineteenth century, things began to change. The fundamental shift was the move to an experimental methodology. It is this which marks the birth of psychology as a science after its lengthy gestation. From this moment of parturition one sees the infant science undergoing a slow process of development and maturation: the successive advances in theory and methodology, the accumulative tradition of experimentation and observation, the elaboration of testable hypotheses and synthesising laws, the cumulative record of crucial experiments, innovatory conceptions, proofs and disproofs. And as psychology begins to be sure of its facts and theories, it becomes able to play its part in the wider society, in a range of applications which assist in those situations where individual abilities or psychological capacities are involved. Not that psychology yet has the unity which can be found in the 'model' sciences of physics and chemistry – this distinction between psychology and its methodological mentors is noted repeatedly. But if psychology is still a heterogeneous discipline, with diverse and competing theories often displacing one another without regard to the proper processes of comparative evaluation, or even subsisting side by side without entering into proper dispute, if there is so little agreement on the investigative procedures proper to psychology and even polemic and controversy concerning the very terms with which the discipline should be defined, nonetheless this is a diversity in unity, characteristic of the youth of any science, healthy and proper to the emergence on to the field of knowledge of a new science of man.

For such histories, the unity of psychology, of its history and its prehistory, is a unity of its object. One can only be seeing, in these discourses of the past, halting attempts to gain access to that which contemporary psychology is now beginning to understand. Such a psychological historiography thus necessarily adopts an empiricist methodology, for it is based upon the premise that it is a given real object which psychology has sought for so long to discover and which it has found at last. This is why so much emphasis is placed upon the role of methodology in establishing the scientificity of psychology. Psychology constituted itself as a science when scientists freed themselves from the distortions and prohibitions imposed by religion, metaphysics and a speculative tradition, and began to engage with the object itself through painstaking observation and experimentation and through subjecting theories and hypotheses to empirical verification. But to make such a claim is to erase the many and varied ways in which the objects of these psychological investigations have been construed, and the social, theoretical and philosophical problems which gave rise to them. The objects of scientific discourses are historical and not ontological; history itself cannot provide any tranquil and unifying antidote to the fractious condition of contemporary psychology.

One might be forgiven for wondering just what the motivation was for a labour of writing which repeats the same tale endlessly, which is so meticulous and yet so impoverished in the insights which it provides into the processes involved in the formation of this new domain of scientific explanation. We should not simply see, in this way of writing the history of psychology, a mistake of methodology, continually repeated due to a lack of analytic awareness or philosophical correctness. These accounts are better understood somewhat differently. They do not occupy a field external to that of the psychological discourse with which they are contemporary. On the contrary, they gain their rationality from the way in which they function internally to psychology itself.

Historiographic discourse in psychology serves to demarcate the field of psychology's modernity and to produce a redistribution of elements within the corpus of past texts. This redistribution effects a distinction between the sanctioned and the lapsed, between those elements which are consonant with the contemporary regime of scientific truth (and may therefore be included within the canon of texts and arguments which have formed the precursors of modernity) and those elements which are discrepant with this regime (which must be expelled to a lapsed history of errors, illusions, false paths and byways, diversions from the forward march of knowledge).[5]

In this sense the texts of psychological historiography are *programmatic*: the object of which they speak – scientific psychology – is both an existence to be ratified and a reality to be produced. Many discourses establish their claim to truth in part through such a construction of a sanctioned history. At one and the same time the discourse is legitimised through the construction of lines of ancestry and descent and its novelty is demonstrated with respect to this filiation. Within scientific discourses themselves this operation has a certain justification. It is, no doubt, vital to distinguish between those concepts, experiments, speculations, bodies of evidence which remain contemporary and those which are obsolete. The former must be taken into account in the formulation of new data, the construction of new arguments and proofs and so forth; the latter are impertinent to the current concerns of scientific activity. History is thus an internally functioning element in the organisation of scientific truth.[6] Scientific discourses are governed by definite norms of truth, and modes of formulations and recognition of true propositions, and this entails a certain conception of the history of these norms and a constant and recurrent evaluation of the transformations which have produced it.

Yet if a standard of truth and falsity functions as a necessary internal element in the recurrent histories which sanction contemporary science, we must nonetheless recognise its consequences for scientific historiography itself. Histories of this type have a horizon which is necessarily that of the contemporary. They are thus unable to grasp the norms according to which the contemporary operates to construct truth, precisely because these norms constitute the very ground and the limit of the historical enterprise. If present norms of truth are deployed as the unquestioned means of evaluation of past norms of truth, such histories must remain unable to think the historicity of truth within the history of psychology. They are condemned to provide a philosophico-historical reprise on the operation of those discourses which are their object. Their histories are teleologies which serve to grant an imprimatur to the psychology of the present.

In posing the question 'what is psychology?', Canguilhem attempts a brief sketch of psychology's past whose rationale is somewhat different.[7] Its objective is not to legitimate the contemporary psychological enterprise, but to cast light upon its problematic character. He suggests that the stresses within present psychology have their foundation in the very different, and contradictory, projects which the discipline welds together. The most ancient of these, in the philosophical systems of classical antiquity, regarded the soul as a natural being, and the physics of the soul shares something with modern psychological neuro-physiology and with psychopathology as a medical discipline: the investigation of the soul as an organ no different in principle from those of respiration or digestion. In the seventeenth century he identifies the birth of psychology as a science of subjectivity centring upon the senses: the external senses and their relation to internal perception; the internal senses and the problem of consciousness; the intimate sense and the issues of wishing and willing. However, he argues that in the nineteenth century, when psychology set itself the project of constituting an objective science of reactions and behaviour, it simultaneously engaged in a fundamental misrecognition of the nature of its object and opened itself up to a role as a social technique. In seeking objective laws of adaptation, Canguilhem argues, psychology denies the incidence of history and society upon the 'adaptiveness' of behaviour, reduces its concept of man to that of a tool, and makes of psychologists the instruments of an instrumentalism which is concerned only with the problems of setting people into place and setting them to work.

Perhaps this provocative, if provisional, assessment enables us to characterise the role played in the constitution of psychological modernity by the events we have been following. The issue of adaptation – of establishing the laws and charting the variations of the relations between individual conducts and social expecta-tions – was central to the project of individual psychology. And the psychology of social adaptation played a matrix role in the formation of the new scientific discipline. Through it, conditions were established within which a scientific discourse and practice of psychology could begin to coalesce: institutional sites; professional agencies; authorised texts; systems for the organisation and dissemination of research and discussion; ways of formulating arguments; relations between psychologists and their subjects; styles of psychological experimentation and adjudication; objects and domains appropriate for psychological judgment. It is true that the formation of the psychology of the individual – with its particular objects of concern, conceptions of norms and normality, techniques of measurement and social aspirations – cannot be regarded as the origin of scientific psychology. But in providing a basis from which psychology could constitute itself as an effective social reality, it allowed these other ways of thinking about, investigating and experimenting upon the soul partially to separate themselves from the disciplines of philosophy, logic, ethics, metaphysics, medicine and biology, and annex themselves to the new discipline of psychology. The fragmentation of contemporary psychology does indeed bear witness to the processes involved in the birth of this new scientific discipline. Contemporary psychology is a chimera: in the stresses which constantly traverse it we can see the signs of the diverse provenance of its constituent parts.

Norms of life, number, and administration

> It is life itself, and not medical judgment, which makes the biological normal a concept of value and not a concept of statistical reality.
>
> Georges Canguilhem, [1943] 1978[8]

One thing at least is certain. Psychology's role as an administrative technology cannot be understood as the application of a psychological knowledge of normality, gained through theoretical reflection or laboratory investigation, to a domain of practical problems. On the contrary, it was through attempts to diagnose, conceptualise and regulate pathologies of conduct that psychological knowledge and expertise first began to establish its claims for scientific credibility, professional status and social importance.

Perhaps it is true that the only lasting contribution to psychological modernity which was made by the psychology of the individual in England over this period was the standardised test of intelligence. And it is also true that individual psychologists were certainly not a socially powerful instance, and their strategies met with rather limited success before the Second World War. But however short-lived the specific doctrines and proposals were, and however tenuous was the toehold that the psychology of the individual gained as a professional instance within the field of social regulation, the importance of these events should not be underestimated. For what they made possible was a scientific technique for the administration of individuals and populations in terms of their mental attributes and capacities.

Such an administrative technique depended upon a particular conception of normality and pathology, and a particular conception of norms. The psychology of the individual grounded itself in the belief that there was a symmetry between three registers of norms – norms of socially desirable conduct, norms of the distribution of psychological characteristics and attributes in the population, and statistical conceptions of the normal distribution of variation in large groups. This mode of conceptualisation was central both to its theory of its object – intelligence, temperament – and to its techniques of assessment and claims to diagnostic ability. How are we to understand the role of norms in clinical judgments, and the peculiar characteristics of the norms of individual psychology?

Georges Canguilhem's doctoral thesis of 1943 consists of an illuminating discussion of the relations between the concept of norm and the sciences of life.[9] Oversimply, one could say that biology and medicine owe their modernity to the way in which they construe the specificity of their object – life. For such discourses a knowledge of life becomes possible through conceiving of life as itself a normative process. Life, in that it consists of processes which are homeostatic and self-regulating, has an inherent normativity. Thus medical and biological discourses could organise their evidence and their concepts and explanations in terms of this essential normativity of their object and its consequences for the analysis of specific phenomena. Two consequences are significant here.

Firstly, normality, and the processes of regulation which tend to return the organism to it, has a very particular status. Normality is equivalent to health; it is the state to which the organism tends by virtue of its organisation; it is its state whilst untroubled. Thus health, for the living organism, is normality and normativity; health cannot be merely a numerical value. Canguilhem is fond of quoting Leriche: health is life in the silence of the organs.

Secondly, disease is an essential problem for the science of life; one that, however conceived, must be understood in relation to the normativity of life itself. In relation to this normativity, and the health which is associated with it, disease is a negative value. It is dis-ease, a certain perversion of normal functioning, a disquiet of the bodily processes. But in relation to *knowledge* of life, disease acquires a positive value, in that the existence of the biological normal is revealed through its infraction. The normativity of the life processes makes itself evident when these are disturbed and seek to re-establish themselves. It is thus to the possibility of disease that we owe the possibility of a scientific awareness of life.

Now it is no doubt true that to derive the normativity of medical discourse and practice from the ontological normativity of its object is to take an epistemological shortcut. It is also to think *internally* to contemporary medical and biological knowledge. It is, of course, necessary to consider the theoretical and social conditions which made it possible to think in normative terms about health and disease, and to be able to examine the historical and cultural variability of such norms, which cannot merely be ascribed to their object. Nonetheless, Canguilhem's argument enables us to distinguish between knowledges which base their *conception* of norms upon the normativity of their object, and those which derive their norms in other ways.

One important condition for the emergence of clinical medicine was undoubtedly the statisticalisation of disease – aetiology, symptomatology, prognosis – that was made possible by the hospital. But even so, one would wish to insist that a medical norm is not merely a statistical value. Medicine does not derive its concepts of its object from a calculation of average levels of functioning. Even those attributes of medical normality – signs of health or indicators of disease – most amenable to quantification have the peculiar character of a double normativity. The normal population values for such diagnostic indicators as pulse rate, temperature, blood pressure and so forth are always linked to a conception of the normal operation of the homeostatic mechanisms of the body itself. Statisticalisation, for clinical medicine, was a condition of discovery of the normativity of life, it was not its foundation.

The rules of formation of the psychology of the individual differ on almost every count. Individual psychology *derives* its conception of its object from the statistical normativity of the population. The norms which it proposes are not those of life but those of large numbers. The possibility of a knowledge of the individual, for the psychology of the individual, is not provided through a conception of the psyche, its processes, its homeostatic mechanisms, the laws of its development and the abnormalities to which they can give rise. It is founded upon a metaphysic of the quantification of qualities and the laws of variation in populations. A knowledge of the individual is possible not on account of the specificity of the psyche and its variability, but precisely because it is conceived of as non-specific. Once this variability can be numerically specified, it differs not at all from the variability of any other quality in large groups. And indeed, on this premise are based the objects, means and techniques of quantification themselves, for those measures of qualities which do not accord with the statistical norms for variability in general can have the status only of errors to be discarded. It is more than merely metaphor which is involved in the assumption of equivalence between populations of numbers and populations of persons. It is the constitutive doctrine of the psychology of the individual.

But individual psychology requires a second level of equivalence of norms. It was founded through the identification of norm in the register of the statistical with norm in the register of the social. The operation which made individual psychology possible was the identification of statistical norms of variation with social norms of expectation. The abnormality which was so crucial in the founding of a medical notion of bodily norms was a disturbance in its object, the body itself. But the abnormality around which individual psychology was organised was not an abnormality of a life process, or one specifiable in terms of ease and dis-ease. It was an abnormality in terms of a norm of functioning specified by particular social apparatuses. The unease which enabled the normativity of individual psychology to be established was constituted by the objectives of government rather than the vicissitudes of the psyche. It was the school, the courts, the police and the army which provided the psychology of the individual with those *whom it would have to be able to construe as abnormal.*

It is true that at its inception the project of measuring intelligence, in both England and France, was linked to a theory of the intellect, and that the techniques devised were thus articulated upon such a theory. Anthropometrics did indeed seek to derive a means of differentiation of individuals from its theory of bodily and mental energy. But the psychology of the individual only began to establish itself as a functioning discourse when it abandoned the purity of anthropometric measures and dirtied its hands with the requirements of educational administration. The statistical techniques developed within anthropometrics were no longer utilised to elucidate and investigate the fundamental laws of mental life. They were now applied directly in an assessment of the degree of conformity between conduct and social expectations. Psychology thus no longer sought to ground the norms of the intellect upon a theory of cognitive functioning. Still less were these norms founded in the normativity of the laws of the vital processes of the psyche itself. The normativity of the object of individual psychology was constructed by a process of extrapolation from norms of a completely different order. Individual psychology got off the ground when it combined norms derived from particular conceptions of population and its regulation with norms derived from a particular conception of numbers and their variation.

The theoretical object which is constituted by the psychology of the individual thus has to conform to a double requirement. Firstly that the variability to which it is subject conforms with the distribution which is *already* known – the judgment of school, court or whatever. Hence, as far as devices of assessment are concerned, items enter or leave the tests on the grounds of their ability to differentiate according to the norms prescribed by the social institution in question. Secondly that the distribution across the population conforms to the demands of statistical theory and the normal distribution curve. The existence of the psychology of the individual depended upon it being able to align norms from the two registers; the whole project of development and standardisation of tests seeks to carry out this task, and does so, paradoxically, in the name of scientific rigour.

Medicine can function as a clinical practice on account of the organic relations which it establishes between its conceptions of normality and pathology. This enables it to operate as both a diagnostic and a therapeutic instance. Individual psychology, equipped with a technique but not a theory, a project but not a concept, and a notion of deviation without an account of normality, was condemned to repeat neurotically the operation which had founded it. This is so, not only in the test of intelligence, but in all those other techniques of assessment which have succeeded it since the Second World War. Hence its destiny was to become not a *clinical* but an *administrative* practice.

From its inception up until today, individual psychology, differential psychology, psychometrics, sought to extrapolate a theory of psychological functioning from a means of differentiation. No wonder the meeting between psychometrics and a theory of cognition has been repeatedly postponed. To derive a theory of normality from a conception of the normativity of a life process and the incidence of pathology is one thing. To derive a theory of normality from the normativity of a statistical average and the incidence of variations from it is another. This problem is exacerbated if it takes place within a practice, and by means of a technique, which depends upon discarding that which individuals share and attending only to that which differentiates them. And the problem is exacerbated further when what counts as abnormality is set by a norm of adaptation to the conventions of a socio-economic order. Health, for the psychology of the individual, is not so much life in the silence of the organs as life in the silence of the authorities.

Notes

Introduction

1 Renan [1890] 1923, quoted in Canguilhem, 1978, pp. 14-15.
2 Hearnshaw, 1964, is the best general account of the history of English psychology.
3 Ibid., p. 211.
4 This psychology also termed itself 'individual psychology', and the present study also uses this term. However it should be pointed out that the phrase 'individual psychology' was appropriated in the 1920s and 1930s by Alfred Adler and his followers to designate his particular doctrines. Except where specified, the present study does not use the term in that sense.
5 For detailed consideration of the methodological bases of this study, see the PhD thesis upon which this book is based, especially Chs 1 and 2. The approach is broadly derived from the 'archaeological' studies of the formation and functioning of the human sciences developed by Michel Foucault (Foucault, 1967, 1970, 1972 and 1973). Archaeology does not provide a systematic analytic machine for 'application' to particular domains; the present study utilises it as a set of conceptual tools which, together with equipment borrowed from elsewhere and a few home-made devices, provides the means for putting together an analysis of the formation of the psychology of the individual.
6 In using this formulation I am deliberately allying myself with the remarks made by Michel Foucault at the close of the preface to his study of medicine, *The Birth of the Clinic* (Foucault, 1973, p. xix).

1 The moral subject of psychology

1 Report on the Progress of Victor of Aveyron, 1806, quoted from Itard, 1972, pp. 157-8.
2 The fullest account of the discovery of the 'Wild Boy of Aveyron' is in Lane, 1977. This also contains a comprehensive discussion of

contemporary writings, and a translation of Bonnaterre's 'Historical Notice of the Sauvage de l'Aveyron', published in 1800, from which this description is drawn.

3 This is the title of an illuminating paper by Georges Canguilhem (Canguilhem, 1980).

4 See Ian Hacking's marvellous book *Representing and Intervening*, 1983, esp. Part B.

5 For some examples see Rousseau [1754] 1913; Von Linne (Linneaus), 1758, Bk 1; Gall and Spurzheim, 1810; Feuerbach [1832] 1833; Evans, 1892; Wasserman [1928] 1973; Zingg, 1940; Dennis, 1941; Gessell, 1941; Singh and Zingg, 1942; Lévi-Strauss, 1966; Bettelheim, 1967; Malson, 1972; Armen, 1974; Maclean, 1977.

6 Lane, 1977, p. 19.

7 Ibid., p. 285.

8 Malson, 1972, p. 36. He is referring to the work reported in Kellogg and Kellogg, 1934.

9 Canguilhem, 1968, p. 21, quoted in Lecourt, 1975, p. 168.

10 Itard [1801] 1972, p. 99.

11 Rousseau, op. cit.; Montesquieu [1748] 1949; Voltaire [1764] 1835; Buffon, 1749; La Mettrie [1751] 1791. On the philosophy of the Enlightenment generally see Cassirer, 1951.

12 Diderot, *Lettres sur les sourds et les muets*; see also his *Lettre sur les aveugles*, both in vol. 1 of *Oeuvres complètes*, 1875-6. Cf. also Diderot, 1857.

13 Cf. Lane, op. cit., pp. 78-82.

14 Condillac [1746] 1971; Locke [1689] 1920. On the problem of knowledge in eighteenth-century philosophy, and the conception of the mind entailed, see Cassirer, op. cit., ch. 3. See also Hacking, 1975. On the issues discussed in the following pages, see Foucault, 1970, esp. pp. 86-92.

15 Condillac, op. cit., p. 122.

16 Cf. Condillac, *Traité des systemes*, 1771; see also *The Logic*, [1780] 1809.

17 Condillac [1754] 1930.

18 Cheseldon's account of some observations of a thirteen-year-old boy who was born blind and had his sight restored was published in 1728, followed by an account of the operation (Cheseldon, 1728a; 1728b). Its implications were widely discussed, and were considered in Buffon's (1749) *Histoire naturelle de l'homme*. The techniques for the removal of cataracts were perfected in Paris by Jacques Daviel, and reported in 1752. Cf. Garrison, 1929, pp. 343 and 349.

19 Condillac, op. cit., n. 17, p. 46.

20 Ibid., p. 3.

21 Ibid.,.p. 89.

22 Ibid., p. 82.

23 Cf. Cheseldon, op. cit., n. 18. On the place of vision in eighteenth-century French philosophical discourse see Hacking, 1975, pp. 32-3 and Foucault, 1973, esp. pp. xiiff.

24 See the discussion of Epée's work later in this chapter.

25 Condillac [1780] 1809, esp. ch. iv.
26 Itard, op. cit., p. 113.
27 Ibid., p. 127.
28 Condillac's own course of education for the Prince of Parma, 1775, which ran in its published form to some sixteen volumes of detailed instruction, was perhaps the first example of this, in the field of scientific pedagogy. For phenomenotechnics see the work of Bachelard, introduced in Lecourt, 1975, and Gaukroger, 1976.
29 Itard [1808] 1972, p. 101.
30 Cf. K. Jones, 1972, p. 100; Skultans, 1975, pp. 10 et seq.
31 Cf. Foucault, 1967, ch. 7.
32 Battie [1758] 1962.
33 Pargeter, 1792, quoted from Leigh, 1961, p. 67. Leigh provides useful material from texts of this period.
34 Quoted from Kraepelin, 1962, p. 76. Kraepelin cites numerous examples of German prophets of moral medicine – Reil, Heinroth, Vering, Neumann and Hoffbauer. Willis's treatment of George III is discussed, rather tendentiously, in MacAlpine and Hunter, 1969.
35 E.g. Zilboorg, 1941, ch. 8. It should be noted at this point that despite what is suggested in currently fashionable accounts (e.g. Scull, 1979; Ingleby, 1981), moral treatment neither originated outside medicine nor opposed it. What was involved was the formation of a new relation between medicine and madness and a new relation between doctor and patient. Cf. also Pinel [1801] 1806; Tuke [1813] 1964.
36 Foucault, 1967, p. 257.
37 Quoted from Kraepelin, op. cit., p. 78.
38 Foucault, 1967, p. 267.
39 For example, see Pinel, op. cit.; Crichton, 1798; and the texts cited in nn. 32, 33 and 34.
40 Itard, op. cit., pp. 174-5.
41 Quoted from Lane, op. cit., n. 1, pp. 57-69.
42 A good discussion of these issues is in Donnelly, 1977, ch. 7, subsequently published as Donnelly, 1983. For a traditional account see Manuel, 1972.
43 Donnelly, 1983.
44 Voltaire, *Oeuvres*, Paris, 1835, vol. 7, p. 472, quoted in Donnelly, op. cit., p. 161.
45 Quoted in Donnelly, op. cit., p. 162.
46 Cf. Foucault, 1973; Temkin, 1963.
47 Foucault, 1973, esp. ch. 6.
48 Foucault, 1973, chs 8 and 9; Canguilhem, 1978.
49 Pinel, 1798. See the discussion in Rosen, 1946.
50 Pinel [1801] 1806.
51 Details from Lane, op. cit., n. 1.
52 Epée [1784] 1801.
53 Sicard in Massieu, 1815, cited in Lane, op. cit., n. 1.
54 Quoted in Lane, op. cit., p. 99.
55 Esquirol [1818] 1965, pp. 446 and 474.

56 For Séguin see his 1866, 1870 and 1876. His work is discussed in
    Lane, op. cit., esp. ch. 10; see also Holman, 1914; Boyd, 1914; and
    Kraft, 1961.
57 Quoted in Boyd, op. cit., p. 91.
58 Séguin, 1866, p. 199.
59 On Montessori see Boyd, op. cit.; Culverwell, 1913; and Fynne,
    1924.

2   The psychology of populations

1   Guy, 1873, p. 472.
2   Colquhoun, 1797, p. 1.
3   Colquhoun, 1800, Preface.
4   Quoted in Critchley, 1967, p. 47.
5   Cf. ibid., p. 7.
6   Cf. Foucault [1975], 1977, pt 1; Hay, 1975; Jeffry, 1968; Parks,
    1976.
7   See Pasquino, 1978, p. 45. See also Rosen, 1953a.
8   Pasquino, op. cit., p. 51. Cf. also Foucault's remarks on biopolitics in
    History of Sexuality [1976], 1979a, and in Foucault, 1979b.
9   Steuart [1767], 1966, vol. 1, p. 15; quoted in Tribe, 1979, p. 83.
    Tribe has an excellent discussion of these issues.
10 Sinclair, 1791-9, vol. xx, p. xix; quoted in Cullen, 1975, p. 10.
11 Foucault, 1979b, p. 17.
12 Cf. on this question Tribe, op. cit., ch. 6.
13 Ibid., p. 111.
14 For a useful discussion of these issues, see Procacci, 1978.
15 Colquhoun, 1806, pp. 7-8. Cf. also Bentham, 1843, Smith [1776],
    1976; Ricardo [1817], 1957-73.
16 Colquhoun, 1806, p. 82. Cf. Procacci, op. cit.
17 On the Old Poor Law see Marshall, 1968 and Poynter, 1969. For
    criticisms of the Poor Laws see Malthus [1798], 1976, p. 97; Smith,
    op. cit., p. 470; Ricardo, op. cit., p. 108. For the Poor Law Report see
    Poor Law Commission, 1834. For criticisms see especially Blaug,
    1963 and Blaug, 1964; these are critically discussed in Williams,
    1981, part 1, as are other contemporary historical discussions of the
    Poor Laws. Coats, 1960, is useful on economic thought and Poor Law
    policy.
18 Poor Law Commission, op. cit., p. 127. On the New Poor Law more
    generally, see Rose, 1972; and Fraser, 1976.
19 Hobsbawm, 1969, p. 233.
20 Cf. Dicey, 1905, p. 305.
21 The key text here is Gareth Stedman Jones's study, *Outcast London*.
    This text, however, utilises a theoretical approach contested in the
    present study, regarding the theory of urban degeneracy as an
    ideology which diverted attention from the real nature of poverty in
    the nineteenth century, which Jones's re-analysis of statistical data
    purports to demonstrate. See Jones, 1976, and the criticisms in

Williams, 1972, and Tomlinson, 1981.

22   For a discussion of the medicine of epidemics see Foucault [1963], 1972; Rosen, 1953a; Rosen, 1953b; Briggs, 1961; Flynn's introduction to Chadwick [1842], 1965.

23   See the Report of the Select Committee of 1838 discussed in Dyos, 1957; cf. Jones, 1976, ch. 8.

24   On Chadwick and social hygiene see Chadwick [1842], 1965; Lewis, 1952. On the role of Farr, see Eyler 1973a, Eyler, 1973b, Eyler, 1979. More generally, see Frazer, 1950; Hodgkinson, 1967; Hodgkinson, 1968. We return to this issue in subsequent chapters.

25   Jones, op. cit., chs 9 and 10.

26   Cf. Harris, 1972.

27   On the work of the Statistical Society, see Abrams, 1968, and Hilts, 1973.

28   Mayhew, 1861-2. See the discussion of Mayhew in Jones, op. cit.; and Williams, 1981. ch. 5.

29   On relief work and the debates over charity in the last half of the nineteenth century see Young and Ashton, 1956; Woodroofe, 1962; De Scheinwitz, 1947, and Gilbert, 1966.

30   Booth, 1892-7, vol. 1, pp. 28-62.

31   Ibid., pp. 156-78. Cf. Jones, op. cit., ch. 6.

32   White, 1886; Llewellyn-Smith in Booth, 1892-7, vol. 3; Marshall, 1890; cf. the discussion in Jones, op. cit. The question of 'alien immigration', which was central to the American debates, was raised in England largely in this context and in relation to the problem of 'sweated labour'. The argument centered around Jewish immigration and was posed differently than in America – it was precisely the superiority of the Jewish intellect, its cynical and calculating nature, the willingness of the Jew to work long hours for little pay and hence displace or drag down native workers that provided the justification for the limiting of rights of entry in the Aliens Act of 1905. See Hobson, 1892, pp. 59ff; White, 1892; Russell, 1900; Royal Commission on Alien Immigration, 1903, and the discussions in Gartner, 1960; Gainer, 1972, and C. Jones, 1977.

33   Booth, op. cit., vol. 1, pp. 43-4.

34   Cf. Barnett and Barnett, 1909; Alden, 1905; Kelly, 1907; and the discussion in Harris, op. cit.

35   Beveridge, 1905, p. 326.

36   Ibid., p. 327. See also Booth, 1892, and the discussion in Harris, op. cit., ch. 1.

37   See Booth, 1892. Cf. Brown, 1968.

38   White, 1806, pp. 28-9; cf. Gareth Stedman Jones, op. cit., ch. 16.

39   Cf. Foucault [1976], 1979a, pp. 118ff.

40   Cf. Bucknill and Tuke, 1858, esp. p. 342.

41   For a clear recent statement, see the account in Smith, 1981, ch. 3. Cf. Spurzheim, 1817; Gall, 1835; Combe, 1831; Carpenter, 1842. There is an extensive secondary literature on this period. In relation to Britain see, for example, Young, 1970; Cantor and Shapin, 1975; Cooter, 1981. A different approach analyses this shift in terms of the

'medicalisation' thesis which reduces these theoretical conditions to rationales for doctors monopolising madness. See especially Scull, 1979. This thesis is contested in ch. 1 of the PhD thesis on which the present book is based.

42 Jacob, 1974, p. 149. Jacob is also a valuable source on the organisation of biological discourse in this period, as is Foucault's *Order of Things* [1966], 1970, especially chs 5 and 8.

43 Cf. Rosenberg, 1974. Cf. also Provine, 1971, and Ludmerer, 1972.

44 Cf. Jacob, 1974, ch. 3.

45 Lucas, 1847-50; Moreau, 1830; Morel, 1957. This account follows Ackernecht, 1969 which depends upon Genil-Perrin, 1913.

46 Burrows, 1828, especially pp. 100-3.

47 Bucknill and Tuke, 1858, esp. ch. 8.

48 Duncan and Millard, 1866.

49 The possibility that criminal behaviour might be the outcome of a diseased mind rather than an evil will was the focus of controversy. For a good discussion of these issues, see Smith, 1981; for the equivalent controversy in France, see Foucault, ed., 1978b.

50 Especially the work of Magnan, see Magnan, 1876. Cf. Ellenberger, 1970, p. 281.

51 This is clear in all his writings. See, for example, Maudsley, 1873.

52 Maudsley, 1874, p. 46.

3 Heredity versus environment

1 Marshall, 1890, pp. 225-6.

2 Galton, 1883, p. 25n. There is an extensive secondary literature on the origin of Galton's eugenic ideas and their social conditions. See especially Buss, 1976; Cowan, 1972; Cowan, 1977; Mackenzie, 1981, ch. 3. See also Pearson 1914-30 and Blacker, 1952. For genetics and eugenics in America, see Pickens, 1968; Kamin, 1977, chs 1 and 2 and the references cited in n. 43 to chapter 2 above.

3 Galton [1892], 1962, p. 41.

4 Galton, 1883, pp. 1-2.

5 Jacob, 1974, p. 174.

6 Galton, 1889, p. 35.

7 Ibid., p. 60.

8 Jacob, op. cit., p. 166.

9 Malthus [1798], 1976.

10 Galton, 1883, pp. 314ff.

11 Darwin [1859], 1968, p. 108.

12 Ibid., p. 117.

13 Ibid., p. 102.

14 Jacob, op. cit., p. 167.

15 Galton, 1883, p. 49.

16 Cf. Galton, 1889, p. 55.

17 Galton, 1883, p. 50.

18 Ibid., p. 52.

19 Galton, 1889, p. 62.
20 Galton, 1869, p. 26.
21 Ibid., p. 36.
22 The first formulation of this is in Galton, 1865. For a useful discussion of the Darwinian theory of blending inheritance, see Vorzimmer, 1963.
23 Pearson, 1898. The debate between biometricians and Mendelians has been much discussed. For an account of the issues see Frogget and Nevin, 1971. For attempts at social explanation in terms of interests and the like, see Farrall, 1975, and Mackenzie, 1981, ch. 6.
24 See especially Darwin, 1868, vol. 2.
25 In this respect he anticipated Weismann's (1893) theory of germ plasm.
26 Galton, 1883, pp. 25, 27.
27 Ibid., pp. 20, 23.
28 Cf. Galton, 1892, passim.
29 White, 1886, p. 49.
30 Galton, 1901.
31 Ibid., p. 664.
32 Ibid., p. 663.
33 Galton, 1907.
34 Galton, 1901, p. 665.
35 Cf. Cowan, 1977.
36 The most extensive discussion, well referenced to the eugenic literature, is Searle, 1976.
37 Cf. Searle, 1978; Norton, 1978; Mackenzie, 1976 and 1981. Some of these papers are gathered together in Webster, 1981. Such accounts often draw upon the theoretical positions developed in Bloor, 1976, and Barnes, 1974, 1977 and 1982. These analyses in terms of 'interests' are criticised in ch. 1 of the PhD thesis upon which this book is based.
38 Schumpeter, 1954, pp. 250-76 has a useful account of debates over population in political and economic discourse. See also Glass, 1978, for a discussion of the eighteenth-century debate.
39 Child, 1690, ch. 10.
40 See Schumpeter, op. cit. and Cullen, 1975.
41 Turgot [1788], 1793, Section 5.
42 Malthus [1798], 1976.
43 Searle, 1971.
44 See White, 1901; Pearson, 1901; Shaw, 1900; Chamberlain, 1903. It should be noted that the link between the fortunes of the nation, competition, efficiency and fitness were not made only by the apologists of imperialism, they also organised the arguments of those who were concerned to oppose imperialism. Thus, for example, Hobson's famous (1902) critique of the economic justification for imperialism (in favour of a theory of underconsumption), the political rationale for imperialism (it was in the interests only of a class of economic parasites, monopolists and militarists) and the moral basis of imperialism (in favour of a 'rational humanism') nonetheless

operated on this terrain when it argued for the substitution of 'rational' for 'natural' selection among nations in a federation of civilised states (cf. ibid., pt II, ch. II).

45 For a discussion of Spencer and the general theme of 'evolution' in social thought see Spencer, 1972, and Burrow, 1966.

46 Lenin [1917], 1964; on the Austro-Marxists see Bottomore and Goode, 1978; for Chamberlain see the speeches collected in Chamberlain, 1903. For a discussion of the links between social imperialism and social reform, see Semmel, 1960.

47 Cf. Shadwell [1896], 1909.

48 White, 1901, p. vii.

49 Ibid., pp. 102-3. For texts elaborating on this theme see also Warren, 1901; Pearson, 1901; Maurice, 1903; Shee, 1903; Horsfall, 1904. See also the discussion in Searle, 1971, ch. 3 and Gilbert, 1966, pp. 88-101.

50 Some of these issues are discussed in Lewis, 1980.

51 Galton, 1883, pp. 318-19.

52 Pearson, 1904, p. 159.

53 For discussion of Pearson and biometrics see Semmel, 1960, ch. 2; Searle, 1976; Norton, 1978; Mackenzie, 1981, ch. 4.

54 Heron, 1906, p. 22.

55 Cf. Mackenzie, 1976; Searle, 1976.

56 Rowntree, 1901, pp. 216-21.

57 These questions are well discussed in Williams, 1981, ch. 8.

58 Rowntree, 1913, pp. 148-9; cf. Williams, op. cit., pp. 34ff.

59 Rowntree, 1914, esp. ch. 5.

60 *British Medical Journal*, 1903, p. 208. One can also locate here the strategy of school clinics, open-air night camps and camp schools whose most notable British proponents were Margaret and Rachel McMillan, cf. McMillan, 1930, and the discussion in Whitbread, 1972. Some of these issues are picked up again in chapter 6 below.

61 Inter-Departmental Committee on Physical Deterioration, 1904, p. 14.

62 The Inter-Departmental Committee's recommendation on the provision of school meals was embodied in permissive legislation in the Education (Provision of Meals) Act 1906; their recommendations on school medical inspection in the Education (Administrative Provisions) Act 1907, which marked the establishment of the School Medical Service; neglect of a child's health by a parent was made a legal offence in the Children Act of 1908, the first maternity clinics and child welfare clinics again were established in this period. These questions are discussed further in chapter 6 below.

63 Webb, 1910, pp. 240-1.

64 Royal Commission on the Poor Laws and the Relief of Distress, 1909, Minority Report.

65 Ibid., p. 1179.

66 Cf. Beveridge, 1909.

67 Ibid., pp. 1188-9.

68 For a discussion of these proposals, see Harris, 1972, ch. 3; cf. also Brown, 1968.

69 Royal Commission on the Poor Laws and the Relief of Distress, 1909, p. 1204.
70 Ibid., p. 1206.

4   The psychology of the individual

1 Burt, 1927, p. 5.
2 The description is that of Sir Robert Blair, Chief Education Officer, on Burt's appointment to a half-time post. Burt quotes it in his autobiographical account (Burt [1952] 1968, p. 64) where he puts it in Blair's scottish accent: 'Young man, ye're the fust official psychologist in the wurrld, and ye've all London at yer feet. Now come back in a week and tell me what ye'r going to do.' Cf. Sutherland and Sharp, 1980.
3 Burt, 1927.
4 Binet and Henri, 1896, translation from Herrnstein and Boring, 1965, p. 428.
5 Ibid., p. 431.
6 Royal Commission on the Care and Control of the Feeble-Minded, 1908, vol. 8, para. 9.
7 Cf. Searle, 1976.
8 Searle, op. cit., tends to imply the former position; Barker, 1982, the latter.
9 There is no adequate account of the history of idiocy. Rosen, Clark and Kivitz, 1976, is a useful collection of source material. Kanner, 1964, and Wolfensberger, 1976, are fairly straightforward institutional histories. The work of Cranefield is useful in providing detailed material on very specific areas: cf. Cranefield, 1961; Cranefield, 1962; Cranefield and Federn, 1967. Other useful discussions are Kanner, 1967, 1975; Haffter, 1968; Neugebauer, 1978, and Ryan and Thomas, 1980, especially ch. 5.
10 Quoted from Matthews, 1954, p. 183.
11 Quoted from Jones, 1972, p. 183.
12 Cf. Howe, 1848.
13 E.g. Sidney, 1854; Millard, 1864; Anon, 1865. cf. Jones, op. cit., and Ryan and Thomas, op. cit.
14 Figures cited in Jones, 1972, p. 183; cf. also Tuke, 1882, p. 310.
15 Cf. Hilliard and Kirman, 1957, ch. 1.
16 Ibid.
17 Charity Organisation Society, 1877, p. 6.
18 Ibid., p. 7.
19 Ibid., p. 50.
20 Cf. Jones, op. cit., p. 185.
21 As, for example, in the case of the Wild Boy of Aveyron, discussed in chapter 1 above.
22 Willis, 1672; cf. Cranefield, 1961.
23 Howe, 1848.

24 Ireland, 1877.

25 Ibid., p. 254.

26 For example, in France, in the programmes of the Ideologues discussed briefly in chapter 1 above. For early English debates over the moralising function of education see Jones and Williamson, 1979. Cf. also Foucault [1975], 1977a, passim.

27 For the history of 'special education' in England, see Pritchard, 1963.

28 See Pritchard, op. cit.; for the history of special education for the 'maladjusted' see Bridgeland, 1971. Cf. also Donzelot [1977], 1979, pp. 128ff.

29 Royal Commission on the Blind, Deaf and Dumb, 1889, paras 709-24; cf. Sutherland, 1977, p. 138.

30 See, for example, Shuttleworth, 1888; Charity Organisation Society, 1893.

31 Education Department (Defective and Epileptic Children) (Committee), 1895, vol. 1, para. 13.

32 Poor Law Schools (Committee), 1893.

33 Charity Organisation Society, 1893. Cf. Keir, 1952, p. 9, and Jones, 1972, p. 186. The COS also sponsored the formation of the National Association for Promoting the Welfare of the Feeble-Minded, in 1896, which we discuss presently, and collated information from such diverse bodies as the Metropolitan Association for Befriending Young Servants and the National Vigilance Society on the difficulties of feeble-minded girls and young men.

34 Warner, 1888. The Scheme was reported in Warner, 1890, pp. 142ff. Doctors continued to use the scheme for many years, and it was still included in the 16th edition of Newsholme and Kerr's *School Hygiene*, published in 1924.

35 Warner, op. cit., p. 659, cf. Potts, 1982.

36 Warner, 1895, and 1896. Cf. also Warner, 1897.

37 Cf. Pritchard, 1963, pp. 132-51; Sutherland, 1977, p. 138.

38 Education Department (Defective and Epileptic Children) (Committee), 1895, vol. 1, para. 14.

39 Ibid., vol. 2, question 106.

40 Quoted in Sutherland, 1977, p. 139.

41 Cf. Pritchard, op. cit.

42 Lake, a London head teacher, had drawn up a record card for documenting the physical, mental and moral characteristics of his pupils in 1885, and apparently used a scheme of tests based on the work of Galton; cf. Barnes, 1901. Sophie Bryant, Headmistress of Camden High School for Girls, published the results of her 'experiments in testing the character of schoolchildren' in 1886 (Bryant 1886 cf. also Cattell and Bryant, 1889) which, according to Keir, 1952, p. 8, had a wide influence. Sully had also stressed the importance of observation and recording of children's behaviour and ability in his *Teacher's Handbook of Psychology*, first published in 1886 and widely used in the training of teachers cf. Keir, op. cit. These questions are discussed further in chapter 5 below.

43 Evidence to Royal Commission on the Care and Control of the

Feeble-Minded, 1908. Cf. Sutherland, 1977, p. 139.

44 See Mary Dendy's appendix to Lapage, 1920.
45 Pinsent, 1903.
46 Ibid., p. 515.
47 Jones, 1972, pp. 194-204, and Searle, 1976, pp. 106-11, give details of the campaign leading up to the passage of the Bill, and the positions taken up by the various forces.
48 Quoted in Jones, 1972, p. 196.
49 Tredgold, 1908.
50 Tredgold, 1910, p. 721.
51 Cf. the accounts in Jones and Searle, cited in n. 47 above. For a contemporary discussion of the Act itself, see Davey, 1913.
52 Royal Commission on the Care and Control of the Feeble-Minded, 1908, vol. 8. Cf. Fry et al., 1909.
53 Royal Commission, 1908, vol. 8, para. 553.
54 Tredgold, 1914, p. 38.
55 Royal Commission, 1908, vol. 8, para. 556.
56 Tredgold, 1914, p. 8.
57 Royal Commission, 1908, vol. 8, para. 556.
58 Ibid., para. 19.
59 Full details of the Act are given in Wormwald and Wormwald, 1913, and in Jones, 1972, pp. 204-9.
60 Jones, 1972, pp. 212-14.
61 Tredgold, 1914, pp. 359-61.

5   The measure of intelligence

1 Oliver Gillie, *Sunday Times*, 25 October 1976, p. 1.
2 Oliver Gillie's public charges in the *Sunday Times* systematised and substantiated doubts about Burt's work which were already fairly widespread. *The Times* followed up Gillie's article with a report headlined 'Theories of IQ pioneer "completely discredited" '. (*Times*, 1976). Burt's twin study data was first questioned by Leon Kamin in 1972; his criticisms were published in Kamin [1974], 1977. These doubts were shared by Jensen, 1974, and Clarke and Clarke, 1974. A full account and judicious assessment of the controversy is given in Hearnshaw's biography of Burt. Hearnshaw concludes that Burt did indeed fabricate much of his twin study data after 1950, the original materials having been destroyed in bombing during the Second World War. He almost certainly invented two collaborators – Miss Howard and Miss Conway – who he claimed had gathered post-war data for him, though he may have based them on real voluntary care workers who had collected information in the inter-war years. The post-war articles supporting Burt's views, written in their names, were certainly penned by Burt himself. Burt fabricated figures on kinship correlations, working back from conclusions to 'data', and those concerning declining rates of scholastic achievement supposedly associated with the introduction of comprehensive education and

'progressive' teaching methods (Hearnshaw, 1979, ch. 9). The charge that, even in his earlier work, Burt often guessed at parental IQ and then treated his guesses as hard data also seems well founded.

3 Especially influential criticisms in the first phase of dispute in the UK after the Second World War were Simon, 1953; Halsey and Gardener, 1953; Heim, 1954. The second phase of dispute was sparked off by the apparent failure of schemes of 'compensatory education', as interpreted by Jensen, 1969, and Eysenck, 1971. This interpretation was criticised in, for example, Kamin [1974], 1977 and the papers collected in Richardson and Spears, 1972.

4 Titchener, 1901-5, vol. 2, pt. 1, p. v.

5 Fechner [1860], 1966.

6 Ibid., p. 7.

7 Wundt [1896], 1897.

8 Galton, 1883, pp. 28-9.

9 Keir, 1952, p. 9.

10 Ibid., p. 10.

11 Galton, 1891.

12 Cf. Keir, 1952, pp. 10-11.

13 Cattell, 1890, p. 373.

14 Ibid.

15 Ibid., pp. 380-1.

16 Spearman, 1904. For the analysis of the prolems of the tests, see Sharp, 1899, and Wissler, 1901.

17 Spearman, 1904, p. 269.

18 McDougall, 1914, p. 302.

19 For details see Hearnshaw's (1979) biography of Burt, p. 27.

20 Spearman, 1915, p. 313.

21 Burt, 1909, p. 169.

22 Ibid., p. 97.

23 Cf. n. 2 above.

24 Hearnshaw, 1979, p. 57.

25 Burt, 1909, p. 176.

26 Board of Education, 1910.

27 Board of Education, 1911, p. 220.

28 Board of Education, 1912, p. 196.

29 Board of Education, 1913, p. 229.

30 Binet and Henri, 1896.

31 Binet's early work on intelligence is discussed in Wolf's (1973) biography, especially chs 3 and 4. A useful source of material in translation is Binet and Simon, 1916.

32 Quoted in Wolf, 1973, p. 140.

33 Binet and Simon, 1905b.

34 This is Wolf's view: see 1973, p. 29.

35 Quoted in Wolf, 1973, p. 141.

36 For an account of this episode, see ibid., pp. 160ff.

37 Ibid., p. 170.

38 Binet and Simon, 1905a, present this investigation in detail immediately before the article in which they first put forward their

scale. Wolf, op. cit., p. 173, refers to it as this 'catalytic agent' which, given the need, the experimental discernment and the hypothesis which Binet already possessed, set off the necessary insight.

39 Binet and Simon [1907], 1914.

40 Binet and Simon, 1908.

41 Binet and Simon, 1908, p. 60; translation quoted from Wolf, op. cit., p. 191.

42 Binet and Simon, 1909, p. 146, translation quoted from Wolf, op. cit., pp. 203-4.

43 Stern [1912], 1914.

44 Cf. Potts, 1982, pp. 1-2.

45 Keir, 1952, p. 10.

46 Sutherland and Sharp, 1980, in a useful examination of some of the primary source material, appear to account for the victory of the doctors in terms of prior incumbency plus high status.

47 Board of Education, 1910, p. 15.

48 On eyesight see Cohn [1883], 1886; Crichton-Brown's report of 1884 to the Education Department on 'mental over-pressure' is discussed in Board of Education, 1910a, pp. 2-4; generally see Dukes, *Health at School*, 1887.

49 Cf. Pritchard, 1963, p. 128. There was also a lengthy debate on the specific effects of education on women and, in particular, upon their fertility.

50 Cf. ibid., p. 128, for a discussion of Bradford and the influence of the Independent Labour Party and Margaret McMillan. Kerr moved to London in 1902 where his relations with Newman were not always harmonious. Cf. Sutherland and Sharp, op. cit., pp. 183f.

51 Cf. Keir, op. cit., p. 10.

52 Local Government Board, 1904. The open-air school movement was clearly within this strategy. The first open-air school was founded in Charlottenburg, outside Berlin, in 1904, and a number of such schools opened in Britain, both for day pupils, and, after 1911, residential. The idea was that dark, overcrowded and ill-ventilated urban schools exacerbated the conditions of nervous, debilitated, undernourished and anaemic or tubercular children, who would recover more quickly in fresh air, but also with wholesome and regular meals and rest. Margaret McMillan pioneered open-air sleeping, in addition to day-time activities. See also Crowley, 1910; Laurie, 1911, esp. article by Drummond. For summaries see Pritchard, op. cit., pp. 171-5 and Department of Education and Science, 1975, pp. 21-2.

53 Board of Education, 1905, vol. 1, pp. 31-2.

54 Of course, these aspects of the organisation of the body had been the concern of many different discourses – religious, moral, texts on manners and so forth – for many centuries. See, for example, the texts discussed by Elias in *The Civilising Process* [1939], 1978. And both philanthropic and medical discourse, especially during the nineteenth century, sought to instil norms of personal conduct into families. But the school is a mechanism which allows the interventions to be universalised and articulated within a technical apparatus – this

transforms the nature and possibility of the strategy. This point is taken up again presently.

55 Newman sought to promote these clinics in his very first Annual Report and regularly reported on their progress.

56 Board of Education, 1910, p. 32. These objectives were laid out in a memorandum from the Board in 1907, Circular 576.

57 Cf. n. 54, and the discussion in chapter 6 below.

58 In his Report for 1909, Board of Education, 1910, p. 15.

59 Education Department (Defective and Epileptic Children) Committee, 1898, passim. Cf. also Royal Commission on the Care and Control of the Feeble-Minded, passim, and Sutherland and Sharp, 1980, p. 182.

60 See, for example, Abelson, 1911; Myers, 1911; Brown, 1911.

61 See, for example, Keir, 1952, p. 14; Burt [1952], 1968, p. 64n.

62 Board of Education, 1910.

63 See the discussion earlier in this chapter.

64 E.g. Kerr, 1928, which is discussed in Potts, 1982.

65 Sutherland and Sharp, 1980, p. 184.

66 For accounts of this episode see Hearnshaw, 1979, ch. 3; Burt, [1952], 1968, pp. 62-4; and Sutherland and Sharp, op. cit.

67 Burt, 1914.

68 Ibid., p. 50.

69 Board of Education, 1924, p. 66.

70 Ibid., p. 72.

71 Burt, 1921, p. 1.

72 For some examples of this copious literature see Ballard, 1920; Ballard, 1922; Brown and Thomson, 1921; Gordon, 1923; Herd, 1930; Peterson, 1925; Richardson, 1922.

73 Ballard, 1920, p. 13.

74 Myers discussed the uses of psychology in his book of 1918, directing attention to its role in industry, drawing on the work of Munsterberg and Taylor (cf. Munsterberg, 1912). The NIIP published the Journal of the National Institute of Industrial Psychology from 1922 onwards; cf. also Myers, 1920; Myers, 1926; and Welch and Myers, 1932, which reviews ten years work of the NIIP. A brief account of this area is contained in Hearnshaw, 1964, pp. 275-82. Unfortunately there is no space to pursue the important issues raised by this field of work.

75 Thomson, 1922; Brown and Thomson, 1921. For Thomson's own account of this, see his article in Boring et al. [1952], 1968; this work is discussed in Sutherland, 1977, and Sutherland, 1981.

76 Sutherland, 1981, and Sutherland and Sharp, 1980, p. 197, n. 37.

77 Most notably the work of Brian Simon — see his 1971, 1974 and 1978.

78 Jones, 1972, pp. 215-17 is a useful account.

79 Board of Education and Board of Control, 1929.

80 Board of Control, 1934. The Board of Control also produced a Report in 1931 on the use of segregation in colonies for mental defectives; Board of Control, 1931.

81 Board of Control, 1934, p. 77.

6 Hygiene and welfare

1 Board of Education, 1914, p. 16.
2 On the new preventive medicine, see Ministry of Health, 1919. See also Haslam, 1930; Williams, 1932; and, for an American comparison, see Hill, 1916. Cf. Armstrong, 1983, ch. 2. On social hygiene and venereal disease, see Weeks, 1981, esp. pp. 214-20 and Bland, 1984.
3 Lewis, 1980; McCleary, 1935.
4 Board of Education, 1914, p. 24. See also Newman's article on child mortality in relation to the health of the State in vol. 30 of the *Journal of the Royal Sanitary Institute*, and Newsholme in Local Government Board, 1910.
5 McCleary, op. cit., p. 36.
6 Books on mothercraft at this time are too numerous to reference. The successive editions of the *Mothercraft Manual*, first published in 1923, were important in the promotion of hygienic principles amongst the literate and well-to-do, in particular the doctrines of Truby King and the Mothercraft Training Society. See Liddiard, 1923. Correct mothercraft, of course, promoted mental as well as physical hygiene. There is a brief discussion of changes in childrearing advice and its relation to psychological conceptions of childhood in Newson and Newson, 1974. Cf. Hardyment, 1983, esp. ch. 4.
7 Board of Education, 1915, p. 25.
8 For an American example, see Hill, 1916, p. 29.
9 Younghusband, 1947; see also Macadam, 1925.
10 Younghusband, op. cit., pp. 80-1.
11 Macadam, 1934, p. 118; see also Hospital Almoners Association, 1932.
12 Macadam, 1925, p. 21. See also Owen, 1977. On Care Committee workers see Board of Education, 1910.
13 Younghusband, 1978, p. 24.
14 Cf. Rooff, 1972; Younghusband, 1978; Timms, 1964; Yelloly, 1980.
15 Cf. Rooff, 1972, p. 139.
16 See the various volumes of the Charity Organisation Quarterly over this period, especially the numerous articles by Pringle, the secretary of the COS from 1914-18 and 1925-36. This theme had been established earlier – see Mowrat, 1961, pp. 114ff.
17 See Deacon, 1976.
18 See Woodroofe, pp. 64-73.
19 See Addison, 1977, p. 39; and Marwick, 1964.
20 See the discussion in texts cited in n. 19.
21 See Orr, 1936; M'Gonigle and Kirby, 1936.
22 Rathbone, 1924. Cf. Macnicol, 1980, and Lewis, 1980.
23 Charles, 1934.
24 Cf. Lewis, 1980, ch. 7.
25 Royal Commission on Lunacy and Mental Disorder, 1926, pp. 16-22.
26 Board of Control, 1918; Royal Commission on Lunacy and Mental Disorder, op. cit.; Feversham Committee, 1939. Cf. Jones, 1972, ch. 9.

27 This account is drawn from the Reports issued annually by the Council. See, for example, National Council for Mental Hygiene, 1924.

28 National Council for Mental Hygiene, 1928, p. 32.

29 Board of Education, 1921, p. 109.

30 Board of Education, 1928, p. 31. Cf. Healy, 1917.

31 Board of Education, 1930, p. 26.

32 The best account is May, 1973, which I have drawn on extensively in the following paragraphs. See also Platt, 1969, chs 2 and 3 and Fox, 1952, ch. 19. A good collection of materials concerning this period, mostly English, is Sanders, 1970. Civil law differed, in that it recognised the status of infancy and the problems it posed with respect to property rights, contract, enfeoffment and so forth. See Anon, 1718, and Bingham, 1816.

33 Blackstone, 1765-9, vol. 4, esp. p. 23. See also Russell, 1819, pp. 3ff. For sample judgments see Sanders, 1970, pp. 10-17, 21-36.

34 Foucault, 1977; Ignatieff, 1978.

35 See Abrams, 1968, on the statistical societies and Jones and Williamson, 1979, on moral topography.

36 Neale, 1840.

37 Carpenter, 1851. See also Hill, 1857; Beames, 1850.

38 See Hall and Pretty, 1908, for a discussion of the Act and its relation to previous legislation.

39 Cf. Holcombe, 1977; McGregor, 1957; Harrison and Mort, 1977. The campaigns which led to the Married Women's Property Acts, discussed in Holcombe, can also be seen in this light.

40 See Pinchbeck and Hewitt, 1973, esp. chs 12 and 13.

41 For a discussion of analogous events in France, see Donzelot, 1979, esp. ch. 4.

42 Board of Education, 1920; Home Office, 1927. The exception was Borstal, first included in legislation in 1908, which was generally commended for children over 16. See Fox, 1952.

43 Home Office, 1927, p. 6.

44 Maurice Hamblin Smith, 1922, cited in William Clarke Hall, 1928, p. 109. Cf. also Burt, 1923, 1925; Goring, 1913.

45 Hall, 1926; he is following Burt, 1923 and 1925.

46 The 'welfare' criterion had been urged by Hall, 1926 and in Home Office, 1927, e.g. p. 121. It was included in the Children and Young Persons Act, 1933, Section 44.

47 Home Office, 1927, p. 5. Cf. Home Office, 1895.

48 Hall, 1926, pp. 64, 59.

49 Burt, 1929, p. 290.

50 Hall, op. cit., p. 58.

51 Urged by Hall, 1926, in Home Office, 1927, and included in the 1933 Act in Section 35. This duty was stressed in the Home Office circular of 9.8.33 which drew attention to the Act, included in Hall and Morrison, 1933.

52 Hall, 1926, p. 96; Burt, 1925, appendix and 1929; Fry, 1924; Smith, 1924; Board of Education, 1920, p. 40; Home Office, 1924, p. 9; National Council for Mental Hygiene, 1924.

53 See also Home Office, 1927, p. 43.
54 See the Fifth Report of the Home Office Children's Branch, 1938.

7   The psychological family

1 For a good account of the early medical literature, see Garrison and Apt, 1965.
2 Underwood, 1797, vol. 3, p. 152. Spurzheim, 1817, p. 106; Burrows, 1828, p. 244; quoted in Browne, 1860, p. 286.
3 Browne, loc. cit. Cf. also West, 1854, p. 189. West introduced a separate lecture on disorders of the mind in childhood in the 3rd edition of his book, apologising for its fragmentary nature due to the lack of access of medical men to information on this type of affliction of early life. He pointed to the similarity between disorders of the mind in childhood and moral insanity – a theme which will be taken up later. See also Albutt, 1892, and Maudsley, 1879, ch. 5.
4 Browne, 1860, pp. 289ff.
5 See Parkinson, 1807; Buchan, 1807.
6 Maudsley, 1879, ch. 3; Clouston, 1892; Craig, 1905; Cole, 1913; Bruce, 1906.
7 Cf. Cole, 1913, p. 287.
8 Henderson and Gillespie, 1927, p. 371.
9 Henderson and Gillespie, 1932, p. vii.
10 Ibid., p. 488.
11 See Armstrong, 1983, pp. 19-31.
12 Cameron, 1919, p. 31.
13 For example Jones's influential *Papers on Psychoanalysis*, first published in 1912; Pfister's *Psychoanalytic Method*, 1917; Low's *Introduction to Psychoanalysis*, 1920. Jones' own reflections on the history of psychoanalysis in Britain are contained in his *Free Associations*, 1959, and in Jones, 1945 and 1957, vol. 3.
14 It was, however, influential in other areas. For a discussion of the influence of psychoanalytic theories of family, kinship and sexuality on marxism and anthropology, see Coward, 1983, chs 6 and 8.
15 The BMA eventually reported favourably and recognised psycho-analysis as an authorised medical speciality. Cf. Yelloly, 1980, p. 35.
16 Hart, 1912; Brown, 1913, discussed in Yelloly, 1980, p. 29. William Brown also wrote some standard texts on mental measurement. See Brown, 1911, Brown and Thompson, 1921, and the discussion in chapter 5 above.
17 Hearnshaw, 1964, pp. 245-6, has a concise account of the debate. See War Office, 1922 and Mott, 1919.
18 In Miller, ed., 1920, p. 62.
19 The collection of papers edited by Hugh Crichton Miller is a good index: Miller, ed., 1920. Among the contributors were H. Crichton Miller, J.A. Hadfield, W.H.R. Rivers, M. Culpin and W. McDougall. Brown also worked with shell-shocked soldiers, as Medical Officer in Charge of the Craiglockhart War Hospital for Neurasthenic Officers.

20 The language is McDougall's, in Miller, 1920.
21 McDougall, 1908; Trotter, 1916; Shand, 1914. Janet's conception was especially promoted in the work of Hart, 1912, and Brown – for example his *Psychology and Psychotherapy*, 1921.
22 Rivers in Miller, ed., op. cit., and also in Rivers, 1920; McDougall in Miller, ed., op. cit.
23 See especially the papers by Hadfield, Culpin and McDougall in Miller, op. cit.
24 Hart, 1912; Tansley, 1920; Hadfield, 1923; McDougall, 1926; Miller, 1921, 1922; Gordon, 1926; MacCurdy, 1923; Raven, 1929. McDougall was the most outspoken protagonist in the opposition of the new psychology to psychoanalysis. See especially his 1926 and 1936. Susan Brierley, who was later – as Susan Isaacs – to return to Freud via Melanie Klein, also contributed. See Brierley, 1921.
25 McDougall, 1923, p. 110. Cf. McDougall, 1908.
26 Shand, 1914.
27 Trotter, 1916.
28 Tansley, 1920, p. 242. Cf. also Miller, 1921, 1922.
29 Cf. Tansley, op. cit., chs 19 and 20 and Miller, 1922, chs 9 and 10.
30 Cf. Hadfield, 1923, chs 2 and 3.
31 Brierley, 1921, p. 40.
32 It should be pointed out that there were texts which attempted to span the gap between orthodox psychoanalysis and the new psychology, by introducing heretical elements into psychoanalysis without recognising any conceptual incompatibility. Flugel's *Psychoanalytic Study of the Family*, 1921, was the most important of these. It was the third volume published in the orthodox International Library of Psychoanalysis, and contained acknowledgments to both Jones and Burt, and favourable references to Hart, Trotter, Shand and McDougall. From the arguments so produced, Flugel derived numerous maxims concerning appropriate parental conduct, together with analyses of the psychical origins of criminality, delinquency and social unrest as a consequence of early familial relations. Orthodox analysts kept a friendly distance from Flugel, but his book sold steadily in Britain year after year and was one of the financial successes of the Hogarth Press, which disseminated orthodox Freudian thought in Britain. (Cf. Coward, 1983, pp. 235-6.)
33 This was established early on, in the work with the shell shocked. E.g. Brown, 1921, ch. 1.
34 Hug-Hellmuth, 1921; Klein, 1923, 1927, 1932; Isaacs, 1928, 1930, 1933. Whilst some analysts objected to the whole principle of child analysis, Klein was initially supported by Jones and others. The initial disputation was with Anna Freud, who had started her own work with older children in Vienna in the early 1920s. Anna Freud's work on child analysis was published in America in 1928, but in England not until 1946. Nonetheless the lines of dispute were laid out in a Symposium on Child Analysis held in London in 1927. Klein disputed Anna Freud's contention that the child could not form a transference neurosis and that child analysis should be educational, seeking to

strengthen a feeble super-ego. She also disagreed with Anna Freud's views that valuable work with children could only be done in the positive transference, and that the interpretation of symbolic meaning of children's play in the 'play technique' was of dubious validity. For present purposes, these disputes achieved significance only after the Second World War, when Anna Freud's ego psychology took hold in England and became influential both in therapeutic practice and in more general conceptions of the role of early mother-child relations in later disturbances. *The Ego and Mechanisms of Defence* was published in translation in England in 1937. A second axis of dispute, involving Klein and Edward Glover in particular, concerned the competence of lay analysts to discuss psychosis.

35 E.g. Isaacs, 1935 ed., 1937.
36 Isaacs, 1930, p. 8. See also 1933, esp. pp. 385-6.
37 See the much reprinted *The Nursery Years*, 1929, the pamphlets cited above n. 35, and the chapter on 'Problems and crises in early development', in 1933.
38 Griffiths, 1935; Lowenfeld, 1935.
39 The problems with this 'folk myth' are well discussed in Riley, 1979. See also Riley, 1983, esp. ch. 5.
40 Bowlby, 1944. See also Bowlby, 1940 and the discussion in Riley, op. cit. For the development of Winnicott's work, see his papers collected in *Through Pediatrics to Psychoanalysis*, 1975.
41 As Burt points out, in his criticism of the concepts of moral insanity and moral imbecility in *The Young Delinquent*, 1925, p. 36, the term 'moral insanity' was first used by Pritchard in 1835, and especially developed in Maudsley's work – see Maudsley, 1868. For the categories of mental defect in the 1913 Act, see the discussion in chapter 6 above.
42 Mercier, 1917; Tredgold, 1917; East, 1923. See also the other contributors to the Symposium held jointly by the Educational and Medical Sections of the *British Psychology Society*, and published in the *British Journal of Medical Psychology* – Shrubsall, 1923; Stoddart, 1923; and Burt, 1923. See for the 'medical' view, Maudsley, 1872, pp. 31-65 and Tredgold, 1914, p. 326. The issue is discussed extensively in Burt, 1925, pp. 34ff.
43 Burt, 1917.
44 Burt, 1923 and, for the most extended discussion, Burt, 1925, ch. 2.
45 Burt, 1925, p. 58.
46 Burt, 1917.
47 Burt, 1918; Sybil Clement Brown, pioneer of psychiatric social work in England, was fond of referring to this lecture – cf. Brown, 1939a, 1939b.
48 Burt, 1918, p. 5.
49 Burt, 1925.
50 Ibid., pp. 399-400.
51 Ibid., pp. 420-537. On reformation see especially pp. 515ff.
52 Ibid., p. 570. Cf. above. The principal sources on psychoanalysis that Burt refers to are Flugel's *The Psycho-analytic Study of the Family*

(1921), Pfister's *Psychoanalytic Method* (1917), Hug-Hellmuth's article on child analysis, 1921, and Melanie Klein's article 'The role of the school in the libidinal development of the child' (1924), as well as Freud's *Introductory Lectures on Psychoanalysis* (1922) and Jones, *Papers on Psychoanalysis* (1923).

53 Burt, op. cit., pp. 4-5.
54 Ibid., pp. 610-11. Burt had first put forward his scheme in a Report to the London County Council on the future organisation of the Psychological Service for Schools.

8   Psychology and the clinic

1 The clinic, which was in Stoke-on-Trent, is reported in the Underwood Report on maladjusted children, Ministry of Education, 1955, p. 8.
2 Cameron, 1919, was based on experience in the Children's Department of Guy's Hospital, London.
3 This account relies on Boll, 1962.
4 My account draws upon Dicks, 1970, and the Reports issued by the Clinic from 1928 onwards – Tavistock Clinic, 1928, etc. The description of Crichton Miller is from Irvine's (1933) sycophantic biography.
5 See for example, Kimmins, 1927.
6 Cf. Home Office, 1932 and Dicks, op. cit.
7 See Miller, 1921, 1922, and Dicks, op. cit.
8 Lord, ed., 1930. Cf. Dicks, op. cit.
9 See, for example, National Council for Mental Hygiene, 1928, p. 27.
10 Ministry of Education, 1955, pp. 7-13; Keir, 1952; Yelloly, 1980, pp. 46-52; Burt, 1955; Burbury et al., 1950.
11 Fry, 1924; Smith, 1924.
12 Strachey, 1926.
13 On English discussions of child guidance in America see Shrubsall, 1927; Crowley, 1928; Fairfield, 1928; Hardcastle, 1933. See also Stevenson and Smith, 1934.
14 Healy, 1915.
15 Quoted in the Underwood Report, Ministry of Education, 1955, p. 10.
16 Burke and Miller, 1929. Miller went on to head the Children's Department of the Tavistock in 1933, when he was active in the move from family investigation to family therapy, discussed below.
17 See the history given in Institute of Child Psychology, 1934.
18 Lowenfeld, 1935. See also the *Institute of Child Psychology News Bulletin*, published from 1936, and renamed *Child Psychology* in 1938, which devoted much of its space to discussion of the genesis of emotional difficulties and the role of play therapy.
19 Pailthorpe, 1932.
20 See Glover, 1944.
21 On the growth of the Prison Psychological Service, see Richards,

1977. For an influential text produced from the ISTD, see Friedlander, 1946.

22 Board of Education, 1955, p. 12.

23 Ibid.

24 This is drawn from the Annual Reports (Child Guidance Council, 1931, etc.), from the Reports of Inter-Clinic Conferences (Child Guidance Council, 1935 and 1937), and from other publications (Child Guidance Council 1938a, 1938b). See also the contributions by the staff of the Tavistock Clinic to the volumes of Probation from 1929-1934 (National Association of Probation Officers, 1929-1934).

25 E. Miller, ed., 1937. The quotes are from Miller's Introduction.

26 See the materials collected in *Advances in Understanding the Child*, Home and Schools Council, 1935. The Library was under the General Editorship of Kimmins. See, for example, Drever and Drummond, 1930.

27 See Glover, 1932, for a discussion of differing medico-psychological conceptions of normality.

28 Burt, ed., 1933. The series also included Jones on the unconscious mind. Cf. also Hadfield, ed., 1935.

29 Moodie, 1931.

30 For a description of this transformation in America, see Hardcastle, 1933, p. 335.

31 E.g. Fox, quoted in Yelloly, 1980, pp. 47-8.

32 E.g. Rees and Robinson, 1930.

33 E.g. Raven, 1925.

34 E.g. Miller, 1929; Gillespie, 1933; Cosens, 1933.

35 Cf. Richmond, 1917; Robinson, 1930.

36 Timms, 1964, p. 48.

37 Cf. Yelloly, 1980, ch. 3. Yelloly argues that *psychoanalysis* had little impact on social work in the 1930s, but her prioritisation of psychoanalysis as the index of social work's modernity obscures the specific rationale of the psychosocial strategy.

38 Brown, 1939a, p. 41.

39 Brown, 1939b.

40 See especially Burt, 1925, chs 1 and 14 and Burt, 1929.

41 MacCalman, in Gordon, ed., 1939, p. 259. Things were a bit different in Scotland, where the clinics grew out of the education service – five out of the eleven Scottish clinics were directed by psychologists.

42 The lines of argument have scarcely changed. See, for example, the papers given to a British Psychological Society Symposium on Psychologists and Psychiatrists in the Child Guidance Service, held in March 1951. Kennedy, 1951, argues the medical case; Davidson, 1952, argues for a division of function and collaboration. McCallum, 1952, shows the educational origin and direction of the Scottish service and suggests that this provides the ideal opportunity for the introduction of psychologists and psychiatrists without conflict. Keir, 1952, reconstructs the history of child guidance to minimise the psychiatric input and locate its roots in biology and education, suggesting something like a medical take over of the movement in the 1930s.

43 See the Annual Reports of the Child Guidance Council over this period; Moodie, 1931; Child Guidance Council, 1935, 1937.

44 Gordon, ed., 1939, esp. chapter by MacCalman.

45 Ibid., n. 44. See also the chapters by E. Miller and Rees of the Tavistock in Culpin, 1931.

46 For these discussions see Child Guidance Council, 1935, 1937, and the remarks on English psychologists made by Hardcastle in his (1933) report on the American situation.

47 Darwin, 1877; Preyer, 1894; Shinn, 1893; Sully, 1895; Claparede, 1911; Stern, 1914. The work of G. Stanley Hall and Mark Baldwin, with its doctrine of recapitulation, was very influential in America – see Hall, 1904, and Baldwin, 1895. For a representative Child Study text in England, see Drummond, 1907. See also the discussion in Caws, 1949.

48 In this connection, it is significant that Jean Piaget's first psychological work was on standardising Binet's tests of intelligence. See Piaget's contribution to Boring et al., ed., 1968.

49 See Gesell, 1925, 1928.

50 See the reviews in Buhler, 1931; Collins, 1939; and Earl, 1939.

51 Bridges, 1931.

52 Isaacs, 1933, p. 6.

53 Isaacs, 1931, p. 5.

54 Cattell, 1946, p. xvii.

55 Cattell, 1936a.

56 Galton, 1883, pp. 133-46. Jung, 1918.

57 Burt, 1925, p. 402.

58 Cf. ibid.

59 Collins, 1925, 1927; Vernon, 1933b.

60 Downey, 1923. Cf. Collins, 1923; Burt, 1925, pp. 403-5; Oates, 1928; Richardson, 1929.

61 Cf. Collins, 1925, Burt, 1925, pp. 405-13.

62 Burt, 1938; Cattell, 1933a; Oates, 1929. Cattell always looked on the bright side, see 1936b, and went on to produce his 16 Personality Factor Test – see, for example, Cattell, 1957. Much could be written on the significance of the Second World War and the demand for a technique for assessing the personalities of recruits.

63 Earl, 1939.

64 Burt, 1925, pp. 414-9; Valentine, 1929. Burt, it appears, may also have considered himself able to assess parental intelligence in this way. Cf. chapter 5, n. 2, above.

65 Burt, 1925, p. 9.

66 Freud, 1928, pp. 184-5.

Conclusion

1 Murphy and Kovach, 1972, p. 3.

2 For 'paradigms' see Kuhn, 1970, and Barnes, 1982. A fairly recent, but somewhat inconclusive debate attempted to apply Kuhn's notion of scientific revolutions to psychology, to establish if it had reached

the stage of 'normal science'. Cf. Palermo, 1971; Warren, 1971; Weimer and Palermo, 1973; Weimer, 1974.

3 Quoted in Boring, 1929, p. vii.

4 E.g. Boring, 1929; Brett, 1912-21; Murphy, 1928; Flugel, 1933.

5 These terms come from Bachelard. See, in particular, Bachelard, 1951 and the accounts given in Lecourt, 1975; Gaukroger, 1976 and Bhaskar, 1975.

6 See especially Canguilhem, 1977.

7 Canguilhem [1956], 1980.

8 Canguilhem [1943], 1978, p. 43.

9 Ibid.

Bibliography

Official Publications are listed at the end.

ANON (1718) *The Infant's Lawyer: or the Law (Ancient and Modern) Relating to Infants* London: J. Nutt for St. John Baker.

ANON (1865) Idiot asylums. *Edinburgh Review* 122, 37-74.

ABELSON, A.R. (1911) The measurement of mental ability of 'backward' children. *British Journal of Psychology*, 4, 268-314.

ABRAMS, Philip (1968) *The Origins of British Sociology 1834-1914* Chicago: University of Chicago Press.

ACKERKNECHT, Erwin H. (1969) *A Short History of Psychiatry* (tr. S. Wolf) London: Hafner.

ADDISON, Paul (1977) *The Road to 1945* London: Quartet.

ADLAM, Diana and ROSE, Nikolas (1981) The Politics of Psychiatry. In *Politics and Power: 3* London: Routledge & Kegan Paul.

ALBUTT, T. Clifford (1892) Insanity in children. In vol. 1 of Daniel Hack Tuke, ed., *A Dictionary of Psychological Medicine*, 2 vols, London: Churchill.

ALDEN, Percy (1905) *The Unemployed, A National Question* London: King.

ALLEN, G. (1976) Genetics, Eugenics and Society: Internalists and externalists in contemporary history of science. *Social Studies of Science*, 6, 105-22.

ARMEN, Jean-Claude (1974) *Gazelle Boy* London: Bodley Head.

ARMSTRONG, David (1983) *Political Anatomy of the Body* Cambridge: Cambridge University Press.

ARNAULD, Antoine [1661] (1964) *The Art of Thinking* (tr. J. Dickoff and P. James) Indianapolis: Bobbs-Merrill.

ASHDOWN, Margaret and BROWN, S. Clement (1953) *Social Service and Mental Health* London: Routledge & Kegan Paul.

ATTLEE, Clement R. (1920) *The Social Worker* London: G. Bell & Sons.

BACHELARD, Gaston (1951) *L'activité rationaliste de la physique contemporaine* Paris: PUF.

BALDWIN, James Mark (1895) *Mental Development in the Child and the Race* New York: Macmillan.

BALLARD, Philip B. (1920) *Mental Tests* London: Hodder & Stoughton.
BALLARD, Philip B. (1922) *Group Tests of Intelligence* London: Hodder & Stoughton.
BARKER, David (1982) How to curb the fertility of the Edwardian unfit. Unpublished paper given to Society for the Social History of Medicine conference on Mental Handicap, 24.4.82.
BARNES, Barry (1974) *Scientific Knowledge and Sociological Theory* London: Routledge & Kegan Paul.
BARNES, Barry (1977) *Interests and the Growth of Knowledge* London: Routledge & Kegan Paul.
BARNES, Barry (1982) *T.S. Kuhn and Social Science* London: Macmillan.
BARNES, Earl (1901) A forgotten student of child study. *The Paediologist*, 3, 120-3.
BARNETT, Samuel A. and BARNETT, Henrietta (1909) *Towards Social Reform* London: Fisher Unwin.
BARTLETT, Frederic C. (1928) Temperament and social class. *Eugenics Review*, 20, 25-8.
BASNETT, M. (1969) *Voluntary Social Action: A History of the National Council of Social Service, 1919-1969* London: National Council of Social Service.
BATTIE, William [1758] (1962) *A Treatise on Madness* London: Dawsons.
BAUDOUIN, Louis Charles (1924) *Suggestion and Auto-suggestion* (tr E. and C. Paul) London: George Allen & Unwin.
BAUMGARTEN, Franziska (1936) Character traits. *British Journal of Psychology*, 36, 289-98.
BEAMES, Thomas (1850) *The Rookeries of London* London: Bosworth.
BECCARIA BONESANA, Cesare (1804) *Elementi de economia publica* Milano.
BENTHAM, Jeremy (1843) Principles of the civic code. In *The Works of Jeremy Bentham* (ed. J. Bowring), vol. 1, Edinburgh: William Tait.
BETTELHEIM, Bruno (1967) *The Empty Fortress* New York: Free Press.
BEVERIDGE, William H. (1905) The problems of the unemployed. *Sociological Papers*, 3, 324-31.
BEVERIDGE, William H. (1909) *Unemployment. A Problem of Industry* London: Longmans.
BHASKAR, Roy (1975) Feyerabend and Bachelard: two philosophies of science. *New Left Review*, 94, 31-55.
BINET, Alfred and HENRI, Victor (1895) La psychologie individuelle. *L'Année psychologique*, 2, 411-65.
BINET, Alfred and SIMON, Theodule (1905a) Sur la nécessité d'établir un diagnostic scientifique des états inférieurs de l'intelligence. *L'Année psychologique*, 11, 163-90.
BINET, Alfred and SIMON, Theodule (1905b) Méthodes nouvelles pour le diagnostic du niveau intellectuel des anormaux. *L'Année. psychologique*, 11, 191-244.
BINET, Alfred and SIMON, Theodule (1908) Le développement de l'intelligence chez les enfants. *L'Année psychologique*, 14, 1-94.

BINET, Alfred and SIMON, Theodule (1909) L'intelligence des imbéciles. *L'Année psychologique*, 15, 1-147.

BINET, Alfred and SIMON, Theodule [1907] (1914) *Mentally Defective Children* (tr W.B. Drummond) London: Edward Arnold.

BINET, Alfred and SIMON, Theodule (1916) *The Development of Intelligence in Children* (translation of articles from *L'Année psychologique* by E.S. Kite) Baltimore: Williams & Watkins.

BINGHAM, Peregrine (1816) *The Law of Infancy and Couveture* London: Butterworth.

BLACKER, Carlos P. (1952) *Eugenics. Galton and After* London: Duckworth.

BLACKSTONE, William (1765-9) *Commentaries on the Laws of England* Oxford: Clarendon Press.

BLAND, Lucy (1984) Cleansing the portals of life: Campaigns against VD in early twentieth century Britain. In *The State and the Crisis of Hegemony 1880-1920*, London: Hutchinson.

BLAUG, Mark (1963) The myth of the Old Poor Law and the making of the new. *Journal of Economic History*, 23, 151-84.

BLAUG, Mark (1964) The Poor Law Report re-examined. *Journal of Economic History*, 24, 229-45.

BLOOR, David (1976) *Knowledge and Social Imagery* London: Routledge & Kegan Paul.

BOLL, Theophilus E. (1962) Mary Sinclair and the Medico-Psychological Clinic of London. *Proceedings of the American Philosophical Society*, 106, 310-26.

BOOTH, Charles (1892) Inaugural address. *Journal of the Royal Statistical Society*, 60, 521-57.

BOOTH, Charles (1892-97) *Life and Labour of the People in London* (10 vols) London: Macmillan.

BORING, Edwin G. (1929) *A History of Experimental Psychology* London: Century Co.

BORING, Edwin G., LANGFELD, Herbert S., WERNER, Heinz, and YERKES, Robert M. (eds) [1952] (1968) *A History of Psychology in Autobiography, Vol IV* New York: Russell & Russell.

BOTTOMORE, Tom and GOODE, Patrick (eds) (1978) *Austro-Marxism* Oxford: Oxford University Press.

BOWLBY, John (1940) *Personality and Mental Illness* London: Kegan Paul.

BOWLBY, John (1944) Forty-four juvenile thieves: their characters and home lives. *International Journal of Psychoanalysis*, 25, 19-53 and 107-128.

BOYD, William (1914) *From Locke to Montessori* London: Harrap & Co.

BRADBY, Mary K. (1919) *Psycho-analysis and its Place in Life* London: Hodder & Stoughton.

BREMNER, R.H. (1956) Scientific philanthropy, 1873-93. *Social Service Review*, 30, 168-73.

BRETT, George S. (1912-1921) *A History of Psychology*, 3 vols, London: Allen & Co.

BRIDGELAND, M. (1971) *Pioneer Work with Maladjusted Children* London: Staples.

BRIDGES, Katherine Banham (1931) *The Social and Emotional Development of the Pre-School Child.* London: Kegan Paul, Trench, Trubner.

BRIERLEY, Susan (afterwards Isaacs) (1921) *An Introduction to Psychology* London: Methuen.

BRITISH MEDICAL JOURNAL (1903) National health and military service. *British Medical Journal,* July 25th 1903, 207-8.

BROWN, J. (1968) Charles Booth and labour colonies. *Economic History Review,* 21, 349-60.

BROWN, S. Clement (1939a) Family case work and mental health. *Charity Organisation Quarterly,* 13, 40-50.

BROWN, S. Clement (1939b) The methods of social case-workers. In F.C. Bartlett, M. Ginsberg, E.J. Lingren and R.H. Thouless (eds), *The Study of Society* London: Kegan Paul, Trench, Trubner and Co.

BROWN, William (1911) *The Essentials of Mental Measurement* London: Cambridge University Press.

BROWN, William (1913) Freud's theory of dreams. *The Lancet,* 19.4.1913, 1182.

BROWN, William (1921) *Psychology and Psychotherapy* London: Edwin Arnold.

BROWN, William (1923) *Talks on Psychotherapy* London: University of London Press.

BROWN, William and THOMSON, Godfrey H. (1921) *The Essentials of Mental Measurement* London: Cambridge University Press.

BROWNE, James Crichton (1860) Psychical diseases of early life. *Journal of Mental Science,* 6, 284-320.

BRUCE, Lewis C. (1906) *Studies in Clinical Psychiatry* London: Macmillan.

BRYANT, Sophie (1886) Experiments in testing the character of schoolchildren. *Journal of the Royal Anthropological Institute,* 15, 338-49.

BUFFON, George-Louis Leclerc, Comte de (1749) *Histoire naturelle de l'homme* Paris: Imprimerie Royale.

BUHLER, Charlotte (1931) The social behaviour of the child. In C. Murchison (ed.), *Handbook of Child Psychology* Worcester, Mass: Clark University Press.

BURBURY, Winifred M., BALINT, E.M. and YAPP, B.J. (1950) *An Introduction to Child Guidance* London: Macmillan.

BURKE, Noel H.M. and MILLER, Emanuel (1929) Child mental hygiene – its history, methods and problems. *British Journal of Medical Psychology,* 9, 218-42.

BURN, John L. (1947) *Recent Advances in Public Health* London: Churchill.

BURNS, Charles L.C. (1933) Child guidance on the continent. *British Journal of Educational Psychology,* 3, 251-67.

BURROW, John W. (1966) *Evolution and Society* London: Cambridge University Press.

BURROWS, George (1828) *Commentaries on Insanity* London: Underwood.

BURT, Cyril L. (1909) Experimental tests of general intelligence. *British Journal of Psychology*, 3, 94-177.

BURT, Cyril L. (1911) Experimental tests and their relation to general intelligence. *Journal of Experimental Pedagogy*, 1, 93-112.

BURT, Cyril L. (1914) The measurement of intelligence by the Binet tests. *Eugenics Review*, 6, 36-50 and 140-52.

BURT, Cyril L. (1915) *General and specific factors underlying the primary emotions.* Manchester: British Association.

BURT, Cyril L. (1917) The unstable child. *Child Study*, 10, 3, 61-79.

BURT, Cyril L. (1918) Individual psychology and social work. *Charity Organisation Quarterly*, 43, 4-19 and 51-60.

BURT, Cyril L. (1921) *Mental and Scholastic Tests* London: London County Council.

BURT, Cyril L. (1923a) The causal factors of juvenile crime. *British Journal of Medical Psychology*, 3, 1-33.

BURT, Cyril L. (1923b) Delinquency and mental defect. *British Journal of Medical Psychology*, 3, 168-78.

BURT, Cyril L. (1925) *The Young Delinquent* (The Sub-Normal School Child, vol. 1) London: University of London Press.

BURT, Cyril L. (1927) *The Measurement of Mental Capacities* The Henderson Trust Lecture, No. VII. Edinburgh: Oliver & Boyd.

BURT, Cyril L. (1929) The psychological clinic. *Howard Journal*, 2, 290-4.

BURT, Cyril L. (1933) *How the Mind Works* London: George Allen & Unwin.

BURT, Cyril L. (1938) The analysis of temperament. *British Journal of Medical Psychology*, 17, 158-88.

BURT, Cyril L. (1949) Recent discussions of juvenile delinquency. *British Journal of Educational Psychology*, 19, 32-43.

BURT, Cyril L. (1955) The historical development of the guidance movement in education – England. In *The Year Book of Education*, 1955, ed R.K. Hall and J.A. Lauwerys, London: Evans.

BURT, Cyril L. [1952] (1968) Cyril Burt. In E. Boring, H. Langfield, H. Werner and R. Yerkes (eds), *A History of Psychology in Autobiography, vol. IV* New York: Russell & Russell.

BURT, Cyril L. et al. (1926) *A Study in Vocational Guidance* Industrial Fatigue Research Board Report No. 33. London: HMSO.

BUSS, A. (1976) Galton and the birth of differential psychology and eugenics: social, political and economic forces. *Journal of the History of the Behavioural Sciences*, 12, 47-59.

CAMERON, Hector C. (1919) *The Nervous Child* London: Oxford University Press.

CAMERON, Hector C. (1955) *The British Paediatric Association, 1928-1952* London: British Paediatric Association.

CANGUILHEM, Georges (1968) *Études d'histoire et de philosophie des sciences* Paris: Vrin.

CANGUILHEM, Georges (1977) *Ideologie et rationalité* Paris: Vrin.

CANGUILHEM, Georges [1943, 1963-6] (1978) *On the Normal and the Pathological* (tr. Carolyn Fawcett) Dordrecht: Reidel.

CANGUILHEM, Georges (1980) What is psychology? (tr. H. Davies) *I & C*, 7, 37-50.

CANTOR, G.N. and SHAPIN, S. (1975) Phrenology in the early nineteenth-century Edinburgh: an historiographic discussion. *Annals of Science*, 32, 195-256.

CARPENTER, Mary (1851) *Reformatory Schools for the Children of the Perishing and Dangerous Classes, and for Juvenile Offenders* London: Gilpin.

CARPENTER, William B. (1842) *Principles of Human Physiology* London: Churchill.

CASSIRER, Ernst (1951) *The Philosophy of the Enlightenment* (tr. F. Koelln and J. Pettigrove) Princeton, New Jersey: Princeton University Press.

CATTELL, James McKeen (1890) Mental tests and measurements (followed by some remarks by F. Galton). *Mind*, 15, 373-80.

CATTELL, James McKeen and BRYANT, Sophie (1889) Mental association investigated by experiment. *Mind*, 14, 230-50.

CATTELL, James McKeen and FARAND, L. (1896) Physical and mental measurements of the students of Columbia University. *Psychological Review*, 3, 618-48.

CATTELL, Raymond B. (1933a) Temperamental tests: 1. Temperament. *British Journal of Psychology*, 23, 308-29.

CATTELL, Raymond B. (1933b) Temperamental tests. 2. Tests. *British Journal of Psychology*, 24, 20-49.

CATTELL, Raymond B. (1936a) *A Guide to Mental Testing for Psychological Clinics, Schools and Industrial Psychologists* London: University of London Press.

CATTELL, Raymond B. (1936b) Temperament tests in clinical practice. *British Journal of Medical Psychology*, 16, 43-62.

CATTELL, Raymond B. (1946) *Description and Measurement of Personality* London: Harrap.

CATTELL, Raymond B. (1957) *Personality and Motivation Structure and Measurement* New York: Harcourt, Brace and World.

CAWS, A.G. (1949) Child study fifty years ago. *Bulletin of the British Psychological Society*, 1, 3, 104-9.

CHADWICK, Edwin [1842] (1965) *Report on the Sanitary Conditions of the Labouring Population of Great Britain* (ed. M.W. Flynn) Edinburgh: Edinburgh University Press.

CHAMBERLAIN, Joseph (1903) *Imperial Union and Tarrif Reform* London: Grant Richards.

CHARITY ORGANIZATION SOCIETY (1877) *Report of a Special Committee on the Education and Care of Idiots, Imbeciles and Harmless Lunatics* and Report of a Deputation on the Subject to the President of the Local Government Board. London: Longmans, Green & Co.

CHARITY ORGANIZATION SOCIETY (1893) *The Feeble-minded Child and Adult* London.

CHARLES, Enid (1934) *The Twilight of Parenthood* London: Watts.

CHESELDON, William (1728a) An account of some observations made by a Young Gentleman, who was born blind, or lost his sight so early, that he had no rememberance of ever having seen, and was couch'd between 13 and 14 Years of age. *Philosophical Transactions*, 35, 447-50.

CHESELDON, William (1728b) Explanation of the Instruments used, in a new operation on the Eyes. *Philosophical Transactions*, 35, 451-2.

CHILD, Josiah (1690) *Discourse about Trade* London: Sowie.

CHILD GUIDANCE COUNCIL (1931) (1932 etc.) *Annual Report for 1931 (1932 etc.)* London: Child Guidance Council.

CHILD GUIDANCE COUNCIL (1935) *Report of the Inter Clinic Conference* London: Child Guidance Council.

CHILD GUIDANCE COUNCIL (1937) *Proceedings of the Inter-Clinic Conference of Great Britain, 1937*, London: Child Guidance Council.

CHILD GUIDANCE COUNCIL (1938a) *What is Child Guidance?* London: Child Guidance Council.

CHILD GUIDANCE COUNCIL (1938b) *Young Offenders and the Courts* London: Child Guidance Council.

CLAPAREDE, E. (1911) *Experimental Pedagogy and the Psychology of the Child* New York: Longmans Green.

CLARKE, A.D.B. and CLARKE, Ann M. (1974) *Mental Deficiency* (3rd edn) London: Methuen.

CLOUSTON, Thomas S. (1892) Developmental insanities and psychoses . . . the insanities of puberty and adolescence. In vol. 1 of Daniel Hack Tuke (ed.) *A Dictionary of Psychological Medicine*, 2 vols, London: Churchill.

COATS, A.W. (1960) Economic thought and poor law policy in the eighteenth century. *Economic History Review*, 2nd series, 13.

COHN, Hermann L. [1883] (1886) *The Hygiene of the Eye in Schools* (tr. W.P. Turnbull) London: Simpkin, Marshall and Co.

COLQUHOUN, Patrick (1797) *A Treatise on the Police of the Metropolis* (5th edn) London: Dilly.

COLQUHOUN, Patrick (1800) *A Treatise on the Police of the Metropolis* (6th edn) London: Mawman.

COLQUHOUN, Patrick (1806) *A Treatise on Indigence* London: Hatchard.

COLE, Robert H. (1913) *Mental Diseases* London: University of London Press.

COLLINS, Mary (1925) Character and temperament tests. *British Journal of Psychology*, 16, 89-99.

COLLINS, Mary (1927) British norms for the Pressey Cross-Out Test. *British Journal of Psychology*, 18, 121-33.

COLLINS, Mary (1939) Modern trends in child psychology. In F.C. Bartlett et al (eds) *The Study of Society*, London: Kegan Paul, Trench, Trubner.

COMBE, Andrew (1831) *Observations on Mental Derangement* Edinburgh: John Anderson.

CONDILLAC, Etienne Bonnot Abbé de [1746] (1971) *Essay on the*

Origin of Human Knowledge (reprinted from the 1756 translation of *Essai sur les origines des connaissances humaines* by T. Nugent) Gainsville, Florida: Scholars Facsimiles.

CONDILLAC, Etienne Bonnot Abbé de [1754] (1930) *Treatise on the Sensations* (tr. of *Traité des sensations*, by G. Carr). London: Favil Press.

CONDILLAC, Etienne Bonnot Abbé de (n.d.) *Principes de la grammaire Francoise* Nantes: Busseuil.

CONDILLAC, Etienne Bonnot Abbé de (1771) *Traité des systèmes* Amsterdam et Leipsick.

CONDILLAC, Etienne Bonnot Abbé de (1775) *Cours d'étude par l'instruction du prince de Parme* Parme: Imprimerie Royale.

CONDILLAC, Etienne Bonnot Abbé de [1780] (1809) *The Logic of Condillac* (tr. of *La Logique*, by Joseph Neef). Philadelphia.

COOTER, Roger (1981) Phrenology and British Alienists. In A.T. Scull, ed., *Mad-Houses, Mad-Doctors and Madmen* London: Athlone.

COSENS, Marjorie (1933) Psychology and social casework. *Charity Organization Quarterly*, 7, 63-73.

COWAN, Ruth S. (1972) Francis Galton's statistical ideas: the influence of eugenics. *Isis*, 63, 509-28.

COWAN, Ruth S. (1977) Nature and nurture: the interplay of biology and politics in the work of Francis Galton. *Studies in History of Biology*, 1, 133-208.

COWARD, Rosalind (1983) *Patriarchal Precedents* London: Routledge & Kegan Paul.

CRAIG, Maurice (1905) *Psychological Medicine* London: Churchill.

CRANEFIELD, P. (1961) A seventeenth-century view of mental deficiency and schizophrenia – Thomas Willis on stupidity or foolishness. *Bulletin of the History of Medicine*, 35, 291-316.

CRANEFIELD, Paul F. (1962) The discovery of cretinism. *Bulletin of the History of Medicine*, 36, 489-511.

CRANEFIELD, Paul F. and FEDERN, Walter (1967) The begatting of fools, translation of Paracelsus, De Generatione Stultorum, with annotated discussion. *Bulletin of the History of Medicine*, 41, 56-74 and 161-74.

CRICHTON, Alexander (1798) *An inquiry into the nature and origins of mental derangement* (2 vols) London: Davies.

CRITCHLEY, Thomas A. (1967) *A History of Police in England and Wales, 1900-1966* London: Constable.

CROWLEY, Ralph H. (1910) *The Hygiene of School Life* London: Methuen.

CROWLEY, Ralph H. (1928) *Child Guidance Clinics, with Special Reference to the American Experience* London: Child Guidance Council.

CULLEN, Michael J. (1975) *The Statistical Movement in Early Victorian Britain* Hassocks, Sussex: Harvester.

CULPIN, Millais (1931) *Recent Advances in the Study of the Psychoneuroses* London: Churchill.

CULVERWELL, Edward, P. (1913) *The Montessori Principles*

and Practice London: Bell.

DARWIN, Charles [1859] (1968) *The Origin of Species* Harmondsworth: Penguin.

DARWIN, Charles (1868) *The Variations of Animals and Plants under Domestication* London: John Murray.

DARWIN, Charles (1877) Biographical sketch of an infant. *Mind*, 2, 285-94.

DAVEY, Herbert (1913) *The Law Relating to the Mentally Defective* London: Stevens & Sons.

DAVIDSON, Mary (1952) The relation between psychologists and psychiatrists in the service of maladjusted adults and children. *British Journal of Educational Psychology*, 22, 1-4.

DEACON, A. (1976) *In Search of the Scrounger: the Administration of Unemployment Benefit in Britain, 1920-1931* London: Bell.

DENNIS, W. (1941) The significance of feral man. *American Journal of Psychology*, 54, 425-32.

DICEY, Albert V. (1905) *Lectures on the Relation between Law and Public Opinion in England during the Nineteenth Century* London: Macmillan.

DICKS, Henry V. (1970) *Fifty Years of the Tavistock Clinic* London: Routledge & Kegan Paul.

DIDEROT, Denis (1857) *A Letter upon the Blind* (tr. C.S. Howe) Boston: Perkin's Institution for the Blind.

DIDEROT, Denis (1895-1877) *Oeuvres complètes* Paris.

DONNELLY, Michael J. (1977) Perceptions of lunacy in early nineteenth century Britain. Unpublished PhD Thesis, London University.

DONNELLY, Michael J. (1983) *Managing the Mind* London: Tavistock.

DONZELOT, Jacques [1977] (1979) *The Policing of Families* (tr. Robert Hurley) London: Hutchinson.

DOWNEY, June E. (1923) *The Will-Temperament and its Testing* London: Harrap.

DOYAL, Lesley (with PENNELL, Imogen) (1979) *The Political Economy of Health* London: Pluto.

DREVER, James and DRUMMOND, Margaret (1930) *The Psychology of the Pre-School Child* London: Partridge.

DRUMMOND, William B. (1907) *An Introduction to Child Study* London: Edward Arnold.

DUKES, Clement (1887) *Health at School* London: Casswell.

DUNCAN, Peter M. and MILLARD, William (1886) *A Manual for the Classification, Training and Education of the Feeble-Minded, Imbecile and Idiotic* London: Longman.

DYOS, H.J. (1957) Urban transformation: a note on the objects of street improvement in Regency and Early Victorian London. *International Review of Social History*, 11, 259-65.

EARL, C.J.C. (1939) Some methods of assessing temperament and personality. In F.C. Bartlett et al. (eds) *The Study of Society* London: Kegan Paul, Trench, Trubner.

EAST, W. Norwood (1923) Delinquency and mental defect. *British Journal of Medical Psychology*, 3, 153-67.

ELIAS, Norbert [1939] (1978) *The Civilizing Process: The History of Manners* (tr. Edmund Jephcott) Oxford: Blackwell.

ELLENBERGER, Henri F. (1970) *The Discovery of the Unconscious: the History and Evolution of Dynamic Psychiatry* New York: Basic Books.

EPÉE, Charles M., Abbé de l' [1784] (1801) *The Method of Educating the Deaf and Dumb Confirmed by Long Experience* (tr. F. Green) London: G. Cooke.

ESQUIROL, Jean E.D. [1818] (1845) *Mental Maladies* (tr. E.K. Hunt) Philadelphia.

EVANS, Elizabeth (1892) *The Story of Caspar Hauser from Original Records*, London.

EYLER, John M. (1973a) William Farr on the cholera: the sanitarian's disease theory and the statistician method. *Journal of the History of Medicine and Allied Sciences*, 28, 79-100.

EYLER, John M. (1973b) Mortality statistics and Victorian health policy: programme and criticism. *Bulletin of the History of Medicine*, 50, 335-55.

EYLER, John M. (1979) *Victorian Social Medicine: The Ideas and Methods of William Farr* Baltimore: Johns Hopkins University Press.

EYSENCK, Hans J. (1971) *Race, Intelligence and Education* London: Temple Smith.

FAIRFIELD, L.D. (1928) *Child Guidance in America* London: London County Council.

FARRALL, Lyndsay A. (1975) Controversy and conflict in science: a case study – the English Biometric School and Mendel's laws. *Social Studies of Science*, 5, 269-301.

FECHNER, Gustav [1860] (1966) *Elements of Psychophysics*, vol. 1 (tr. H.E. Adler) New York: Holt, Rinehart & Winston.

FEUERBACH, Anselm von [1832] (1833) *Caspar Hauser* (tr. H.G. Lindberg) London.

FEVERSHAM COMMITTEE (1939) *Report on the Voluntary Mental Health Services* London: Feversham Committee.

FLUGEL, John C. (1921) *The Psychoanalytic Study of the Family* London: Hogarth Press.

FLUGEL, John C. (1933) *A Hundred Years of Psychology, 1833-1933* London: Duckworth.

FOUCAULT, Michel [1961] (1967) *Madness and Civilization* (tr. Richard Howard) London: Tavistock.

FOUCAULT, Michel [1966] (1970) *The Order of Things* (tr. Alan Sheridan) London: Tavistock.

FOUCAULT, Michel [1969] (1972) *The Archaeology of Knowledge* (tr. Alan Sheridan) London: Tavistock.

FOUCAULT, Michel [1971] (1972) Orders of discourse (tr. Richard Swyer) *Social Science Information*, 10, 7-30.

FOUCAULT, Michel [1963] (1973) *The Birth of the Clinic* (tr. Alan Sheridan) London: Tavistock.

FOUCAULT, Michel [1954] (1976) *Mental Illness and Psychology* (tr. Alan Sheridan) New York: Harper and Row.

FOUCAULT, Michel [1975] (1977a) *Discipline and Punish* (tr. Alan Sheridan) London: Allen Lane.

FOUCAULT, Michel [1971] (1977b) Nietzsche, genealogy, history (tr. Donald Bouchard) in Donald F. Bouchard (ed.) *Language, Counter-Memory, Practice* Oxford: Blackwell.

FOUCAULT, Michel (1978) Politics and the analysis of discourse (tr. Colin Gordon). *Ideology and Consciousness*, 3, 7-26.

FOUCAULT, Michel (ed.) [1973] (1978) *I, Pierre Riviere . . .* Harmondsworth: Penguin.

FOUCAULT, Michel [1976] (1979a) *The History of Sexuality, vol. 1.* (tr. Robert Hurley) London: Allen Lane.

FOUCAULT, Michel (1979b) On governmentality. *Ideology and Consciousness*, 6, 5-21.

FOUCAULT, Michel [1977] (1980) Truth and power (tr. Colin Gordon). In Colin Gordon (ed.) *Power/Knowledge* Brighton: Harvester.

FOUCAULT, Michel (1982) The subject and power. Afterword to H.L. Dreyfus and P. Rabinow *Michel Foucault: Beyond Structuralism and Hermeneutics* Brighton: Harvester.

FOX, Lionel W. (1952) *The English Prison and Borstal Systems* London: Routledge & Kegan Paul.

FRASER, Dereck (ed.) (1976) *The New Poor Law in the Nineteenth Century* London: Macmillan.

FRAZER, William M. (1950) *The History of English Public Health 1834-1939* London: Baillière, Tindall & Cox.

FREUD, Anna (1928) *Introduction to the Techniques of Child Analysis* (tr. L.P. Clark) New York: Nervous and Mental Diseases Publishing Co.

FREUD, Sigmund (1909) *Selected Papers on Hysteria* (tr. A.A. Brill) New York: Journal of Nervous and Mental Diseases Publishing Co.

FREUD, Sigmund (1910) *Three Contributions to the Sexual Theory* (tr. A.A. Brill) New York: Nervous and Mental Diseases Publishing Co.

FREUD, Sigmund (1913) *The Interpretation of Dreams* (tr. A.A. Brill) London: George Allen.

FREUD, Sigmund (1914) *The Psychopathology of Everyday Life* (tr. A.A. Brill) London: Fisher Unwin.

FREUD, Sigmund (1920) *A General Introduction to Psychoanalysis* (tr. A.A. Brill) New York: Boni and Liveright.

FREUD, Sigmund (1922) *Introductory Lectures on Psycho-analysis* (tr. J. Riviere) London: Allen & Unwin.

FREUD, Sigmund (1927) *The Problem of Lay Analysis* (tr. A.P. Maerker-Brandon) London: Brentano's.

FRIEDLANDER, Kate (1946) *A Psychoanalytic Approach to Juvenile Delinquency* London: Kegan Paul, Trench, Trubner.

FROGGART, P. and NEVIN, N.C. (1971) The 'Law of Ancestral Heredity' and the Mendelian-Ancestrian controversy in England, 1889-1906. *Journal of Medical Genetics*, 8, 1-36.

FRY, Edward et al. (1909) *The Problem of the Feeble-Minded:* an abstract of the Report of the Royal Commission with an introduction by Sir E. Fry. n.p.

FRY, Margery (1924) A Belgian psychological laboratory. *Howard Journal*, 1, 121-9.

FYNNE, Robert J. (1924) *Montessori and her Inspirers* London: Longmans & Co.

GAINER, Bernard (1972) *The Alien Invasion: The Origins of the Aliens Act of 1905* London: Heinemann.

GALL, Franz J. and SPURZHEIM, J.C. (1810) *Anatomie et physiologie du système nerveau en général et du cerveau en particulaire* Paris.

GALL, Franz J. (1835) *On the Functions of the Brain and Each of its Parts* (tr. W. Lewis) Boston: Marsh, Capen & Lyon.

GALTON, Francis (1865) Hereditary talent and character. *Macmillan's Magazine*, 12, 157-66 and 318-27.

GALTON, Francis (1869) *Hereditary Genius*: an enquiry into its laws and consequences. London: Macmillan.

GALTON, Francis (1883) *Inquiries into Human Faculty and its Development* London: Macmillan.

GALTON, Francis (1889) *Natural Inheritance* London: Macmillan.

GALTON, Francis (1891) Retrospect of the work of the Anthropometric Laboratory. *Journal of the Anthropological Institute*, 21, 32-5.

GALTON, Francis (1901) The possible improvement of the human breed under the existing conditions of law and sentiment. (Second Huxley Lecture of the Anthropological Institute, delivered 29.10.1901) *Nature*, 64, 1670, 659-65 (Oct. 31. 1901).

GALTON, Francis (1907) *Probability, the Foundation of Eugenics:* The Herbert Spencer Lecture. Oxford: Clarendon Press.

GALTON, Francis [1892] (1962) *Hereditary Genius* (reprint of 2nd edn) London: Fontana.

GARRISON, Fielding H. (1929) *An Introduction to the History of Medicine* Philadelphia: Saunders.

GARRISON, Fielding H. and APT, Arthur F. (1965) *Apt-Garrison History of Pediatrics* Philadelphia: Saunders.

GARTNER, Lloyd P. (1960) *The Jewish Immigrant in England, 1870-1914* London: George Allen & Unwin.

GAUKROGER, Stephen (1976) Bachelard and the problem of epistemological analysis. *Studies in History and Philosophy of Science*, 7, 189-244.

GAUKROGER, Stephen (1979) *Explanatory Structures* Hassocks, Sussex: Harvester.

GENIL-PERRIN, Georges (1913) *Histoire des origines et de l'évolution de l'idée de dégénéréscence en médecine mentale* Paris.

GESELL, Arnold (1925) *The Mental Growth of the Pre-School Child* New York: Macmillan.

GESELL, Arnold (1928) *Infancy and Human Growth* New York: Macmillan.

GESELL, Arnold (1941) *Wolf Child and Human Child* New York: Harper.

GILBERT, Bentley B. (1966) *The Evolution of National Insurance in Great Britain: The Origins of the Welfare State* London: Joseph.

GILLESPIE, Robert D. (1933) Psychiatric social work. *Charity Organization Quarterly*, 7, 108-14.

GILLIE, Oliver (1976) Pioneer of IQ faked his research findings. London: *Sunday Times*, 24.10.76, pp. 1-2.

GLASS, David V. (1978) *Numbering the People* London: Gordon & Cremonesi.

GLOVER, Edward (1932) Medico-psychological aspects of normality. *British Journal of Psychology*, 23, 152-66.

GLOVER, Edward (1944) *The Diagnosis and Treatment of Delinquency. Clinical Report on the Work of the ISTD, 1937-41* London: Institute for the Study and Treatment of Delinquency.

GORDON, Colin (1979) Other Inquisitions. *Ideology and Consciousness*, 6, 23-46.

GORDON, Colin (1980) The normal and the biological – a note on Georges Canguilhem. *I&C*, 7, 33-6.

GORDON, Colin (ed.) (1980) *Power/Knowledge* Brighton: Harvester.

GORDON, Hugh (1923) *Mental and Scholastic Tests among Retarded Children* Education Pamphlet No. 44. London: Board of Education.

GORDON, Ronald G. (1926) *Personality* London: Kegan Paul.

GORDON, Ronald G. (1939) *A Survey of Child Psychiatry* London: Child Guidance Council.

GORING, Charles (1913) *The English Convict* London: HMSO.

GRIFFITHS, Ruth (1935) *A Study of Imagination in Early Childhood and its Function in Mental Development* London: Kegan Paul.

GUY, William A. (1873) Inaugural address, *Journal of the Statistical Society*, 36, 467-85.

HACKING, Ian (1975) *Why Does Language Matter to Philosophy?* Cambridge: Cambridge University Press.

HACKING, Ian (1983) *Representing and Intervening* Cambridge: Cambridge University Press.

HADFIELD, James A. (1923) *Psychology and Morals* London: Methuen.

HADFIELD, James A. (ed.) (1935) *Psychology and Modern Problems* London: University of London Press.

HAFFTER, C. (1968) The changeling: history and psychodynamics of attitudes to handicapped children in European folklore. *Journal of the History of Behavioural Sciences*, 4, 55-6.

HALL, G. Stanley (1904) *Adolescence* New York: Appleton.

HALL, William Clarke (1917) *The State and the Child* London: New Commonwealth Books.

HALL, William Clarke (1926) *Children's Courts* London: George Allen & Unwin.

HALL, William Clarke and PRETTY, Arnold (1908) *The Children Act, 1908* London: Stevens.

HALL, William Clarke and MORRISON, A.C.L. (1934) *The Law Relating to Children and Young Persons* London: Butterworth.

HALLIDAY, R.J. (1971) Social Darwinism: a definition. *Victorian Studies*, 14, 389-405.

HALSEY, A.H. and GARDNER, L. (1953) Selection for secondary education. *British Journal of Sociology*, 4, 60-75.

HARDCASTLE, D.N. (1933) The child guidance clinic in America: its condition and future development. *British Journal of Psychology (Medical Section)*, 13, 328-53.

HARDYMENT, Christina (1983) *Dream Babies: Childcare from Locke to Spock* London: Cape.

HARRIS, Jose (1972) *Unemployment and Politics: a Study in English Social Policy* London: Oxford University Press.

HARRISON, Rachel and MORT, Frank (1977) Patriarchal aspects of nineteenth century state formation. In P. Corrigan (ed.) *Capitalism, State Formation and Marxist Theory* London: Quartet.

HART, Bernard (1912) *The Psychology of Insanity* Cambridge: Cambridge University Press.

HARWOOD, J. (1976) The race-intelligence controversy: a sociological approach. I – professional factors. *Social Studies of Science*, 6, 369-94.

HASLAM, John F.C. (1930) *Recent Advances in Preventive Medicine* London: Churchill.

HAY, Douglas (1975) Property, authority and the criminal law. In D. Hay, P. Linebaugh, J. Rule, E. Thompson and C. Winslow (eds) *Albion's Fatal Tree* London: Allen Lane.

HEALY, William (1915) *The Individual Delinquent* Boston: Little Brown.

HEALY, William (1919) *Mental Conflicts and Misconduct* London: Kegan Paul, Trench, Trubner.

HEARNSHAW, Leslie S. (1964) *A Short History of British Psychology 1840-1940* London: Methuen.

HEARNSHAW, Leslie S. (1979) *Cyril Burt, Psychologist* London: Hodder & Stoughton.

HEIM, Alice (1954) *The Appraisal of Intelligence* London: Methuen.

HENDERSON, David K. and GILLESPIE, Robert D. (1927) *A Textbook of Psychiatry* (1st edn) London: Oxford University Press.

HENDERSON, David K. and GILLESPIE, Robert D. (1932) *A Textbook of Psychiatry* (3rd edn) London: Oxford University Press.

HERD, Henry (1930) *The Diagnosis of Mental Deficiency* London: Hodder & Stoughton.

HERON, David (1906) *On the Relation of Fertility in Men to Social Status* Drapers' Company Research Memoirs. Studies in National Deterioration 1. London: Dulau and Co.

HERRNSTEIN, Richard J. and BORING, Edwin G. (1965) *A Source Book in the History of Psychology* Cambridge, Mass.: Harvard University Press.

HILL, Hibbert W. (1916) *The New Public Health* New York: Macmillan.

HILL, Matthew Davenport (1857) *Suggestions for the Repression of Crime* London.

HILLIARD, Leslie T. and KIRMAN, Brian H. (1957) *Mental Deficiency* London: Churchill.

HILTS, V. (1973) Statistics and social science. In R.N. Giere and R.S. Westfall (eds) *Foundations of the Scientific Method: the Nineteenth Century* Bloomington: University of Indiana Press.

HOBSBAWM, Eric J. (1969) *Industry and Empire* Harmondsworth: Penguin.

HOBSON, John A. (1891) *Problems of Poverty* London: Methuen.

HOBSON, John A. (1902) *Imperialism: A Study* London: James Nisbet.

HODGKINSON, Ruth G. (1967) *The Origins of the National Health Service: The Medical Services of the New Poor Laws 1834-1871* London: Wellcome Historical Medical Library.

HODGKINSON, Ruth G. (1968) Social medicine and the growth of statistical information. In *Medicine and Science in the 1860's* London: Wellcome Institute of the History of Medicine.

HOLCOMBE, Lee (1977) Victorian wives and property reform. In M. Vicinus (ed.) *A Widening Sphere* Bloomington, Indiana: Indiana University Press.

HOLLAND, Eardley, JEWSBURY, R.C. and SHELDON, Wilfred (1933) *A Doctor to a Mother* London: Edward Arnold.

HOLMAN, Henry (1914) *Seguin and His Psychological Method of Education* London: Pitman.

HOME AND SCHOOL COUNCIL OF GREAT BRITAIN (1935) *Advances in Understanding the Child* London: Home and Schools Council.

HORSFALL, Thomas C. (1905) *The Relation of National Service to the Welfare of the Community* Manchester: Sherratt & Hughes.

HOSPITAL ALMONERS' ASSOCIATION (1931) *The Hospital Almoner* np: Hospital Almoners' Association.

HOWE, Samuel G. (1848) *The Causes of Idiocy* Edinburgh: Maclachlan & Stewart.

HUG-HELLMUTH, Hermione von (1921) On the technique of child analysis (tr. R. Gabler and B. Low). *International Journal of Psychoanalysis*, 2, 287-305.

HUNTER, Richard and MACALPINE, Ida (1963) *Three Hundred Years of Psychiatry* London: Oxford University Press.

IGNATIEFF, Michael (1979) *A Just Measure of Pain* London: Macmillan.

INSTITUTE OF CHILD PSYCHOLOGY (1934) (1935 etc.) *Annual Report for the Year 1933* (1934 etc.) London: Institute of Child Psychology.

IRELAND, William W. (1877) *On Idiocy and Imbecility* London.

IRELAND, William W. (1898) *Affections of Children, Idiocy, Imbecility and Insanity* London: Churchill.

IRVINE, Elizabeth F. (1963) *A Pioneer of the New Psychology: Hugh Crichton-Miller* Chatham: Ward J. Mackay.

ISAACS, Susan (1928) The mental hygiene of the pre-school child. *British Journal of Medical Psychology*, 8, 186-93.

ISAACS, Susan (1929) *The Nursery Years* London: Routledge.

ISAACS, Susan (1930) *Intellectual Growth in Young Children* London: Routledge.

ISAACS, Susan (1933) *Social Development in Young Children* London: Routledge.

ISAACS, Susan (1935) *The Psychological Aspects of Child Development* London: Evans.

ISAACS, Susan (ed.) (1935) *Concerning Children* London: University of London Institute of Education and Home and Schools Council.

ISAACS, Susan (1937) *The Educational Guidance of the School Child* London: Evans.

ITARD, Jean [1799, 1806] (1972) *The Wild Boy of Aveyron* (tr. E. Fawcett, P. Ayrton and J. White) London: New Left Books.

JACOB, François (1974) *The Logic of Living Systems. A History of Heredity* (tr. B. Spillmann) London: Allen Lane.

JARRETT, Mary (1919) The psychiatric thread running through all social work. *Mental Hygiene*, 3, 210-19.

JEFFRY, C.R. (1968) The development of crime in early English society. In W.R. Chambliss (ed.) *Crime and the Legal Process* New York: McGraw Hill.

JENSEN, Arthur R. (1969) How much can we boost IQ and scholastic achievement? *Harvard Educational Review*, 39, 1-123.

JENSEN, Arthur R. (1974) Kinship correlations reported by Sir Cyril Burt. *Behavioural Genetics*, 4, 1-28.

JONES, Caroline (1977) *Immigration and Social Policy in Britain* London: Tavistock.

JONES, Ernest (1913) *Papers on Psychoanalysis* (1st edn) London: Bailliere, Tindall & Cox.

JONES, Ernest (1923) *Papers on Psychoanalysis* (3rd edn) London: Balliere, Tindall & Cox.

JONES, Ernest (1959) *Free Associations* London: Hogarth Press.

JONES, Ernest (1945) Reminiscent notes on the early history of psychoanalysis in English speaking countries. *International Journal of Psychoanalysis*, 26, 8-10.

JONES, Ernest (1957) *Sigmund Freud, Life and Work* vol. 3. London: Hogarth Press.

JONES, Gareth Stedman (1976) *Outcast London* Harmondsworth: Penguin.

JONES, Karen and WILLIAMSON, Kevin (1979) The birth of the schoolroom. *Ideology and Consciousness*, 6, 59-110.

JONES, Kathleen (1972) *A History of the Mental Health Services* London: Routledge & Kegan Paul.

JUNG, Carl G. (1918) *Studies in Word Association* (tr. M.D. Eder) London: Heinemann.

KAMIN, Leon J. [1974] (1977) *The Science and Politics of IQ* Harmondsworth: Penguin.

KANNER, Leo (1964) *A History of the Care and Study of the Mentally Retarded* Illinois: C.C. Thomas.

KANNER, L. (1967) Medicine in the history of mental retardation, 1800-1965. *American Journal of Mental Deficiency*, 72, 165-70.

KEIR, Gertrude (1952) A history of child guidance (with the assistance of Sir Cyril Burt and other members of the British Psychological Society). *British Journal of Educational Psychology*, 22, 5-29.

KELLOGG, Winthrop N. and KELLOGG, Luella A. (1933) *The Ape and the Child* New York: McGraw Hill.

KELLY, Edmond (1907) *The Unemployables* London: King.

KENDREW, Emily N. (1930) A further attempt to measure the strength of instincts. *British Journal of Psychology*, 21, 160-74.

KENNEDY, Alexander (1951) Psychologists and psychiatrists and their general relationship. *British Journal of Educational Psychology*, 21, 167-71.

KERR, James (1926) *The Fundamentals of School Health* London: George Allen & Unwin.

KIMMINS, Charles W. (ed.) (1927) *The Mental and Physical Welfare of the Child* London: Partridge.

KLEIN, Melanie (1923) The role of the school in the libidinal development of the child. *International Journal of Psycho-Analysis*, 5, 312-31.

KLEIN, Melanie (1926) The psychological principles of infant analysis. *International Journal of Psychoanalysis*, 8, 25-37.

KLEIN, Melanie (1932) *The Psychoanalysis of Children* (tr. Alix Strachey) London: Woolf & Institute of Psycho-analysis.

KRAEPELIN, Emil [1917] (1962) *One Hundred Years of Psychiatry* (tr. W. Baskin) London: Peter Owen.

KRAFT, Ivor (1961) Edward Seguin and the 19th century moral treatment of idiots. *Bulletin of the History of Medicine*, 35, 393-418.

KUHN, Thomas (1970) *The Structure of Scientific Revolutions* (2nd edn) Chicago: Chicago University Press.

LAKATOS, Imre (1971) History of science and its rational reconstruction. In R. Buck and R.S. Cohen, *PSA 1970: In Memory of Rudolph Carnap* Dordrecht: Reidel.

LA METTRIE, Julien O. de [1751] (1791) Traité de l'âme. In *Oeuvres philosophiques* London: Nourse.

LANE, Harlan (1977) *The Wild Boy of Aveyron* London: George Allen & Unwin.

LAPAGE, C. Paget (1920) *Feeblemindedness in Children of School Age* (with an appendix on the colony at Sandlebridge by Mary Dendy) Manchester: Manchester University Press.

LAURIE, Arthur P. (ed.) (1911) *The Teacher's Encyclopaedia*, vol. IV London: Caxton.

LECOURT, Dominique [1969, 1972] (1975) *Marxism and Epistemology: Bachelard, Canguilhem, Foucault* (tr. B. Brewster) London: New Left Books.

LEIGH, Denis (1961) *The Historical Development of British Psychiatry* vol. 1: *18th and 19th Century* Oxford: Pergamon Press.

LENIN, Vladimir I. [1917] (1964) Imperialism, the highest state of capitalism. In *Selected Works in Three Volumes*, vol. 3. London: Lawrence & Wishart.

LÉVI-STRAUSS, Claude (1966) *The Elementary Structures of Kinship* London: Weidenfeld & Nicolson.

LEWIS, Jane (1980) *The Politics of Motherhood* London: Croom Helm.

LEWIS, Richard A. (1952) *Edwin Chadwick and the Public Health Movement* London: Longmans, Green & Company.

LIDDIARD, Mabel (1923) *The Mothercraft Manual* London: Churchill.

LLEWELLYN-SMITH, Hubert (1892-7) The Influx of Population. In C. Booth, *Life and Labour of the People in London*, vol. 3. London: Macmillan.

LOCKE, John [1689] (1920) *An Essay Concerning Human Understanding* London: Ward, Lock.

LOMBROSO, Cesare [1898] (1911) *Crime: Its Causes and Remedies* (tr. Henry P. Horton) Boston: Little, Brown.

LONG, Constance (1920) *The Psychology of Phantasy* London: Baillière, Tindall & Cox.

LORD, John R. (ed.) (1930) *Report of the Proceedings of the Conference on Mental Health* London: National Council for Mental Hygiene.

LOW, Barbara (1920) *Psycho-analysis* London: George Allen & Unwin.

LOWENFELD, Margaret (1935) *Play in Childhood* London: Gollancz.

LUCAS, Proper (1847-50) *Traité philosophique et physiologique de l'hérédité naturelle*. Paris: Corbeil.

LUDMERER, Kenneth M. (1972) *Genetics and American Society: a Historical Appraisal* Baltimore: Johns Hopkins University Press.

MACADAM, Elizabeth (1925) *The Equipment of the Social Worker* London: George Allen & Unwin.

MACADAM, Elizabeth (1934) *The New Philanthropy* London: Unwin Bros.

MACALPINE, Ida and HUNTER, Richard (1969) *George III and the Mad Business* London: Allen Lane.

McCALLUM, Catherine M. (1952) Child guidance in Scotland. *British Journal of Educational Psychology*, 22, 79-88.

McCLEARY, George F. (1935) *The Maternity and Child Welfare Movement* London: King.

MacCURDY, John T. (1923) *Problems in Dynamic Psychology* Cambridge: University Press.

MacCURDY, John T. (1925) *The Psychology of Emotion, Morbid and Normal* London: Kegan Paul.

McDOUGALL, William (1908) *Introduction to Social Psychology* London: Methuen.

McDOUGALL, William (1914) Psychology in the service of eugenics. *Eugenics Review*, 5, 295-308.

McDOUGALL, William (1920) *Introduction to Social Psychology* (15th edn) London: Methuen.

McDOUGALL, William (1923) *An Outline of Psychology* London: Methuen.

McDOUGALL, William (1926) *An Outline of Abnormal Psychology* Boston: Scribner.

McDOUGALL, William (1936) *Psychoanalysis and Social Psychology* London: Methuen.

M'GONIGLE, George C.M. and KIRBY, John (1936) *Poverty and Public Health* London: Gollancz.

McGREGOR, Oliver R. (1957) *Divorce in England* London: Heinemann.

MACKENZIE, Donald (1976) Eugenics in Britain. *Social Studies of Science*, 6, 499-532.

MACKENZIE, Donald (1981a) *Statistics in Britain, 1865-1930: The Social Construction of Scientific Knowledge* Edinburgh: Edinburgh

University Press.

MACLEAN, Charles (1977) *Wolf Children* London: Allen Lane.

MacNICOL, John (1980) *The Movement for Family Allowances* London: Heinemann.

McMILLAN, Margaret (1930) *The Nursery School* London: J.M. Dent.

MAGNAN, Jacques J.V. (1876) *On Alcoholism: the Various Forms of Alcoholic Delirium and their Treatment* (tr. W.S. Greenfield) London.

MALSON, Lucien (1972) *Wolf Children* London: New Left Books.

MALTHUS, Thomas [1798] (1976) *An Essay on the Principle of Population* Harmondsworth: Penguin.

MANUEL, Frank (1972) From equality to organicism. In *Freedom from History and Other Untimely Essays* London: University of London Press.

MARSHALL, Alfred (1890) *Principles of Economics*. vol. 1 London: Macmillan.

MARSHALL, John D. (1968) *The Old Poor Law, 1795-1834* London: Macmillan.

MARWICK, Arthur (1964) Middle opinion in the thirties: Planning, progress and political 'agreement'. *English Historical Review*, 79, 285-98.

MASSIEU, Jean (1815) *Recueil des définitions et résponses les plus remarquables de Massieu et Clerc* (including English translation by J.H. Sivrae) London: Cox & Bayles.

MATTHEWS, Frank B. (1954) *Mental Health Services* London: Shaw & Sons.

MAUDSLEY, Henry (1868) *The Physiology and Pathology of the Mind* (2nd edn) London.

MAUDSLEY, Henry (1873) *Body and Mind* London: Macmillan.

MAUDSLEY, Henry (1874) *Responsibility in Mental Disease* London: King.

MAUDSLEY, Henry (1879) *The Pathology of Mind* London: Macmillan.

MAURICE, Frederick (1903) National health: a soldier's study. *Contemporary Review*, 83, 41-56.

MAY, Margaret (1973) Innocence and experience: the evolution of the concept of juvenile delinquency in the mid-nineteenth century. *Victorian Studies*, 17, 7-29.

MAYHEW, Henry (1861-2) *London Labour and the London Poor* 4 vols London: Griffin, Bohn.

MERCIER, Charles A. (1917) Moral imbecility. *The Practitioner*, 99, 301-8.

MESURIER, L. Le (ed.) (1935) *A Handbook of Probation and Social Work of the Courts* London: National Association of Probation Officers.

MILLARD, William (1864) *The Idiot and his Helpers* Colchester: Essex Hall Idiot Asylum.

MILLER, Emanuel (ed.) (1937) *The Growing Child and its Problems* London: Kegan Paul, Trench and Trubner.

MILLER, Hugh Crichton (ed.) (1920) *Functional Nerve Disease: An Epitome of War Experience* London: Oxford University Press.

MILLER, Hugh Crichton (1921) *The New Psychology and the*

Teacher London: Jarrolds.

MILLER, Hugh Crichton (1922) *The New Psychology and the Parent* London: Jarrolds.

MILLER, Hugh Crichton (1929) The unconscious motive of the juvenile delinquent. *Probation*, 1, 12-14.

MINSON, Jeffrey (1980) Review of Ignatieff: A Just Measure of Pain and Scull: Museums of Madness. *Sociological Review*, 28, 195-8.

MITCHELL, Juliet (1974) *Psychoanalysis and Feminism* London: Allen Lane.

MITCHELL, Thomas W. (1927) *Problems of Psychopathology* London: Kegan Paul.

MONTESQUIEU, Charles de Secondat [1748] (1949) *The Spirit of the Laws* (tr. T. Nugent) New York: Heffner.

MOODIE, William (1930) The Child Guidance Clinic. *The Magistrate*, 2, 391-2.

MOODIE, William (1931) *Child Guidance by Team Work* London: Child Guidance Council.

MOREAU (de Tours) Jacques J. (1830) *De l'influence du physique relativement au disordre des facultés intellectuelles* Paris.

MOREL, Benedict A. (1857) *Traite des dégénéréscences physiques, intellectuelles et morales de l'espèce humaine, et des causes qui produisent ces variétés maladies* Paris.

MORGAN, C.D. and MURRAY, H.A. (1935) A method for investigating fantasies: the Thematic Apperception Test. *Archives of Neurology and Psychiatry*, 34, 289-306.

MORRISON, William (1896) *Juvenile Offenders* London: T. Fisher Unwin.

MOSELEY, William W. (1838) *Eleven Chapters on Nervous and Mental Complaints* London: Simpkin, Marshall & Co.

MOTT, Frederick W. (1919) *War Neuroses and Shell Shock* Oxford: Oxford Medical Publications.

MOWAT, Charles Lock (1961) *The Charity Organization Society 1869-1913* London: Methuen.

MUNSTERBERG, Hugo (1912) *Psychology and Industrial Efficiency* London: Constable.

MURPHY, Gardner (1928) *An Historical Introduction to Modern Psychology* London: Kegan Paul.

MURPHY, Gardner and KOVACH, Joseph K. (1972) *An Historical Introduction to Modern Psychology* (6th edition) London: Routledge & Kegan Paul.

MYERS, Charles S. (1911) The pitfalls of 'mental tests'. *British Medical Journal*, 1, 195.

MYERS, Charles S. (1918) *Present Day Applications of Psychology* London: Methuen.

MYERS, Charles S. (1920) *Mind and Work* London: University of London Press.

MYERS, Charles S. (1926) *Industrial Psychology in Great Britain* London: Jonathan Cape.

NATIONAL ASSOCIATION OF PROBATION OFFICERS (1929-1934)

Probation: the Journal of the National Association of Probation Officers London.

NATIONAL COUNCIL FOR MENTAL HYGIENE (1924) *First Report 1923-1924* London: National Council for Mental Hygiene.

NEALE, William Beaver (1840) *Juvenile Delinquency in Manchester* Manchester.

NEUGEBAUER, R. (1978) Treatment of the mentally ill in medieval and early modern England: a reappraisal. *Journal of the History of the Behavioural Sciences*, 14, 158-69.

NEWSHOLME, Arthur and KERR, James (1924) *School Hygiene* (16th edn) London: George Allen & Unwin.

NEWSON, John and NEWSON, Elizabeth (1974) Cultural Aspects of Childrearing in the English-speaking World. In M.P.M. Richards (ed.) *The Integration of a Child into a Social World* Cambridge: Cambridge University Press.

NICOLL, H. Maurice (1917) *Dream Psychology* Oxford: Oxford Medical Publications.

NORTON, Bernard J. (1978) Karl Pearson and statistics: the social origins of scientific innovation. *Social Studies of Science*, 8, 3-34.

OATES, David W. (1928) An experimental study of temperament. *British Journal of Psychology*, 19, 1-30.

OATES, David W. (1929) Group factors in temperamental qualities. *British Journal of Psychology*, 20, 118-36.

ORR, John Boyd (1936) *Food, Health and Income* London: Macmillan.

OWEN, David E. (1965) *English Philanthropy, 1660-1960* Cambridge, Mass.: Harvard University Press.

OWEN, Grace M. (1977) The Development of Health Visiting as a Profession. In Grace M. Owen (ed.) *Health Visiting* London: Ballière Tindall.

PAILTHORPE, Grace W. (1932) *Studies in the Psychology of Delinquency*: Medical Research Council Special Report No. 170. London: HMSO.

PALERMO, David S. (1971) Is a scientific revolution taking place in psychology. *Science Studies*, 1, 135-55.

PARGETER, William (1792) *Observations on Maniacal Disorders* Reading.

PARKINSON, James (1807) *Observations on the Excessive Indulgences of Children, Particularly Intended to Show its Injurious Effects on their Health and the Difficulties it Occasions in their Treatment during Sickness* London: Symonds et al.

PARKS, E.L. (1976) From Constabulary to Police Society. In W.J. Chambliss and M. Mankoff (eds) *Whose Law, What Order?* New York: Wiley.

PASQUINO, Pasquale (1978) Theatrum politicum. The genealogy of capital – police and the state of prosperity. *Ideology and Consciousness*, 4, 41-54.

PAST AND PRESENT SOCIETY (ed.) (1978) *The Roots of Sociobiology* London: Past and Present Society.

PEARSON, Karl (1898) Mathematical contributions to the theory of evolution: On the law of ancestral heredity. *Proceedings of the Royal Society*, 62, 386-412.

PEARSON, Karl (1901) *National Life from the Standpoint of Science* London: A. & C. Black.

PEARSON, Karl (1904) On the laws of inheritance in man, II. *Biometrika*, 3, 131-90.

PEARSON, Karl (1914-1930) *The Life, Letters and Labours of Francis Galton* (3 vols) Cambridge: Cambridge University Press.

PETERSON, Joseph (1925) *Early Conceptions and Tests of Intelligence* Yonkers, N.Y.: World Books.

PFISTER, Oscar (1917) *Psychoanalytic Method* (tr. C.R. Payne) London: Kegan Paul.

PICKENS, Donald K. (1968) *Eugenics and the Progressives* Nashville: Vanderbilt University Press.

PINCHBECK, Ivy and HEWITT, Margaret (1973) *Children in English Society, Vol. 2* London: Routledge & Kegan Paul.

PINEL, Phillipe (1798) *Nosographie philosophique, ou la méthode de l'analyse appliquée à la médicine* Paris: Maradan.

PINEL, Phillipe [1801] (1806) *A Treatise on Insanity* (tr. D.D. Davis) London: Cadell & Davies.

PINSENT, Ellen F. (1903) On the permanent care of the feeble minded. *The Lancet*, 21.2.1903, 513-15.

PLATT, Anthony (1969) *The Child Savers* Chicago: University of Chicago Press.

POPPER, Karl [1934] (1972) *The Logic of Scientific Discovery* London: Hutchinson.

POTTS, Patricia (1982) Medicine, morals and mental deficiency: the contribution of doctors to the institutionalisation of special education in England, 1890-1930. Unpublished paper given to the Society for the Social History of Medicine Conference on Mental Handicap, 24.4.1982.

POYNTER, John R. (1969) *Society and Pauperism* London: Routledge & Kegan Paul.

PREYER, W. [1882] (1894) *Mental Development in the Child* (tr. H.W. Brown) London: Arnold.

PRICHARD, James C. (1835) *A Treatise on Insanity* London.

PRIDEAUX, D. (1921) Expression of emotion as shown by the psychogalvanic reflex. *British Journal of Medical Psychology*, 2, 23-46.

PRITCHARD, David G. (1963) *Education and the Handicapped 1760-1960* London: Routledge & Kegan Paul.

PROCACCI, Giovanna (1978) Social economy and the government of poverty. *Ideology and Consciousness*, 4, 55-72.

PROVINE, William B. (1971) *The Origins of Theoretical Population Genetics* Chicago: Chicago University Press.

RATHBONE, Eleanor (1924) *The Disinherited Family* London: Arnold.

RAVEN, Alice (1925) The use of psychology in social work. *Charity Organization Quarterly*, no. 14, 251-5.

RAVEN, Alice (1929) *An Introduction to Individual Psychology* Cambridge: Heffer.

REES, John R. and ROBINSON, Doris (1930) Modern psychiatry and social work. In *Hospital Almoners' Association Year Book*, 1930, London.

RENAN, Ernest [1890] (1923) *L'avenir de la science* (translated as *The Future of Science*, Boston: Roberts, 1891) Paris: Calmann-Levy.

RIBOT, Theodule A. [1873] (1875) *Heredity: A Psychological Study of its Phenomena, Laws, Causes and Consequences* London: King.

RICARDO, David [1817] (1951-73) The Principles of Political Economy and Taxation. In *The Works and Correspondence of David Ricardo* (ed. P. Sraffa) vol. 1. Cambridge: Cambridge University Press for the Royal Economic Society.

RICHARDS, Barry (1977) Psychology, prisons and ideology. *Ideology and Consciousness*, 2, 9-25.

RICHARDSON, Cyril A. (1922) *Methods and Experiments in Mental Tests* London: Harrap.

RICHARDSON, Cyril A. (1929) The measurement of conative factors in children and their influence. *British Journal of Psychology*, 19, 405-12.

RICHARDSON, Ken and SPEARS, David (eds) (1972) *Race, Culture and Intelligence* Harmondsworth: Penguin.

RICHMOND, Mary E. (1917) *Social Diagnosis* New York: Russell Sage.

RIESE, Walther (1969) *The Legacy of Phillipe Pinel* New York: Springer.

RILEY, Denise (1979) War in the nursery. *Feminist Review*, 2, 82-108.

RILEY, Denise (1983) *War in the Nursery* London: Virago.

RIVERS, William H.R. (1920) *Instinct and Unconscious* Cambridge: Cambridge University Press.

ROBINSON, Virginia P. (1930) *A Changing Psychology in Social Casework* Chapel Hill, Carolina: University of North Carolina.

ROOFF, Madeline (1972) *A Hundred Years of Family Welfare* London: Michael Joseph.

ROSE, Michael E. (1972) *The Relief of Poverty 1834-1914* London: Macmillan.

ROSE, Nikolas (1979) The psychological complex: mental measurement and social administration. *Ideology and Consciousness*, 5, 5-68.

ROSE, Nikolas (1984) The formation of the psychology of the individual in England 1870-1939. PhD Thesis, University of London.

ROSEN, George (1946) The philosophy of ideology and the emergence of modern medicine in France. *Bulletin of the History of Medicine*, 20, 328-39.

ROSEN, George (1953a) Cameralism and the concept of medical police. *Bulletin of the History of Medicine*, 27, 21-43.

ROSEN, George (1953b) Economic and social policing in the development of public health. *Journal of the History of Medicine*, 8, 406-30.

ROSEN, George (1968) *Madness in Society* Chicago: University of Chicago Press.

ROSEN, Marvin, CLARK, Gerald and KIVITZ, Martin (eds) (1976) *The History of Mental Retardation* Baltimore: University Park Press.

ROSENBERG, Charles E. (1974) The bitter fruit: heredity, disease and social thought in nineteenth-century America. *Perspectives in American History*, 8, 189-235.

ROWNTREE, B. Seebohm (1901) *Poverty. A Study of Town life* (1st edn) London: Macmillan.

ROWNTREE, B. Seebohm (1913) *Poverty: A Study of Town Life* (2nd edn) London: Nelson.

ROWNTREE, B. Seebohm (1914) *The Way to Industrial Peace and the Problem of Unemployment* London: T. Fisher Unwin.

RUSSELL, Charles (1900) The Jewish Question in the East End. In C. Russell & H.S. Lewis (eds) *The Jew in London* London.

RUSSELL, William O. (1819) *A Treatise on Crimes and Misdemeanours* (2 vols) London: Butterworth.

RYAN, Joanna and THOMAS, Frank (1980) *The Politics of Mental Handicap* London: Penguin.

SANDERS, Wiley B. (1970) *Juvenile Offenders for a Thousand Years* Chapel Hill, Carolina: University of Carolina Press.

SCHARLIEB, Mary (1927) *Psychology of Childhood: Normal and Abnormal* London: Constable.

SCHUMPETER, Joseph A. (1954) *History of Economic Analysis* New York: Oxford University Press.

SCHWEINITZ, Karl De (ed.) (1947) *England's Road to Social Security 1349-1947* London: Oxford University Press.

SCULL, Andrew T. (1975) From madness to mental illness: medical men as moral entrepreneurs. *Archives Européenes de Sociologie*, 16, 218-61.

SCULL, Andrew T. (1979) *Museums of Madness: the Social Organisation of Insanity in 19th Century England* London: Allen Lane.

SEARL, M.N. (1933) Play, reality and aggression. *International Journal of Psychoanalysis*, 14, 310-20.

SEARLE, Geoffrey R. (1971) *The Quest for National Efficiency* Oxford: Blackwell.

SEARLE, Geoffrey R. (1976) *Eugenics and Politics in Britain 1900-1914* Leyden: Noordhoff International.

SEARLE, Geoffrey R. (1978) Past and Present Society, *The Roots of Sociobiology*. Proceedings of Conference held 29.9.78. Oxford: Past and Present Society.

SÉGUIN, Edouard (1866) *Idiocy and Its Treatment by the Physiological Method* New York.

SÉGUIN, Edouard (1870) *New Facts and Remarks Concerning Idiocy* New York.

SÉGUIN, Edouard (1876) Report on Education. In R.H. Thurston (ed.) *Report of Commissioners to Vienna International Exhibition, 1873* Washington.

SEMMEL, Bernard (1960) *Imperialism and Social Reform: English Social-Imperial Thought, 1895-1914* London: George Allen & Unwin.

SHADWELL, Arthur [1906] (1909) *Industrial Efficiency* (2nd edn) London: Longmans.

SHAND, Alexander F. (1914) *The Foundations of Character* London: Macmillan.

SHAPIN, Steven and BARNES, Barry (1979) Darwin and Social
Darwinism: Purity and History. In B. Barnes and S. Shapin (eds)
Natural Order: Historical Studies of Scientific Culture Beverly Hills
& London: Sage.

SHARP, Stella E. (1899) Individual Psychology: a study in psychological
method. *American Journal of Psychology*, 10, 329-91.

SHAW, George Bernard (ed.) (1900) *Fabianism and the Empire* London:
Fabian Society.

SHEE, George F. (1903) The deterioration in the national physique.
Nineteenth Century, 53, 797-805.

SHINN, Milicent (1893) *Notes on the Development of a Child* University
of California Studies.

SHRUBSALL, F.C. (1923) Delinquency and mental defect. *British Journal
of Medical Psychology*, 3, 179-87.

SHRUBSALL, F.C. (1927) Notes on the investigation and treatment of
'difficult' children in the United States of America. *Mental Welfare*, 8,
41-8.

SHUTTLEWORTH, George E. (1888) The education of children of
abnormally weak mental capacity. *Journal of Mental Science*, 34,
80-84.

SIDNEY, Edwin (1854) *Teaching the Idiot* London: Society for the
Encouragement of Arts, Manufacture and Commerce.

SIMON, Brian (1953) *Intelligence Testing and the Comprehensive School*
London: Lawrence & Wishart.

SIMON, Brian (1971) *Intelligence, Psychology and Education* London:
Lawrence & Wishart.

SIMON, Brian (1974) *The Politics of Educational Reform* London:
Lawrence & Wishart.

SIMON, Brian (1978) Classification and Streaming. In *Intelligence,
Psychology and Education* (revised edition) London: Lawrence &
Wishart.

SINCLAIR, John (1791-1799) *The Statistical Account of Scotland* (21
vols) Edinburgh.

SINGH, Joseph A.L. and ZINGG, Robert M. (1942) *Wolf Children and
Feral Man* New York: Harper.

SKULTANS, Vieda (1975) *Madness and Morals* London: Routledge &
Kegan Paul.

SKULTANS, Vieda (1979) *English Madness* London: Routledge & Kegan
Paul.

SMITH, Adam [1776] (1976) *An Inquiry into the Nature and Causes of
the Wealth of Nations* (ed. R.H. Campbell and A.S. Skinner) (2 vols)
London: Oxford University Press.

SMITH, Maurice Hamblin (1922) *The Psychology of the Criminal*
London: Methuen.

SMITH, Maurice Hamblin (1924) The medical examination of
delinquents. *Howard Journal*, 1, 115-21.

SMITH, Roger (1981) *Trial by Medicine: Insanity and Responsibility in
Victorian Trials* Edinburgh: Edinburgh University Press.

SMITH, Walter Whately (1922) *The Measurement of Emotion* London:
Kegan Paul.

SPEARMAN, Charles (1904) 'General Intelligence': objectively determined and measured. *American Journal of Psychology*, 15, 201-92.

SPEARMAN, Charles (1915) The measurement of intelligence. *Eugenics Review*, 6, 312-13.

SPENCER, Herbert (1972) *On Social Evolution* (ed. J.D.Y. Peel) Chicago: Chicago University Press.

SPURZHEIM, Johann G. (1817) *Observation on the Deranged Manifestations of the Mind or Insanity* London: Baldwin, Craddock & Joy.

STERN, William [1912] (1914) *The Psychological Methods of Testing Intelligence* (tr. G.M. Whipple) Baltimore: Warwick & York.

STEUART, James [1767] (1966) *An Inquiry into the Principles of Political Oeconomy* (ed. A.S. Skinner), 2 vols Edinburgh: Oliver & Boyd.

STEVENSON, George S. and SMITH, Geddes (1934) *Child Guidance Clinics: A Quarter Century of Development* New York: Commonwealth Fund.

STODDART, W.H.B. (1923) Delinquency and mental defect. *British Journal of Medical Psychology*, 3, 188-93.

STRACHEY, J. St. Loe (1926) American juvenile courts and children's courts in England. *The Magistrate*, 1, 117-18.

SULLY, James (1886) *Teacher's Handbook of Psychology* London: Longman.

SULLY, James (1895) *Studies in Childhood* London: Longmans, Green.

SUTHERLAND, Gilliam (1977) The magic of measurement: mental testing and English education, 1900-1940. *Transactions of the Royal Historical Society*, 27, 135-53.

SUTHERLAND, Gillian (1981) Measuring Intelligence: English Local Authorities and Mental Testing, 1919-1939. In C. Webster (ed.) *Biology, Medicine and Society: 1840-1940*, Cambridge: Cambridge University Press.

SUTHERLAND, Gillian and SHARP, Stephen (1980) 'The fust official psychologist in the wurrld': aspects of the professionalisation of psychology in early twentieth century Britain. *History of Science*, 17, 181-208.

TALBOT, Eugene S. (1898) *Degeneracy: Its Causes, Signs and Results* London: Scott.

TANSLEY, Arthur G. (1920) *The New Psychology and its Relation to Life* London: Allen & Unwin.

TAVISTOCK CLINIC (1928) (1929 etc.) *Report for the Years 1920-1927 (1927-1929 etc.)* London: Tavistock Clinic.

TEMKIN, Oswei (1963) The Scientific Approach to Disease: Specific Entity and Individual Sickness. In A.C. Crombie (ed.) *Scientific Change* London: Heinemann.

THOMSON, Godfrey H. (1922) *The Northumberland Mental Tests* London: Harrap.

TIMES (1976) Theories of IQ pioneer completely discredited. London: *The Times*, 25.10.76, p. 3.

TIMMS, Noel (1964) *Psychiatric Social Work in Great Britain, 1929-1962* London: Routledge & Kegan Paul.

TITCHENER, Edward B. (1901-1905) *Experimental Psychology*, 2 vols London: Macmillan.

TOMLINSON, Jim (1981) *Problems of British Economic Policy, 1870-1945* London: Methuen.

TREDGOLD, Alfred F. (1908) *Mental Deficiency (Amentia)* London: Balliere, Tindall & Cox.

TREDGOLD, Alfred (1910) The feeble-minded. *Contemporary Review*, 97, 717-27.

TREDGOLD, Alfred F. (1914) *Mental Deficiency (Amentia)* (2nd edn) London: Ballière, Tindall & Cox.

TREDGOLD, Alfred F. (1917) Moral imbecility. *The Practitioner*, 99, 43-55.

TRIBE, Keith (1978) *Land, Labour and Economic Discourse* London: Routledge & Kegan Paul.

TURGOT, Robert J. [1788] (1793) *Reflections on the Formation and Distribution of Wealth* London: Good.

TROTTER, Wilfred (1916) *Instincts of the Herd in Peace and War* London: Fisher Unwin.

TUKE, Daniel Hack (1882) *Chapters in the History of the Insane in the British Isles* London: Kegan Paul.

TUKE, Daniel Hack (ed.) (1892) *A Dictionary of Psychological Medicine* (2 vols) London: Churchill.

TUKE, Samuel [1813] (1964) *Description of the Retreat* London: Dawsons.

UNDERWOOD, Michael (1797) *A Treatise on the Disorders of Childhood Adapted to Domestic Use* (3 vols) London.

VALENTINE, C.W. (1929) The relative reliability of men and women in instinctive judgments of character. *British Journal of Psychology*, 19, 213-38.

VERNON, Philip E. (1929) Tests of temperament and personality. *British Journal of Psychology*, 20, 97-118.

VERNON, Philip E. (1933a) The American and the German methods of approach to the study of temperament and personality. *British Journal of Psychology*, 24, 156-77.

VERNON, Philip E. (1933b) The Rorschach inkblot test. *British Journal of Medical Psychology*, 13, 89-118, 179-205 and 271-95.

VOLTAIRE [1764] (1835) *Dictionnaire Philosophique* in *Oeuvres*, vol. 7. Paris.

VORZIMMER, Peter (1963) Charles Darwin and blending inheritance. *Isis*, 54, 371-90.

WARNER, Francis (1888) A method of examining children in schools as to their development and brain condition. *British Medical Journal*, 22nd September 1888, 659-60.

WARNER, Francis (1890) *Lectures on Mental Faculty* Cambridge: Cambridge University Press.

WARNER, Francis (1895) *Report on the Scientific Study of the Mental and Physical Conditions of Childhood, with particular reference to*

Children of Defective Constitution and with Recommendations as to Education and Training London: Royal Sanitary Institute.

WARNER, Francis (1896) Mental and physical conditions among fifty thousand children. *Journal of the Royal Statistical Society*, 59, 125-62.

WARNER, Francis (1897) *The Study of Children and their School Training* London: Macmillan.

WARREN, Charles (1901) Some lessons from the South African War. *National Review*, 38, 181-96.

WARREN, Neil (1971) Is a scientific revolution taking place in psychology? Doubts and reservations. *Science Studies*, 1, 407-13.

WASSERMAN, Jakob [1928] (1973) *Kaspar Hauser* London.

WEBB, Edward J. (1915) *Character and Intelligence.* British Journal of Psychology Monograph Supplement 3. Cambridge: Cambridge University Press.

WEBB, Sidney (1907) *The Decline in the Birth Rate. Fabian Tract No 131* London: Fabian Society.

WEBB, Sidney (1910) Eugenics and the Poor Law: the minority report. *Eugenics Review*, 2, 233-41.

WEBSTER, Charles (ed.) (1981) *Biology, Medicine and Society: 1840-1940* Cambridge: Cambridge University Press.

WEEKS, Jeffrey (1971) *Sex, Politics and Society* London: Longmans.

WEIMAR, Walter B. (1979) The history of psychology and its retrieval from historiography. Parts I and II. *Social Studies*, 4, 235-58 and 367-96.

WEIMAR, Walter B. and PALERMO, David S. (1973) Paradigms and normal science in psychology. *Science Studies*, 3, 211-44.

WEISMANN, August (1893) *The Germ Plasm: A Theory of Heredity* New York: Scribner.

WELCH, Henry J. and MYERS, Charles S. (1932) *Ten Years of Industrial Psychology* London: Pitman.

WEST, Charles (1854) *Lectures on the Diseases of Infancy and Childhood* (3rd edn) London: Longman.

WHITE, Arnold (1886) *The Problems of a Great City* London: Remington.

WHITE, Arnold (1892) *The Destitute Alien in Great Britain* London: Swann Sonnenschein & Co.

WHITE, Arnold (1901) *Efficiency and Empire* London: Methuen.

WHITEBREAD, Nanette (1972) *The Evolution of the Infant-Nursery School: A History of Infant and Nursery Education in Britain, 1800-1970* London: Routledge & Kegan Paul.

WILLIAMS, J.H. Harley (1932) *A Century of Public Health in Britain, 1832-1929* London: Black.

WILLIAMS, Karel (1981) *From Pauperism to Poverty* London: Routledge & Kegan Paul.

WILLIS, Thomas (1672) *De Anima Brutorum* London.

WILSON, Bryan (ed.) (1970) *Rationality* Oxford: Blackwell.

WINNICOTT, Donald W. (1975) *Through Pediatrics to Psychoanalysis* London: Hogarth Press.

WINSLOW, Forbes (1854) *Lettsomian Lectures on Insanity* London: Churchill.

WISSLER, Clark (1901) The correlation of mental and physical tests. *Psychological Review Monograph Supplements*, 3.

WOLF, Theta H. (1973) *Alfred Binet* Chicago: University of Chicago Press.

WOLFENSBERGER, Wolf (1976) *The Origin and Nature of our Institutional Models* New York: Human Policy Press.

WOODROOFE, Kathleen (1962) *From Charity to Social Welfare in England and the United States* London: Routledge & Kegan Paul.

WORMWALD, John and WORMWALD, Samuel (1913) *A Guide to the Mental Deficiency Act, 1913* London: P.S. King.

WUNDT, William [1896] (1897) *Outlines of Psychology* (tr. C.H. Judd) London: Macmillan.

YELLOLY, Margaret A. (1980) *Social Work Theory and Psychoanalysis* New York: Van Nostrand Reinhold.

YOUNG, Agnes, F. and ASHTON, Elwyn T. (1956) *British Social Work in the 19th century* London: Routledge & Kegan Paul.

YOUNG, Robert M. (1970) *Mind, Brain and Adaptation in the Nineteenth Century: Cerebral Localisation and its Biological Context from Gall to Ferrier* Oxford: Clarendon Press.

YOUNGHUSBAND, Eileen (1947) *Report on the Employment and Training of Social Workers* Edinburgh: Carnegie UK Trust.

YOUNGHUSBAND, Eileen (1951) *Social Work in Britain* Edinburgh: Carnegie UK Trust.

YOUNGHUSBAND, Eileen (1978) *Social Work in Britain: 1950-1975* (vol. 1) London: George Allen & Unwin.

ZILBOORG, Gregory (1941) *History of Medical Psychology* New York: Norton.

ZINGG, Robert M. (1940) Feral man and extreme cases of isolation. *American Journal of Psychology*, 53, 487-517.

Official Publications

BOARD OF CONTROL (1918) *Fourth Annual Report* (for the year 1917) London: HMSO.

BOARD OF CONTROL (1931) *Colonies for Mental Defectives* London: HMSO.

BOARD OF CONTROL (1934) *Report of the Departmental Committee on Sterilisation*, Cd 4485 [The Brock Committee] London: HMSO.

BOARD OF EDUCATION (1905) *Report of the Inter-Departmental Committee on Medical Inspection and Feeding of Children attending Public Elementary Schools* London: HMSO.

BOARD OF EDUCATION (1910) (1911 etc.) *Annual Report for the Chief Medical Officer of the Board of Education for 1908 (1909 etc.)* London: HMSO.

BOARD OF EDUCATION (1920) *Report of the Juvenile Organizations Committee on Juvenile Delinquency* London: HMSO.

BOARD OF EDUCATION (1924) *Report of the Consultative Committee on Psychological Tests of Educable Capacity and their Possible Uses in the Public System of Education* London: HMSO.

BOARD OF EDUCATION AND BOARD OF CONTROL (1929) *Report of the Joint Departmental Committee on Mental Deficiency* [The Wood Committee] 3 vols London: HMSO.

DEPARTMENT OF EDUCATION AND SCIENCE (1975) *The School Health Service 1908-1974* London: HMSO.

EDUCATION DEPARTMENT (DEFECTIVE AND EPILEPTIC CHILDREN) (COMMITTEE) (1898) Vol. I: *Report* Cd 8746; Vol. II: *Minutes of Evidence* Cd 8747. London: HMSO.

HOME OFFICE (1895) *Report from the Departmental Committee on Prisons* C. 7702. London: HMSO.

HOME OFFICE (1923) (1924, 1925, 1928, 1938) *First (Second, Third, etc.) Report on the Work of the Children's Branch* London: HMSO.

HOME OFFICE (1927) *Report of the Departmental Committee on the Treatment of Young Offenders* Cmd 2831. London: HMSO.

HOME OFFICE (1932) *Report of the Departmental Committee on Persistent Offenders* London: HMSO.

HOME OFFICE (1946) *Training in Child Care* Interim Report of the Care of Children Committee [Chairman, Myra Curtis]. London: HMSO.

LOCAL GOVERNMENT BOARD (1904) *Report of the Inter-Departmental Committee on Physical Deterioration* 3 vols Cd 2175. London: HMSO.

LOCAL GOVERNMENT BOARD (1910) *Supplement to Report of Medical Officer on Infant and Child Mortality* Cd 5263 London: HMSO.

MINISTRY OF EDUCATION (1955) *Report of the Committee on Maladjusted Children* [Chairman, J. Underwood]. London: HMSO.

MINISTRY OF HEALTH (1919) *An Outline of the Practice of Preventive Medicine* A memorandum by Sir George Newman, Chief Medical Officer, Ministry of Health. Cmd 363 London: HMSO.

POOR LAW COMMISSION (1834) *Report from His Majesty's Commissioners for Inquiry into the Administration and Practical Operation of the Poor Laws.* London: HMSO.

POOR LAW SCHOOLS (COMMITTEE) (1896) *Report of the Departmental Committee appointed by the Local Government Board to Inquire into the Poor Law Schools* 3 vols C. 8027, C. 8032 and C. 8033 London: HMSO.

ROYAL COMMISSION ON THE BLIND, DEAF AND DUMB (1889) *Report*, 4 vols C. 5781. London: HMSO.

ROYAL COMMISSION ON ALIEN IMMIGRATION (1903) *Report* Cd 1743 London: HMSO.

ROYAL COMMISSION ON THE CARE AND CONTROL OF THE FEEBLE MINDED (1908) vols I-IV: *Minutes of Evidence* Cd 4215, 4216, 4217, 4218; vol. V: *Appendix Papers* Cd 4219; vol. VI: *Reports on Medical Investigations* Cd 4420; vol. VII: *Report on Visit of Certain Commissioners to America* Cd 4221; vol. VIII: *Report* Cd

4202 London: HMSO.
ROYAL COMMISSION ON THE POOR LAWS AND RELIEF OF
DISTRESS (1909) *Report* Cd 4499. London: HMSO.
ROYAL COMMISSION ON LUNACY AND MENTAL DISORDER
(1929) *Report* Cmd 2700 London: HMSO.
WAR OFFICE (1922) *Report of the Committee of Enquiry into 'Shell
Shock'* London: HMSO.

Index